1000 YEARS OF CAREER ADVICE

based on

100 Interviews with…

Graduates 10 Years Out of University:

their Career Paths and Lessons Learned

by

Paul Murphy

1000 Years of Career Advice by Paul Murphy

Print ISBN: 978-1-9999750-2-9

www.1000yearsofcareeradvice.com

For my parents, Anita and Jim Murphy

ACKNOWLEDGMENTS

To not only the 100 interviewees in this book, but the many more that didn't make it into the book. This book wouldn't have been possible without you. I especially thank the people whose stories and advice I found particularly inspiring and insightful: Paul, Joel, Suzanne, Colm, Hawwa, Nasir, Claire, Gareth, Lorcan, Emma, Dan, Mary, Niall, Rick, Jennifer, Charlotte, Niamh, Richie, Sarah, Shane, Gemma, Rachel, Laura, Colin, Kevin, Neasa, and Wayne.

The people interviewed at the very end, who were approached so that the book would be more balanced, your time and effort is hugely appreciated. You didn't have to help, some of you I hadn't seen in years, it was extremely good of you. The friends who tried to recruit their friends, you know who you are – you are awesome!

Lastly to all my friends and family who helped: Hawwa, Claire, Deborah, Jean, Denise, Nick, Josue, Sajni, Sushila, Tawhid, Rhys, Chris, Oisin, Tony, Dan, Paul, Mark, Killian, Feidhlim, Mark, Roisin, Paul, Mossy, Eoin, Andy, David, Moira, Sean, Michael, Shaun, Conor, Georgie, Siofra, Shane, Sam, Michael, Giulia, Feidhlim, Rick, Niall, Waz, German, Lorcan, Niamh, Natasha, and Suzanne. Thank you for your time, advice, and willingness to help, it's massively appreciated.

TABLE OF CONTENTS

WHO THIS BOOK IS FOR

This book is predominantly aimed at school leavers, A level/university students, graduates, and young people in general.

However, as it is 100 people telling you about the early part of their careers, I think it is beneficial to lots of people. Those who work in careers, those who feel stuck in their career, those looking for inspiration, and especially parents who are trying to offer advice to their kids.

Ultimately, there is some tremendous life advice given regardless of your age, what stage you are at in your career or what you do for a living.

HOW TO USE THIS BOOK

A few points to note, this book is NOT:

- Research into what careers graduates end up working in.
- A showcase of every possible career path that is open to you.
- Magically going to tell you what your next career move should be.
- An academic paper trying to prove a theory.
- A detailed look at the professions talked about.

The aims of this book are to:

- Pique your interest in a career path so that you can research it more.
- Open your eyes to a new way of thinking about your career.
- To help you emulate the successes, and avoid the mistakes of an older generation.

This book can't tell you your next move. It can't research possible paths for you, and it can't get in touch with someone a few years your senior and ask them to go for a coffee. It is meant to be a reference guide to show how 100 young people have faced career decisions, and what they've learned from them.

The book is written in two parts:

Part 1: The Career Paths of 100 Graduates

Many of these people were very similar, 18-year-olds starting out in university. They each have made decisions that have led them down very different paths. Those decisions in your 20s are very important, as they will shape your whole life. The aim is for the reader to see a broad spectrum of the different paths available to them, and how peoples' paths ten years out from university can be very different from a few years after graduating.

Part 2: The Advice of 100 Graduates

This is the advice collated into recurring themes that kept coming up again and again. It's wisdom that has been learned the hard way, by doing difficult roles, by making mistakes, and by seeing other people do better in their careers. It's wisdom that you seldom get when you are navigating your way through your 20s.

Personally, I'm not a huge fan of my chosen career. I've tried very hard to figure out my possible career paths by researching extensively and asking people who are older than me. I'm just figuring out a lot of this stuff in my 30s and looking back I wish someone would have told me a few key things earlier. It would have saved me a lot of time and effort!

INTRODUCTION

Career paths are difficult to figure out, for everybody, not just young people. I know this because I have battled with a career in finance for the last ten years. I looked at my bosses, and their bosses over the years and really didn't want to be doing their jobs in 5-10 years.

I've also witnessed numerous friends/colleagues over the years have a tough time figuring out their career paths. Some of my peers are unhappy with their chosen paths and don't know how to change, don't want to change or simply have no idea what else they would do.

Problem:

I believe a lot of this unhappiness is down to a fundamental problem: **Young people are under-prepared for the working world.**

<u>University versus the working world:</u>

Looking back on my career, it struck me how different what I've done for the last ten years is to what I learned in school and university. I'm not sure students these days have a good grasp of how different the working world is versus the world of academia; I know my generation didn't.

<u>The advice young people get:</u>

Nobody tells you the important things you need to know, career-wise when you are in your teens and 20s. The advice you get is very much geared towards what you study in university. It's also very prescriptive, risk-averse advice given by an older generation whose working world is very different to the one for entry-level graduates. Universities do offer great careers services, but I'm not sure students get the most out of them.

<u>Lack of defined path:</u>

When you are in your final year, lots of you have no idea what you want to do. For the first time in your lives, there is no defined path. You must find your way at a time when you aren't that mature, you are still young and love to party, but you need money to support yourself. It can be an overwhelming time.

Impact:

Graduates' perceptions of the working world:

Lots of young people graduate thinking they deserve to get a good job and to earn a good salary. They are starting all over again, with little or no knowledge of how the working world works. The 100 interviewees had no idea of the industries, companies, and varied roles/careers paths available to them coming out of university.

A lot of the people interviewed also didn't realise the time and effort it would take to become a qualified lawyer, doctor, accountant, etc. They thought working hard to get a good degree would set them up to practice in their chosen profession. In reality, they had years of hard training/professional exams ahead of them. Often your degree doesn't qualify you to do a job; it's just to get your foot in the door of a company.

Poor decisions:

The people in this book will admit they didn't spend enough time researching possible career paths in their 20s. They spent all their time focused on their exams and neglected to seek career advice from people who had been in their shoes. Coming out of university, young people start applying for jobs; often they take the first one they get. If this is with a badly run company or a bad role, then this can set the tone for their whole career.

People getting stuck in careers they don't like:

Lots of my friends did degrees which they thought would lead to very enjoyable careers, only to embark on their chosen profession and not like it. It took a few years working for them to come to this realisation. By that time, they were accustomed to a certain standard of living and were reluctant to go back to university, take on more debt, be a poor student, and start all over again. They become stuck in a job they don't like, not wanting to take a risk and change paths.

Possible solutions:

<u>Demonstrate the difference between university and the workplace:</u>

This book shows you how different peoples' careers are to what they studied so that you can better prepare for the working world. To do this, I've sought out 100 of my friends across 16 different disciplines and asked them about their career paths. This way you can read a hundred different stories, see what they did in university, and how that relates to what they do now.

<u>Show the poor decisions that people have made:</u>

This book asks 100 people what they would have done differently and the advice they would give young people, so that you can easily navigate through the same pitfalls in your career. From reading the interviews, it is clear what regrets people have, and what they would try and change if they could go back. The advice given is with the benefit of hindsight, which is something often we can't tap into. It's really a collection of 100 peoples' career lessons learned for your benefit.

<u>Show the evolution of peoples' career paths:</u>

The book seeks to show young people how what you choose for a career in your 20s doesn't have to be what you do for the rest of your life. Lots of the 100 interviewees are doing something completely different than they were at university or even five years ago. Also, a lot of people who were unhappy have successfully switched careers. Seeing how these peoples' careers have unfolded is meant to pique your interest in different options and inspire you to research them.

PART 1: THE CAREER PATHS OF 100 GRADUATES

ACCOUNTING

What I knew before the interviews:

- It gives you great exposure to how different companies are run.
- It pays well compared to other professions, especially as you get more senior.
- The hours are not too bad, likely to be 9am - 5/6pm, in comparison to banking which is likely to be 9am – 7pm.
- It's not much fun compared to other departments in a company.

What I learned from the interviews:

- You don't need to necessarily go to university to have just as a successful career as someone who did. Wayne didn't go to university. He did his own thing travelling and working from ages 18-22. He is now one of the most successful people in a multinational media company.
- The big 4 really is a great foundation to build on. Conor worked in the same small department as me, and he pointed out that all the people who worked with us are doing very different careers now.

CAROLINE, 32

1. Accounting Lecturer, University, Riyadh, Saudi Arabia

What is your degree in?
Bachelor of Business (Accounting and Finance)
Master of Accounting
Ph.D. in Accounting

Why did you do the degree you did?
I was interested in a career in accounting as I liked accounting and business studies while doing my Leaving Certificate (A levels).

Why did you embark on the career you did?
I had always wanted to be a lecturer but wanted to get a professional qualification in accounting first. That way I would have at least worked in the area before I began to teach the subject.

When you came out of university did you seek advice from anyone?
Yes, I spoke to my lecturers in university and an accountant I knew from a small firm.

Did you know what your day-to-day role entailed starting off in your career?
I was blind about the importance of research. My job is very little about teaching in the classroom. It's predominately about research and getting publications. That is a full-time job so to add teaching on top of that makes the job extremely demanding.

What percentage of what you learned in university have you used in your day-to-day roles?
I would say 30%.

With the benefit of hindsight, if you were 18 again now would you do anything differently degree-wise?
No

What are the jobs you've done since graduating? And what have they entailed?

2013 – 2018

Programme Director/Lecturer, National University, Saudi Arabia

Managing a team of academics as well as lecturing on a range of accounting and finance modules.

2010 – 2013

Lecturer, National University, Dublin

Accounting lecturer at undergraduate/postgraduate level, specialising in the areas of financial accounting and auditing.

2007 – 2010

Audit Senior, Big 4 Accounting Firm, Dublin

Auditing and testing companies accounts to ensure they adhere to accounting standards.

What are the things you most like about your job, and the things you don't like?

Like:

1. Working with high profile clients in a very professional environment (big 4).
2. Contributing to the education of women in one of the most conservative counties in the world (Saudi Arabia).
3. Developing educational initiatives in Saudi Arabia to help raise the profile of women in local communities.

Don't like:

1. The unprofessionalism of working in the public sector.
2. The lack of opportunities to excel in an academic career, especially when you want to pursue interests other than research.
3. The lack of work-life balance in academia (the general perception that it is an easy job is very ill-informed)

Which would you prefer to work for: a small company or a big company, and why?

If I was going back into industry/practice I would prefer to work for a large company. In the big 4, there were endless opportunities to progress your career in different directions given the size of the organisation.

Have you worked long hours over the years?
Yes – consistently.

Have you had much fun over the years?
I loved working in the big 4 as the work environment and the people around me made it a very enjoyable experience. I also love teaching accounting. There is great satisfaction from helping students understand something that they were previously struggling with. Researching accounting topics can be interesting at times.

If you could start over and you were 22, but you know all you know now, would you do anything differently career-wise?
I would probably have tried to finish my Ph.D. sooner by taking a year out from work. I am still doing it (part-time) after four years, and am finding it very difficult given the demands of my job in the Middle East. This is stalling my progress in my career, but hopefully, it will be worth it when it's finished.

What career advice would you give a young person now?
Try lots of different things. Travel as much as you can and use every opportunity as a learning opportunity. Always give your best effort both in university and your job. Build a good network of contacts around you as this is invaluable in your future career.

What advice would you give a young person who wanted to do what you do?
- If you are thinking about a career in academia, be prepared to do a Ph.D. knowing the focus of your job will be on research even though you will also spend a lot of time in the classroom. The more experience you have the better you will be in the classroom. Don't make the move too quickly

if you are not sure, as it's much harder to move back into practice/industry after a few years away from it.
- That said, if you do move into this career early, make sure you have a realistic plan to get your Ph.D. started and finished as soon as possible. Your career in academia doesn't start until you are over that hurdle.
- You should also maintain strong links with industry as this is very important for an accounting lecturer. I do this by delivering professional training courses for the big 4, judging published accounts awards, and setting up the Irish business network in Saudi Arabia. I have enjoyed my academic career to date, but this has been mainly due to the experience of working in the Middle East. Hopefully when the Ph.D. is finished more opportunities will open up.

***

MARY, 32

2. Internal Audit Manager, Travel Company, Dublin

What is your degree in?
Bachelor of Commerce

Why did you do the degree you did?
I enjoyed studying business and accountancy in secondary school, and they were both subjects I did well in. Studying commerce seemed like the natural progression to make. I wasn't that interested in studying other courses. Maybe I hadn't carried out enough research into other areas at age 16/17?

Did you have any idea about an internal audit career path at the time?
- Having focused my studies in accountancy in the second and final year of my course, studying for a professional qualification seemed like the natural next step. I had gone through the 'milk round' with the big 4 accountancy firms. PwC appealed to me more due to how they described the varied work graduates would do, and the opportunities for working abroad.

- Beyond the graduate programme, I hadn't fully figured out what steer my career would or could take. This even took a few years after I completed the graduate programme to figure out and is something that constantly evolves.

When you came out of university did you seek advice from anyone?
- I spoke to some friends who had gone through the big 4 graduate programme route in different firms (both current employees and programme graduates).
- I spoke to two lecturers in my final year to discuss options and seek advice (accountancy lecturer and corporate strategy). Again, joining one of the big 4 firms to pursue an accountancy graduate programme seemed like a good route to follow with lots of career options.

Did you know what your day-to-day role entailed starting off in your career?
In truth, I felt a little blind starting off on the graduate programme. I wasn't aware of what exemptions I had from exams (if any) and was a little vague on what the day-to-day would involve. I would put this down to my lack of detailed research, I could have considered this more. My accountancy lecturer and friends had advised slightly on this – but mainly at a high level.

What percentage of what you learned in university have you used in your day-to-day roles?
I'm not sure if anything I learned in university I use in my day-to-day roles. The subjects I studied helped me understand a certain business language, so terms used didn't seem unfamiliar to me. Studying finance subjects also helped when it came to preparing for the professional accountancy exams.

With the benefit of hindsight, if you were 18 again now would you do anything differently degree-wise?

Yes, I would have done a language with my course and ideally have spent a year abroad on Erasmus*. Never underestimate the benefits of studying a language, and living and studying abroad.
(*The Erasmus Programme is a European Union (EU) student exchange programme.)

What are the jobs you've done since graduating? And what have they entailed?
2017 – 2018
Internal Audit Manager, Travel Company, Dublin
Planning and carrying out audits for the various departments of the company.
2014 – 2016
Senior Internal Auditor, Financial Trading Company, Dublin
Testing the companies' process and controls to ensure there were no weaknesses ahead of the external audit.
2013 – 2014
Financial Analyst, Telecoms Company, Dublin
Analysing sets of data and reporting to senior management
2010 – 2013
Senior Manager, Big 4 Auditing Firm, Dublin
Same as below with more responsibility for winning clients, budgets, and people management
2006 – 2009
Audit Senior, Big 4 Auditing Firm, Dublin
Inspecting and testing companies accounts to ensure there were no weaknesses.

What are the things you most like about your job, and the things you don't like?
Like:
1. The people I have worked with.
Good people you meet along the way will always make your job more enjoyable.
2. Travelling to interesting places for work, exciting projects.

3. Going to talks/external presentations and listening to inspiring professional speakers.

Don't like:
1. Timesheets.
2. Knowing you have challenging meetings with executives ahead is not something I look forward to – although there is a lot to learn from them.
3. Working weekends.

Which would you prefer to work for: a small company or a big company, and why?

- I was glad to have worked for a big company and would recommend it if the opportunity arose to anyone. A lot of excellent professional training is provided (whether the value of it is appreciated at the time I'm not sure). You get training in email writing, client engagement, time management, etc. The benefits of which you can particularly see when you move beyond practice and notice others who have not had the same level of training!
- When applying for certain roles, job descriptions would often describe seeking a candidate who was big 4 trained. This immediately gives you an advantage over the other candidates. The chances are future employers will have connections with the big 4 firm you trained in.
- Study leave is also very generous with big 4 firms when it comes to professional exams. Smaller firms that cannot afford to give more time off than the minimum standard as they don't have the staff. This is very helpful and allows for ample time to prepare for exams.
- I had the opportunity to work on several foreign secondments in great cities (San Francisco, New York and L.A.). They were opportunities I don't think would have been possible in a smaller practice.
- Above all, the greatest benefit for me was meeting lots of other graduates. Joining the programme felt like an extension of university, starting with nearly 200 others around the same age. The social life was great, and I got to know lots of people, many of which I am still great friends with today!

- In relation to accountancy specifically, I always felt there was a great benefit to working in a small company. You get to really understand the theory of what was being studied and put it into practice. I didn't always feel like what we studied we put into practice in our day-to-day roles in the big 4.

Have you worked long hours over the years?
- Yes. It was made clear to me on day one of joining the programme that there would be a busy season and I would be expected to work overtime and long hours. This didn't bother me too much as in my case it wasn't always entirely excessive, and once I was prepared for it, it was manageable. Overtime hours had to be worked to earn study leave for exams, which seemed fair. Anything in excess of study leave requirements could be used as annual leave which was great as I could take extended time off.
- When I worked in the States on one secondment, I worked on average 80 hours a week for nearly two and a half months. (working weekends and until 2am was standard).
- Since leaving practice, I haven't worked particularly long hours continuously. It was one of the first things I think you notice when you start working in industry – people, in general, work standard hours. When people come out of graduate programmes the first question they often ask each other is 'what are the hours like?'. It seems ingrained in people that hours are excessively long in all companies which is not the case.

Have you had much fun over the years?
I've enjoyed it, but that is largely down to the people I have been lucky to work with, that generally make the job fun. I couldn't necessarily say the job is always fun. My jobs have certainly been interesting (and boring) over the years. I think it depends on what you are working on that determines if something is fun/enjoyable/interesting.

If you could start over and you were 22, but you know all you know now, would you do anything differently career-wise?

I don't think I would change anything. I was happy with the decisions I made. I would advise not to be afraid to communicate to your manager/mentor what you are looking for in your career (roles /promotions you want). Don't assume that employers will always know or notice that this is what you want. Without saying it explicitly – they may not know. Don't be afraid of self-promotion.

What career advice would you give a young person now?

- Enjoy every summer off that you have. You are unlikely to get the time back again once you start working, go away every summer you can, live in a different city/country and enjoy it. Depending on the role you may want to spend a summer working in a field you are interested in to get experience in it, although I think I would avoid that. Have the fun jobs working in bars and beach clubs when you are young; you will be working in an office for long enough.
- Get involved in extra-curricular activities in university. Join clubs, even if you are joining them by yourself, get involved and meet as many people as you can.
- Don't think or worry that whatever decision you make out of university you are bound to that for the rest of your life. It can seem daunting that you must make a very definite decision on your next steps out of university. However, it does not mean that is it for the rest of your working years. I have seen plenty of friends who have gone through graduate programmes, obtained professional qualifications and then change career completely after. They say most people change their career at least four or five times in their working life.

What advice would you give a young person who wanted to do what you do?

- The internal audit career path is a very sociable role. A lot of it involves sitting and meeting with people across an entire organisation right up to senior management and executives. Being able to communicate with people without being disruptive to their day job allows you to build good relationships across the business.

- If you are unsure of what your next career step is the internal audit career path is a great way to learn about all areas of an organisation. It helps you understand what is involved in the different roles of an organisation and the work can be quite varied. It allows you to see if there are areas you want to work in further or may not be interested in. You get an opportunity to talk to directors who are over those areas which gives you an added in if you want to pursue your career in a different direction.

***

LOUISE, 30

3. Audit Manager, Big 4 Accounting Firm, Dublin

What is your degree in?
Bachelor of Accounting and Finance
Master of Accounting

Why did you do the degree you did?
I liked maths and accounting in school and wanted to become an accountant.

When you came out of university did you seek advice from anyone?
No, not until I came out of the graduate programme in the big 4 firm. I did the 'milk rounds' in university and followed the path that all graduates do. Once I became qualified, that is when I sought advice and moved departments in the big 4 firm.

Did you know what your day-to-day role entailed starting off in your career?
I had a little insight as my cousin did it too but I took a different route to her so was a little bit blind in that regard.

What percentage of what you learned in university have you used in your day-to-day roles?
30%.

With the benefit of hindsight, if you were 18 again now would you do anything differently degree-wise?
I possibly would have gone into primary school teaching.

What are the jobs you've done since graduating? And what have they entailed?
2015 – 2018
Audit Manager, Big 4 Accounting Firm, Dublin
Responsible for winning new clients, ensuring audits are done on time and to budget.
2011 – 2014
Audit Senior, Big 4 Firm, Dublin
Looking for weaknesses in companies' internal financial controls and processes.

What are the things you most like about your job, and the things you don't like?
Like:
1. On the job learning – have learned a lot about different clients and industry.
2. Have a lot of responsibility and have progressed in my career and enjoy my current role.
3. Enjoyed working with the people I know.

Don't like:
1. I didn't enjoy the late nights (until 2/3am) and weekends doing audit for four years (that came with a lot of pressure).
2. Studying for my final exams and working during the busy season, it is definitely a tough year.
3. Struggling to come up with a third – that must be a good sign?

Which would you prefer to work for: a small company or a big company, and why?
I'd prefer working for a big company for several reasons:

1. There is scope to gain experience in other areas of the firm and change career paths.
2. There is a good support network in that there will be someone who can help and will have experience in different areas.
3. You meet a lot of people – I would get bored working with the same people all the time if it is a very small team.
4. There are international secondments you can apply for.
5. Big firms are usually well known by several people, and the experience you gain is invaluable to your career.
6. Although people say big firms/big 4 work people to the ground, it is not necessarily true. People in smaller companies face the same thing. I feel that big firms recognise this and there are social events to say thanks and meet colleagues and network.

Have you worked long hours over the years?

I would have worked long hours before I graduated when I was in audit. After I moved departments I haven't worked the same long hours.

Have you had much fun over the years?

I have worked in risk assurance for the last 2 years and I do enjoy it. I feel like I have learned a lot and I can see where I've added value to clients which is rewarding. Also, we do have a lot of social events as a department which are always great fun.

If you could start over and you were 22, but you know all you know now, would you do anything differently career-wise?

If I had to answer this just finishing my graduate programme and finishing my final exams, I would have said I would go into teaching and not do this again. Now that it is all behind me I probably wouldn't change as my day differs each day which I enjoy and gives me a challenge.

What career advice would you give a young person now?

- Talk to people before you decide what you want to do.
- Don't worry and put yourself under necessary pressure to pick the right career (particularly when you're 18 and don't know what you want to do).

There are ways to get where you want. I am a big believer in things happening for a reason. In my experience, even when people are set up in their career, they still may not know what they want to do, so it is ok not to know what you want to do.
- Also, try and pick something you enjoy.

What advice would you give a young person who wanted to do what you do?
Know what you are getting yourself into. The exams can be tough so if you want to become an accountant, talk to people first. It can be a long road to become qualified but it is worth investing in.

***

MOIRA, 32

4. Director, Big 4 Accounting Firm, Dublin

What is your degree in?
Bachelor of Commerce

Why did you do the degree you did?
My sister had also done commerce. To be honest, I didn't think much about it at that point all I wanted was a course to get me into university and to Dublin.

Why did you embark on the career you did?
I liked numbers - which is funny because it's a very small part of my role now.

When you came out of university did you seek advice from anyone?
Not really, I just followed what the others in my class were doing ... it was almost a three-step process - commerce - accounting - big 4! Lucky for me as I probably wouldn't have got there otherwise!

Did you know what your day-to-day role entailed starting off in your career?
Not a clue, and to be honest for the first three years I was still clueless!

What percentage of what you learned in university have you used in your day-to-day roles?
I only use the soft skills I learned – the ability to get on with people, build relationships, etc., basically nothing academic.

With the benefit of hindsight, if you were 18 again now would you do anything differently degree-wise?
I would have chosen a longer degree and opted to do a Masters afterwards. I think I'd still stay in business and possibly specialised in tax.

What are the jobs you've done since graduating? And what have they entailed?
2004 – 2018
Audit Junior rising to Director, Big 4 Accounting Firm, Dublin
Responsible for attracting new business, managing audits from start to finish.

What are the things you most like about your job, and the things you don't like?
Like:
1. The people side of things.
2. Flexibility.
3. The social side.

Don't like:
1. Feeling under appreciated.
2. Long hours.
3. Pressure and what it does to you.

Which would you prefer to work for: a small company or a big company, and why?
I'd prefer a big company; they have more money to invest in you and your career. I also think that being a small fish in a well-known big pond is better than being a big fish in a pond no one knows about!

Have you worked long hours over the years?
Yes, 24-hour days at times, weekends, etc. I don't do them as much now.

Have you had much fun over the years?
The people side is fun. You work with people all day every day, the more senior you get it becomes all about people management.

If you could start over and you were 22, but you know all you know now, would you do anything differently career-wise?
I would have probably done tax.

What career advice would you give a young person now?
- Establish what your key goals in life are, happiness, health, success, power, money, family. Pick your top three and choose a career that will enable you to achieve those. If it's success, define what success is to you and work back as to how to get there. Don't think about the in-between; it will work itself out.
- Also, spend as long as you can in university and travel the world!

What advice would you give a young person who wanted to do what you do?
Do a couple of internships, look at the senior people in the organisation and ask yourself if you see yourself doing what they do. If the answer is yes, keep your eye on the prize and don't sweat the small stuff! If not, move on!

***

PAUL, 35

5. Head of Finance, Media Company, London

What is your degree in?
Bachelor of Accounting

Why did you do the degree you did?
In New Zealand where I grew up, you must decide what you want to do for a career and then study that at university. I was 17 and had to choose. I knew I didn't want to be a builder or a teacher which is what my parents were. I was reasonably good at accounting and knew it paid well, so that's the career I picked.

When you came out of university did you seek advice from anyone?
Before I went to university, I spoke to a career guidance counsellor. I did a test, it turned out I was good with numbers, and that accounting would have been a good career for me.

Did you know what your day-to-day role entailed starting off in your career?
No, I just imagined you were behind a computer crunching numbers for some company. I had no idea what it entailed.

What percentage of what you learned in university have you used in your day-to-day roles?
10% - I still use my debits and credits but nothing else.

With the benefit of hindsight, if you were 18 again now would you do anything differently degree-wise?
I would have tried to pursue a different option and then have accounting in reserve.

What are the jobs you've done since graduating? And what have they entailed?
2016 – 2018

Head of Finance, Media Company, London
Day-to-day accounting, cashflow, budgeting, project analysis, strategic decisions.
2014 – 2015
Financial Controller/Interim CFO, Media Company, London
From board level decisions to managing a team of financial accountants
2011 – 2014
Finance Manager, International Music Company, London
Being involved in a project to carve up a global music company and sell it to competitors.
2009 – 2010
Finance Manager, Energy Company, New Zealand
Preparing statutory accounts, month end reporting, budgeting, etc.
2004 – 2009
Audit Senior, Big 4 Accounting Firm, New Zealand
Planning and carrying out audits of companies in various industries.

What are the things you most like about your job, and the things you don't like?
Like:
1. Some of the people I've worked with.
The quality of people you have around you is really important.
2. The travel when I was in audit.
I got to go to Ireland, Australia, and the Pacific Islands.
3. The career development that working in finance offers.
4. The money, it gives me a good lifestyle.

Don't like:
1. Being an accountant – it's not the most exciting job in the world. If you can cut through the repetitive financial accounting it can be cool.
2. The routine – once you have finalised the monthly accounts, you must do it all over again.
3. Some of the people that I've met not acting with integrity. They will lie and do anything to get ahead of you, that can be a pain.

Which would you prefer to work for: a small company or a big company, and why?

I would say a small company. In a small company, you get much more visibility of how the business works. You get much more exposure to everyone in the company. The processes in a small company aren't going to be as good. However, I enjoy identifying where the problems are, fixing them and adding real value.

Have you worked long hours over the years?

I very rarely work crazy hours. In the big 4 it was long hours, and during month end now it can be long hours.

If you could start over and you were 22, but you know all you know now, would you do anything differently career-wise?

- Sometimes I think what would have happened if I didn't leave the big 4, would I be an audit partner now?
- I would be more aware of how important relationships are. I would have tried to keep in touch with people, once you leave a company it's very easy to fall out of contact with someone. I've worked with some amazing people in the past, yet I can't pick up the phone to them and ask them for advice now, which is a real shame.

What career advice would you give a young person now?

- I think the key thing these days is to have other interests. Be the treasurer of your sports club, organise charity events. I think you should have other things to differentiate your CV coming out of university.
- I would say try and get into a big 4 firm; it sets your career apart from your peers.
- Don't be afraid to take a chance to get where you want to go. Too many people fear making a change and need the job security. I've changed jobs as I found the opportunities. I've had five or six different jobs in the last 10 years, that's why I have such great experience on my CV.
- One thing I've learned through the years is that you are one of the smartest people in the room. If you don't know the answer, then people

more senior than you probably don't either, it's just they are better at bluffing than you. It's all about being confident and believing in yourself.

***

WAYNE, 33

6. Financial Controller, Media Company, London

What is your degree in?
N/A

Why did you embark on the career you did?
Once I finished my A levels, I couldn't figure out whether I wanted to go to university or not. I thought about it, and the only reason I wanted to go to university was to enjoy myself. I thought I could do that myself by working and doing some travelling. So, I worked in a few office jobs on temp contracts and did some travelling for a few years!

Did you find you had a head-start on graduates when they came out of university?
- I found it straightforward to get my first permanent job in London as I had a lot of experience compared to my peers.
- I was training the new graduates up, as I had more experience. They had more pure accounting experience coming from their degrees, but you don't use much of that in the working world.

Would you be an advocate of taking a year out?
- I think it might be a different world now, maybe you need a degree to get your foot in the door of a company, but in any role, you will just learn on the job.
- My cousin secured a local job in a local accounting firm when she was 17 and still in school. It didn't matter what A levels she got, as she had the job lined up already. She's already passed two professional exams and she is only turning 19! When she is 21, she will have passed her professional accountancy exams - she will be approximately four years

ahead of her peers. This may be a very rare case; you would need to be certain that you want to be an Accountant if you go down that path.
- The negative of the gap year is you might end up doing nothing at all.
- From my point of view, I would have been going to university for the wrong reasons. I would have scraped a pass but I wouldn't have excelled. I also didn't know what course to do - I didn't have a clue!

When you came out of university did you seek advice from anyone?
My sister did her professional accountancy (ACCA) exams, she had a good lifestyle and seemed to be doing well. Also, working with numbers appealed to me, and she gave me some good advice.

Did you know what your day-to-day role entailed starting off in your career?
- If I had my time again, I think I might have gone into insurance. I have some friends working in it, and they seem to have a nice life. They get to travel, there is a big social side, and the money is very good.
- You can also do a professional qualification with the Chartered Insurance Institute (ACII). I would maybe have explored that route if I knew about it, I fell into accounting rather than having a keen interest. I don't think they advise you in school as to what your options really are.

What are the jobs you've done since graduating? And what have they entailed?
2016 – 2018
Financial Controller, Media Company, London
Responsible for ensuring the statutory accounts are prepared correctly with no audit issues.
2013 – 2015
Finance Manager, International Media Company, London
Controlling costs of the charitable foundation of the company.
Working with the programme managers on their spending/forecasting.
2011 – 2013
Corporate Controller, International Media Company, London

Ensuring month end processes and year-end accounts were correct for the external Auditors.

2005 – 2011

Financial Accountant, International Property Company, London

Accounts payable clerk, statutory accounts, tax returns.

What are the things you most like about your job, and the things you don't like?

Like:

1. The variety of my role. I'm responsible for quite a big team: payroll, tax, accounts payable and involved with different regions around the world.
2. The numbers and analytical side of it, projecting what sales/costs are going to be.
3. The number of options you have working in finance. You can go down different routes: tax, credit control, management accounting, financial accounting.

Don't like:

1. Nothing really, I enjoy working in finance.

Which would you prefer to work for: a small company or a big company, and why?

- A big company is the best in terms of career progression. However, it's key to have a good team around you, as if you don't it's easy to get isolated in your little area of the company.
- In a small company the atmosphere is brilliant, everyone knows everyone. You feel a lot more valued as part of a 5-man team than as part of a 150-man team. You also get more exposure and experience in a small company.

Have you worked long hours over the years?

The company I work for now has a good work-life balance. My hours are 9–5, and I can work a couple of days from home which is good.

Have you had much fun over the years?

Yes, lots of fun, all the companies (real estate, media) I've worked in have had a good social side. Lots of young people, lots of work nights out, free bars, great Christmas parties, etc. The culture of the company is important.

What career advice would you give a young person now?

- You need to decide what area you are going to go into. Go into an area where you can study for professional exams. That way even if you are not getting a promotion through work, you can leverage the qualifications you are doing outside work.
- If you are not progressing or not getting support, don't just sit in a job, don't be scared to move. Once you get more senior it's harder to jump around, but when you are young it's much easier. I'd advise moving around when you are in your 20s until you find a company that you feel valued in, then stay there and work your way up.
- Also, decide if you want to work in the public or private sector as they are very different.

What advice would you give a young person who wanted to do what you do?

I'd think hard before you decide on going down the audit route, it seems to be very long hours, and not enjoyable. I'd go the route I went down, go straight into a company and then do your professional exams.

BUSINESS OWNER/ENTREPRENEUR

What I knew before the interviews:

When I thought of entrepreneurs, I always thought of older people with established and well-known businesses. It turns out I know quite a few. I always thought setting up your own business was too hard, too risky, and not for me, that I was better off in the comfort of a big company.

What I learned from the interviews:

- You are your own boss and can reap the rewards of your hard work.
- There can be a lack of support, and it can be difficult to delegate.
- The pay can vary, some do very well, others struggle to break even.
- You are never off the clock.
- It sounds like a lot of fun, doing something you are passionate about.
- All the people interviewed are happy to step out of their comfort zone.
- It can be quite stressful as the business depends on you.
- The interviews inspired me to think differently about my career. If these guys can make a go of their own business, why can't I?

BRIAN, 35

7. Owner, Recruitment Company, London

What is your degree in?
Bachelor of Marketing
Master of Marketing

Why did you do the degree you did?
I had a passion for marketing. The career guidance counsellor wasn't good, he should have told me if I was interested in marketing to do psychology.

What percentage of what you learned in university have you used in your day-to-day roles?
Quite a high percentage I would say - presentation skills are a big thing that I use on a day-to-day basis, networking skills, reading people, etc.

Why did you embark on the career you did?
I worked for a fair-trade company in Edinburgh, at the time it was the dotcom boom. Then I did well at a computer company in sales but was told I'd have to take a €20k pay reduction to get into marketing.

Did you know what you wanted to do career-wise?
Yes, I always knew I wanted to do some sort of marketing.

If you could start over and you were 22, but you know all you know now, would you do anything differently career-wise?
As I work in financial recruitment, I would have become an accountant. However, it's very hard to go back the later you go on in life, as you have different commitments. I would do a professional qualification; you've got that stamp that will always be behind you.

What are the jobs you've done since graduating? And what have they entailed?
2011 – 2018

Owner, Recruitment Company, London
Helping people find their ideal jobs.
2003 - 2011
Manager, Recruitment Company, London
Sourcing candidates for roles.
2002 – 2003
Sales Consultant, Dublin
Entry level sales position.

What are the things you most like about your job, and the things you don't like?
Like:
1. The autonomy.
2. The opportunity to work with who I want, when I want, how I want.
3. The diversity of my role.

Don't like:
1. Working on your own can be tough, you can't bounce ideas of people.
2. The uncertainty of the market.

Have you worked long hours over the years?
8am - 6/7pm would be the standard. I'm technically never off the clock.

Have you had much fun over the years?
Yes, I've worked with Coke, FA, BBC, Olympics, etc.

Which would you prefer to work for: a small company or a big company, and why?
- It's great to start out in a big company. It teaches you a huge amount, you get a ready-made support network.
- A lot comes down to the individual; if you want more autonomy, you will like working with a small company.
- I believe there is a time and a place for everything, you can switch and work in both.

What career advice would you give a young person now?
- Networking is key, if you've got a good work ethic and you network well, align yourself to someone who is going places.
- Always hire someone who is better than you.

What advice would you give a young person who wanted to do what you do?
Treat everybody the way you'd want to be treated, answer every call, etc.

***

COLIN, 31

8. Managing Director, Bespoke Furniture Company, London

What is your degree in?
Bachelor of Science (Furniture Technology)
Master of Design and Manufacturing Management

Why did you do the degree you did?
I just had an interest in furniture when I was younger. I would have been making bits of furniture at home when I was young, so it was a natural path to take.

Did you know what your day-to-day role entailed starting off in your career?
For my work placements, I did two stints in furniture workshops in America. So yes, I knew what was involved, those placements were with big established companies, so you got to see what they did, what they didn't do.

What percentage of what you learned in university have you used in your day-to-day roles?
60% - the degree was geared to what I do now for a living.

With the benefit of hindsight, if you were 18 again now would you do anything differently degree-wise?

I thought about maybe becoming an architect, but now that I've started up on my own and it's all going well, I wouldn't change.

What are the jobs you've done since graduating? And what have they entailed?

2015 – 2018

Managing Director, Bespoke Furniture Company, London

Responsible for winning new work, managing jobs, but also doing the accounts, and hiring and firing.

2010 – 2015

Operations Manager, Joinery Company, London

In charge of all jobs, pricing, everything from the design right through to implementation.

2007 – 2009

Workshop Manager, Furniture Making Company, London

Managing various furniture making jobs/cabinet maker.

What are the things you most like about your job, and the things you don't like?

Like:

1. I love the whole process of progression, new roles, more responsibility.
2. Seeing what you can achieve on your own.
3. Meeting new clients. The sense of achievement you get out of winning work, and getting repeat work, as they trust you.

Don't like:

1. People management is the hardest part of my job. I've had to reduce peoples' wages because they are not living up to my expectations, that can be tough. You can tell people what to do, but you nearly have to write it down for them.

Have you worked long hours over the years?

7am – 7pm in my own company, but when I was working for someone else hours were 8am – 4pm.

If you could start over and you were 22, but you know all you know now, would you do anything differently career-wise?
I wouldn't because it has all worked out ok! I think I went out on my own at the right time. If I went out on my own five years ago, I would not have had the contacts. Also, if you are too young starting out people wouldn't trust you with big projects.

What advice would you give a young person trying to start their own business?
Travel as much as you can before you set it up, as having your own business really ties you down. If you are thinking about setting up on your own and have the funds to do it, just do it, don't hesitate - you will learn so much even if you fail.

What advice would you give a young person who wanted to do what you do?
You need to know what you are doing. It's a specialised role, you have to be interested in it.

Was doing your Masters worthwhile in hindsight?
Nothing I learned in my Masters massively benefitted me. The only thing is it looks good on your CV, especially when you are trying to win work. It gives prospective clients that bit more confidence in you.

***

COLM, 35

9. Hostel Owner, Cusco, Peru

What is your degree in?
Bachelor of Business
Master of Accounting

Why did you do the degree you did?
It was broad, I felt that I was blind going into the next step after university, so I thought it'd be wise to keep it general.

When you came out of university did you seek advice from anyone?
I went to two uncles - one who worked in the bank, the other one prepped people for interviews. They gave me good advice, one of them was pushing me down the accounting road. He told me once you get into the big 4 you are sorted, your experience won't be as complete but ultimately, you will get better jobs.

Did you know what your day-to-day role entailed starting off in your career?
I wasn't completely blind because of the Masters. If I went into the big 4 from my degree, I would have been. Like any new job, I found it exciting, I didn't find it an eye-opener. I found that there were so many different departments in a big 4 firm - tax, consultancy, business development. I was just a tiny part of it all.

Why did you embark on the career you did?
I had an idea I wanted to go down the accounting route, it was either marketing or accounting. I did the Masters to make the professional exams easier. I'm delighted that I did it that way, I knew I might struggle working and studying, but that I could get through the final four exams.

What percentage of what you learned in university have you used in your day-to-day roles?
- What I learned in the degree was more applicable to setting up my own business. The cost accounting came in very useful; it was real accounting, i.e. staff costs, food costs, drink costs, etc.
- I did company law basics in university as well, which gave me a little bit more confidence that you are not diving into something completely new. It all comes down to self-belief, the degree gave me the confidence that I could handle the marketing, accounting, and people management.

With the benefit of hindsight, if you were 18 again now would you do anything differently degree-wise?

- No, but if I were to go back, I'd love to have a go at physiotherapy. I was always fascinated with sports injuries, and how the body worked in general, but I couldn't get the results for it in my Leaving Certificate (A levels). You could do physio through other ways, i.e. switching degrees, but I wasn't prepared to do that at the time.
- I couldn't have asked to do any better out of my degree, to be honest.

What are the jobs you've done since graduating? And what have they entailed?

2011 – 2018

Hostel/Bar/Entrepreneur, Peru

Running a 180-bed hostel, bar, and travel agent in Cusco, Peru

2005 – 2009

Audit Assistant Manager, Big 4 Firm, Ireland

Testing processes and inspecting accounts of companies across various industries.

What are the things you most like about your job, and the things you don't like?

1) The big 4

Like:

1. The big 4 was a young vibrant, extension of university. There were 500 people between ages of 22 and 25, everyone was young, and at a similar stage of their lives – it was great!
2. The opportunities that came from working with the big 4, the second move after you left the firm was never going to be difficult.
3. How they treated the staff, there were lots of nights out, weekends away, etc.
4. I made some lifelong friends out of the big 4.

Don't like:

1. The work. I did it because it was a job, I thought you just had to do it, turns out you can love your work, I didn't know that at the time.

2) Hostel

Like:

1. Helping people, I was the main point of contact for everybody. If people lost their bank card, I'd give them my own money. People were a long way from home, I was there to say 'don't worry we can figure it out'.
2. I was proud of Cusco and proud of the hostel – try this food, have a look at that view. It was easy, I used to love my job – you'd have the same 180 beds, but 180 different personalities, and different problems with that. When they look back on their time away, I wanted Cusco to be the highlight of their trip
3. I learned so much about the Peruvian culture, by the fourth year there they all loved me, you had to integrate into the culture.

Don't like:

1. The corruption - it was easy to get rid of as you paid everyone off but it was a hassle.
2. The massive drugs scene - it was an uphill battle every week to keep the hostel clean.
3. I had a bit of a rogue partner; she made me feel a bit isolated being a foreigner.

Have you worked long hours over the years?

- When I was running the hostel - I had one day off a week – every Sunday. Mon to Sat – you were talking 9am to 2am. You must meet everyone at check-in, you want to be there at check-out, as you are the face of the hostel. Then you want to be there for the bar activities at night. The last two years I had a good manager, so my hours were more than 9am – 6pm.

Have you had much fun over the years?

- It was the best time of my life - I didn't see it as work. My day was doing interviews, emails, accounts, I was helping people having the time of their life. I'd never managed a team of chefs, cleaners, receptionists, I found managing the whole project fantastic!

If you could start over and you were 22, but you know all you know now, would you do anything differently career-wise?

- Not sure I would do too much different, I always wanted a degree, I always wanted a professional qualification, I always wanted to have a bar! You talk about people who find something they love, but it doesn't pay well, I found both!

What career advice would you give a young person now?

Don't be afraid, get your qualification, you can end up in the most unexpected of jobs from that. Just because you studied social work or accounting, doesn't mean you are going to be a social worker or an accountant.

What advice would you give a young person who wanted to do what you do?

- Get a solicitor, make sure all the contracts are water tight, and correct from the start, if someone can just take it away from you easily then what's the point?
- Take a loan, and just do it. Don't leave it behind, don't be 50 years of age with regrets. You can always do it if you want it bad enough – just look at me!

Which gets you further in a career – knowing people or being good at your job?

Knowing people only gets you so far, but it won't last, being good at your job will stand the test of time. Nobody suffers fools too long.

What are the pros and cons of living and working abroad?

Pros:

1. You are out chasing the world.
2. You are experiencing new cultures, new people, new perspectives. You get to spend time out there, immerse yourself in the culture.
3. You are developing yourself; it's great to get out and see what's there.

Cons:

1. You are far away from your family. You are not in the same circle of friends anymore.
2. You become distant from what you believe are the things you miss. Then you realise you don't actually miss them.
3. Your friends move on and they are not there when you move back.

***

FEARGHAL, 34

10. Entrepreneur, Various Start-ups, Los Angeles

What is your degree in?
Bachelor of Arts (Management Science and Information Systems)

Why did you do the degree you did?
I was good at maths and interested in business, I thought it was a good mix of the two. The other commerce courses didn't really appeal to me. It was tough to get into as well, so it sounded a good course to do.

Did you know what you wanted to do career-wise?
No, I had no idea, I just wanted to keep my options open, the degree did that for me.

Why did you embark on the career you did?
My dad was an accountant. He was very supportive of me doing an accounting qualification. It is a great qualification to have, you have job security for life, and you can work in any country in the world. I thought it was a good way of getting exposure to big companies, which looking back might not have been the case. In hindsight, the learning curve was shallow, I think other jobs you might learn more and learn faster.

With the benefit of hindsight, if you were 18 again now would you do anything differently degree-wise?
I suppose my degree choice has worked out well – I've learned some cool stuff, and it has opened doors for me. However, I do think maybe I should have done a more established traditional degree, I think

engineering would open as many if not more doors. If you have good results on your CV in engineering, people recognise it around the world. With management science, people don't really know how hard it was. You learn the business/role on the job anyway.

Did you know what your day-to-day role entailed starting off in your career?

I was completely blind, even three or four months into my first job, I didn't really know what an auditor did. It was quite a slow progression, as you are molly coddled a little bit coming in from university.

When you came out of university did you seek advice from anyone?

No, no advice from people in university. In my final year, I knew some guys one year ahead of me, and they spoke well about the big 4 and said it was good fun.

What are the jobs you've done since graduating? And what have they entailed?

2014 – 2018

Entrepreneur, Various Start-Ups, Los Angeles

Designing/building the platform, attracting new customers, and marketing for two of my own start-up companies.

2011 – 2014

Market Risk Analyst, Global Bank, New York

Assessing whether the bank is at risk of losing a lot of money with any of the trades that it does every day.

2006 – 2011

Auditor, Big 4 Accounting Firm, Dublin

Inspecting companies financial accounts to ensure that they are doing everything as they should be.

What are the things you most like about your job, and the things you don't like?

Like:

1. Finance – getting to know new people.

2. Start-up – flexibility, I can work when I want without having to get permission from a manager.
3. Start-up – you are working for yourself and see all the rewards of your work.

Don't like:
1. Start-up – you are on your own, it's a bit suffocating.
2. Start-up – you are never off the clock, always reacting to issues and stuff that inevitably goes wrong.
3. Banking – there are difficult characters and can be tension between departments. People might not be that helpful. The culture is very different in banking.
4. Banking – I was in operations, you are in a no-win situation, people expect things to run smoothly. Inevitably things will go wrong, and that's when people will start to know about you. It's a thankless task.
5. Big 4 – learning curve was shallow, compared to some of my friends who were thrown in the deep-end, I think that's the best way to learn.

Have you worked long hours over the years?
- I was lucky; it depends on your team. In the big 4 firm, I worked in, some friends of mine were nailed with long hours. I think you need to make it clear you need to be gone by 8pm, come in early to make up for it, etc.
- Banking was a standard 8am - 7pm.
- Start-ups: you are never really off the clock, but when it's your baby you don't mind putting in the hours. Even though its long hours I think you enjoy it more and you can basically work from anywhere. You can travel and work almost full time if you want!

Have you had much fun over the years?
Yeah good fun, in the big 4 firm and banking, in start-ups not so much.

Which would you prefer to work for: a small company or a big company, and why?

- Starting off I think you should go big as you learn how to do things well, get good training and make loads of contacts/friends. However now I would lean more towards a medium-sized company, or a quick moving, innovative company where you can make a change and see it happen. With the big banks, things stay broken for years.
- I have friends who work for smaller companies where they make suggestions and see it implemented quickly which is great.

If you could start over and you were 22, but you know all you know now, would you do anything differently career-wise?
- The accounting qualification has given me a huge amount of options. However, management consultancy would have been better to see how companies make money, instead of auditing where you don't get any insight into that.
- I always think what if I did investment banking straight out of university. At the time, I was told if you get a good accounting qualification you can then join a big investment bank and get a great job, which is not the case. If you get a good degree in university, you should just apply straight off to the big banks.

What career advice would you give a young person now?
Try to keep your options open, but that has downsides, I tried to keep my options open, even now, but at some point, you need to pick a route and go for it. Don't worry; there are lots of different routes. Do well at school and university, and always keep an eye out for opportunities.

What advice would you give a young person who wanted to do what you do?
- I'd advise them to tell as many people as possible about their idea. Get as much feedback as possible. Some guys are scared to tell people for fear they will steal it, that will never happen. People will be very honest with you, as you might think it's the best idea in the world, but people will challenge it and tell you whether they agree or not.
- Then do a lot of planning before you spend a penny on it; what's your plan to market? How much will it cost? How are you going to do it? etc.,

doesn't have to be fancy graphs, just simple planning, then weigh up the pros and cons, if you think it all makes sense, just do it. I know people who have ideas for three to four years and never do anything about it.

Which gets you further in a career – knowing people or being good at your job?
Knowing people, not necessarily the old boy's network. Grow your network at work, get to know the managers, and even your peers. They will all move on after a few years and get cool roles in different companies which can open doors for you.

***

FREYA, 29

11. Founder, Hat Making Company, Dublin

What is your degree in?
Diploma in Dress Design

Why did you do the degree you did?
Didn't get great results in my A levels and didn't know what else to do!

Why did you embark on the career you did?
I went to London to work in fashion because there was a bigger market for my skills, and I got a job as a fashion intern for one and a half years.

With the benefit of hindsight, if you were 18 again now would you do anything differently degree-wise?
I would want to go to a bigger university, as the college I went to was just 30 girls, everyone just came in, did their work and went home again. With a bigger university, I would have got to know more people and benefitted from a wider network.

When you came out of university did you seek advice from anyone?
Yes, I worked with a company in Ireland and asked people for advice there. I had a fair idea of what working in fashion was about.

What percentage of what you learned in university have you used in your day-to-day roles?
I have used an awful lot of it. My course was great for learning technical and dress making skills. However, if I went to a bigger university, I would have had that and I would have got to know a network of people.

Was doing the internship worthwhile?
Most definitely, I wouldn't have got the job without the internship and working for free for six months.

What are the jobs you've done since graduating? And what have they entailed?
2017 – 2018
Creative Director, Hat Making Company, Dublin
Designing, making and selling hats.
2012 – 2016
Fashion Production Manager, Clothing Company, London
I supplied stores with the clothes we made.
2009 - 2011
Studio Assistant (Intern), Various Fashion Companies, London
Assisting with clothes production.

What are the things you most like about your job, and the things you don't like?
Like:
1. Working with people.
2. Working with my hands, fabrics, and textiles.
3. Working for luxury brands, which is exciting.

Don't like:
1. The low pay.
2. You could be replaced very easily.
3. The routine, I hated having to go to the same place 9-5 every day.

Have you worked long hours over the years?
Very long hours, oh my god, easily 9am – 8pm every day.

Have you had much fun over the years?
Yes, it was still fun because it was creative, there were lots of perks, i.e. going to Paris Fashion Week.

Is fashion a very competitive industry?
Yes, there is lots of bitchiness and lots of standing on people's toes to get ahead. I worked with lots of women; there are hardly any guys.

Which would you prefer to work for: a small company or a big company, and why?
A small company, as you get exposure to so much more, and you feel more important and valued.

If you could start over and you were 22, but you know all you know now, would you do anything differently career-wise?
I would be more assertive, rather than let myself be pushed around.

What career advice would you give a young person now?
Get out there and meet lots of different people, be friendly as possible as you never know when you will encounter them again.

What advice would you give a young person who wanted to do what you do?
- The best route is interning but be prepared to be broke!
- Aim for the top, and learn from them, try to work with the best companies.
- Try and get a paid internship, one year is loads as you should be able to get a job after one year interning.
- Use your common sense; there are so many idiotic girls.
- Be clever – when tidying the studio, tidy it so only you know where the stuff is.
- Always ask 'can I help,' be keen as mustard, and have a great attitude.

Which gets you further in a career – knowing people or being good at your job?
Knowing people, because they can get you in the door a lot quicker, even if you know the basics, you will get ahead a lot quicker through the people you know.

What advice would you give someone going out on their own?
Be prepared to be a little broke and lonely but try and keep the bigger picture in mind!!!

***

JESS, 35

12. Business Owner/Yoga Teacher, Dublin

What is your degree in?
Bachelor of Arts in European Studies
Diploma in Fashion, Buying and Merchandising

Why did you do the degree you did?
I didn't have a clue what I wanted to do, and European studies seemed a bit more focused than a general arts degree.

Why did you embark on the career you did?
My family are all into fashion, so thought that could be an option. I don't really know though, looking back on it there wasn't much of a thought process, I didn't think about careers at the time.

With the benefit of hindsight, if you were 18 again now would you do anything differently degree-wise?
I wish I studied physiotherapy, as I'm working with a lot of people through injury or age who ask me 'Why can't I move?' … and I know very little about the anatomy.

Did you know what your day-to-day role entailed starting off in your career?
I had no idea, you learn a little bit, but it doesn't really prepare you for the business side of it, the cut throat culture, and the bitchiness. You still must learn everything on the job.

What percentage of what you learned in university have you used in your day-to-day roles?
0%, I wouldn't rely on my degree for a lot.

What are the jobs you've done since graduating? And what have they entailed?
2016 – 2018
Business Owner/Yoga Teacher, Dublin
2012 – 2016
Fashion Production Manager, London
Overseeing production of clothes and ensuring they reach the store on time.
2011 – 2012
Buying Administration Assistant, London
Supporting your buyer, getting prices of garments, getting delivery dates.

What are the things you most like about your job, and the things you don't like?
Like:
1. I liked the clothes, it was interesting.
2. I enjoyed managing people, working with them.
3. The organisation of it all, when it works it works, when it doesn't – oh god!

Don't like:
1. The ruthlessness that comes with fashion.
2. The hierarchy, when you are junior, they really let you know it.
3. The stress.
4. The crap money, for the work you put in, you get paid very badly.

Have you worked long hours over the years?
Yes, fashion is always long hours.

Have you had much fun over the years?
Yes, lots of fun, the girls you work with are always good fun, you have such a laugh!

If you could start over and you were 22, but you know all you know now, would you do anything differently career-wise?
I'd start yoga younger, and I'd do physio. However, I'm not sure I'd change the fashion stuff!

What career advice would you give a young person now?
Go live in a foreign country, as it really made me, don't be worried about joining the rat race!

What advice would you give a young person who wanted to do what you do?
Get into a big company as an intern or the bottom of the chain as a BAA (buyers admin assistant). Expect to work your ass off! Just apply to every fashion company, look online and send your CV out!

What advice would you give a young person trying to start their own business?
Get a part-time job, as you will have some income from that, and do a business course!

Which gets you further – knowing people or how good you are at your job?
Both! I know I'm good at yoga, but I also know that a lot of what I've done is down to my connections and being a real people person!

***

PAUL, 33

13. Managing Director, Investment Holding Company, Dubai

What is your degree in?
Bachelor of Commerce
Master of eCommerce

Why did you do the degree you did?
- I didn't really know what I wanted to do; no one helped me with that process. I don't think you have a clue what the working world is like when you are at high school, and nobody tells you. There was no logic to my decision to do commerce, not sure why I picked it. You go to career guidance counsellors; they fill you with rubbish, stuff that makes no logical sense.

How can young people try to figure out what to do if they don't know?
I do a lot of coaching young people now and get them to do psychometric testing. At the end of it, they get a 70-page booklet telling them about their characteristics, interests, etc. to help guide them.

Did you know what you wanted to do career-wise?
I had no idea. I did know I wanted to get out of Ireland but wasn't sure where. I applied for jobs; one was a marketing intern role for a hotel group based in Dubai, the monthly salary was only £1k a month. I didn't even know how to look after myself, as I still lived with my folks up until that point. I didn't really know anything back then. I knew no one in Dubai. I remember thinking what am I going to do with my life?

With the benefit of hindsight, if you were 18 again now would you do anything differently degree-wise?
- The degree gave me a reference point to be able to say I can talk business, but the theory I learned, is not applicable to the real world. If you follow the accountancy path then it makes sense to do business, but some of the other specialisms they have no application in the real world.

The economics you study at university is so far away from the real world. I think it gives you a basic understanding of supply and demand, but it's so far removed from reality. I remember thinking how rubbish our marketing classes were in university.
- In my first job working as a marketing intern, I remember thinking 'wow, this is what marketing is.' If I was 21 again, I would take an internship in any company, at every possible chance. I think it's better to do eight internships than any degree.
- I remember coming out of university; I had very high expectations. I thought I deserved a good job and nice salary, but you don't deserve any of that - you don't know anything. I also didn't want to go on the perceived ladder that you need to go through to progress your career back home, the peer pressure to conform is overwhelming.

What are the jobs you've done since graduating? And what have they entailed?
2016 – 2018
Managing Director, Investment Holding Company, Dubai
Specialising in breakthrough digital technologies and online business in the Middle East and North Africa.
2015 – 2018
Executive Coach, Dubai
Business coaching for C-level executives and governments
2013 – 2015
Co-Founder and CEO, Online Travel Company, Dubai
2010 – 2014
Founder and CEO, E-Commerce Company, Dubai
Raised $1.4m and started my own company, grew turnover to $33m, and sold it for $40m.
2010 – 2010
Marketing Consultant, Global Airline Company, Dubai
Responsible for online marketing globally.
2009 – 2010
Assistant Digital Marketing Manager, Events Company, Dubai
Developed marketing plans, responsible for all digital marketing.

2007 – 2009
Marketing Manager, International Hotel Group, Dubai
Discovered how to do big real large-scale marketing.
2005 – 2007
Business Development Executive, Book Shop/Art Gallery, Ireland
This was my best education, as I was surrounded by entrepreneurs.

What are the things you most like about your job, and the things you don't like?
Like:
1. Trying to do stuff that other people would never try and do - I thrive on that.
2. Learning. Lots of people would be scared to do things where they are uncomfortable. I can honestly say I've no idea what I'm doing still, I just keep trying.
3. People. I love working with people. I absorb so much energy from it. I'm the worst when I'm stuck behind a desk, I don't add value to anything.

Don't like:
1. The more you grow, the more problems you encounter.

What career advice would you give a young person now?
- The most successful people in the world, are the people who make a lot of decisions. All the people that I profile, and work with that are very successful are all highly decisive. If I was 18, and I was very insecure, and I was controlled by my environment be it, friends or family, I would say be comfortable being the odd one out, by making decisions that your friends wouldn't make.
- Also, don't be afraid to ask. I do a lot of speaking tours of universities for free, I don't want any money for my time, but most universities would never even ask. People ask how do I get a mentor? People never even ask! If I were 18 again, I would go balls out and ask every single person in the world, one person might answer yes, and you never know how that might end up.

What are the best ways to develop yourself as a young person starting out in your career?

Anything that you can do in high school or university that makes you uncomfortable, I'd highly recommend doing. Be the class rep, be the one who organises things, raise money for charity, be the one who asks questions, be the odd person. If you make yourself uncomfortable across several things that's how you will develop and grow.

How did you set goals for yourself in your 20s?

I didn't, now I do. I believe opportunities never come twice, so the second I saw an opening, I ran after it. Early in your career when an opportunity comes take it, don't worry about the risk. The worst thing that can happen is you end up back where your status quo is currently.

Did you have any mentors?

- I didn't have any mentors in the early part of my career; I thought that I was an employee. I thought there was something wrong with me, as I was asking other people who were employees for advice, and what they said made no sense to me. It was only at the age of 27 that I got a mentor that was an entrepreneur and I realised up until that point I had been asking the wrong people.
- People find comfort in following a defined path, being the employee, being comfortable. I wonder all the time am I doing the right thing, am I taking the best approach, but often you are first walking on the road. You must find what works for you.

What advice would you give a young person who wanted to do what you do?

Often when you are trying to launch your own business, you are trying to have all the bases covered. You think you have what you perceive as a perfect product in the market place. I would say try and have your first company before you launch, if you can sell it to three people before you launch then you have a business. Proof of validation is key.

***

RICHIE, 34

14. Managing Director, Advertising Company, Dubai

What is your degree in?
Bachelor of Arts (Economics and German)
Diploma in Digital Marketing

Why did you do the degree you did?
I wanted to be a football coach and thought that this would be a good degree to do. Some of the top modern football coaches did business and economics subjects. However, I hated economics and German; I was really bad at them.

Did you know what you wanted to do career-wise?
Yes, when I graduated, I had an epiphany that advertising would suit me, and I knew social media was big, from reading papers and Facebook starting up, etc.

With the benefit of hindsight, if you were 18 again now would you do anything differently degree-wise?
- I really should have done history, and maybe some IT subjects as that was what I liked. I picked a business subject and a language as I thought that was what the world needed, and that was stupid, but you are young at the time you don't know. Maybe if I'd have done a marketing degree I'd be more creative, although I'm not sure do I want to be anywhere different then I am now, so would I have changed? It's hard to say.
- University is meant to be fun; I struggled, I failed exams. I repeated in the summer, it wasn't fun for me, I should have picked things that I like.
- Looking back, when I graduated I still thought I wanted to be a coach. I did a national coaching course, and the older coaches were intellectually dumb. It wasn't like what we see in the media; I'm glad I tried that and know I have no regrets. What I loved about football is the management style. Everything I've ever read about management when I was trying to get ahead in football, I apply in my company now today.

If you did history, do you think you'd still be where you are today?

- I have a drive from somewhere and that's why I do what I do.
- I did German in university and I applied for a load of marketing jobs in Germany, and I didn't get any of them. In a weird way, if I did get them, I'd still be doing something similar, maybe just not in Dubai. I'd still be running something, and be passionate about social media.
- I do think if I dropped out of my degree I mightn't be where I am now. Lasting the three or four years is important, that's why I don't give people jobs (or rarely) if they haven't done a degree.

Did you know what your day-to-day role entailed starting off in your career?

In Ireland 2006/7 there was hardly any courses for social media. There was one Diploma in Digital Marketing. I paid €1,500 to do the course, I knew more than the lecturer did, and got 92% in my thesis. I sponged everything up, just like when I would read the sports pages, I just loved it.

When you came out of university did you seek advice from anyone?

- No, it was impossible, nobody did what I wanted to do.
- I applied for thousands of jobs; I had no marketing degree. I got a job out beside Dublin Airport doing something slightly German related.
- I got a job doing outdoor media, ads on bins, outdoor billboards, etc., it was all very hard starting out.

What percentage of what you learned in university have you used in your day-to-day roles?

- I ask about degrees in interviews all the time, what did you study? It's so important as it shapes the way you think about things.
- Behavioural economics is so important. Even though I was rubbish at economics, it gave me the principles and a good grounding in why people make the decisions they do. I think your degree is so important as it influences how you think and look at things.

What are the jobs you've done since graduating? And what have they entailed?

2016 – 2018

Managing Director, Advertising Agency, Dubai

Set up my own company, employing 11 people, we advise companies in the Middle East on their social media strategy.

2012 – 2015

Social Media Director, Global Advertising Agency, Dubai

Building a social media department for the Middle East office.

2010 – 2012

Senior Account Manager, Digital Marketing Company, London

This was more strategic client facing work, more involvement with pitching and campaigns (London Olympics was a client).

2007 – 2009

Account Executive, Digital Marketing Company, London

I was the point person for day-to-day admin work relating to digital marketing clients.

What are the things you most like about your job, and the things you don't like?

Like:

1. Problem-solving for clients.
2. The pace of media in general, lots of travel, lots of excitement.
3. The opportunities I've had, pitching for telco clients in Iraq, working all over Middle East.

Don't like:

1. Financially it can be a struggle. Sometimes you work like a slave and I'm not sure you are really rewarded. I'm not sure you are ever rewarded unless you go out on your own.
2. There is a lot of bitchiness and backstabbing. I got pushed out of my first company as my boss was a bully and we didn't get on. It was a huge blow to my confidence. Then I went to London, and I saw that it was only that boss and that company. When you are young, it's very easy to get pushed around.

Have you worked long hours over the years?
Yes, I've done long hours, just as long as any other entrepreneur in the Middle East, it's a real slog.

Have you had much fun over the years?
Yes, it's been lots of fun working, travelling, pitching to clients, working on cool accounts, etc.

Which would you prefer to work for: a small company or a big company, and why?
Both. Small companies are amazing. I've also had some fantastic periods in big companies where there was no tension, and we were having so much fun inside and outside work.

If you could start over and you were 22, but you know all you know now, would you do anything differently career-wise?
- When I was 25 I had this business plan with a mate, but I didn't have the confidence to set up an agency at the time. Now, I've done my 10,000 hours/10 years and I'm very confident in my ability. I'm working with him now on a different project, but I do wonder what would have happened if I backed myself back then.
- I put in as many hours as anyone; it's incredibly hard, it's brutal. I had a difficult first year starting up my company, and I had to get through it, but now two years on I feel invincible. I'm not sure if I have any regrets.

What career advice would you give a young person now?
- If you can be a little bit more focused, if I were 18-20 again, I would have said 'GO FOR IT' to my younger self, and I might have achieved these things a bit earlier. Now, my aim is for my company to be listed on the stock market.
- Believe in yourself a bit earlier, read some self-development books. Think big, set goals and work towards those goals, it's scary what you can achieve if you want it bad enough. I have a friend who is an air hostess who is obsessed with owning a £7m apartment in New York. She reads

a success book every week, and she applies those principles to trying to get that apartment. If I had a little bit more of the self-development principles in me when I was younger, I would be way more successful now.

What advice would you give a young person who wanted to do what you do?
Sometimes to start a new company you think you need to reinvent the wheel, you don't. I thought I needed to be different. You just need to be passionate about it and be a little bit innovative. Don't feel daunted, if you think you can deal with the stress and hours, then go for it!

Which gets you further in a career – knowing people or being good at your job?
I hear it all the time over here in Dubai; it's who you know. Of course, relationships are important. However, I'd hate to think young people use it as an excuse. Look at me; no-one put me anywhere – so connections are bollocks!

***

TOM, 29

15. Property Director, Property Company, UK

What is your degree in?
Bachelor of Science (Geography)

Why did you do the degree you did?
My tutor said that I should do geography, as it was my best subject at A level. His reasoning was geography would keep doors open, as its quite a bland and open-ended degree.

Why did you embark on the career you did?
- My first job was in a mortgage valuation team, it had nothing to do with law, and nothing to do with geography. I called up a recruitment agent and they got me that job.

- It's only in the last few years that I realised an interest in architecture, soon after I started working in property. It would really have helped if I knew about architecture, how to plan a room conversion etc.

When you came out of university did you seek advice from anyone?
No.

Did you at any point want to work in the family business?
No, not all, that was never the intention.

With the benefit of hindsight, if you were 18 again now would you do anything differently degree-wise?
I think I would have done different A levels, as they really shaped my degree choice. My A level subjects were business studies, geography, and biology. I think if I went back I probably would have done something artsy, maths/physics, and then business studies. They would be more focused towards architecture.

What are the jobs you've done since graduating? And what have they entailed?
2015 – 2018
Property Director, Family Property Company, UK
Acquiring, renovating and letting student accommodation.
2012 – 2015
Business System Owner, Financial Regulatory Body, London
Working with the business to understand their requirements, designing and implementing a new IT system.
2009 – 2011
Mortgage Valuation Officer, National Bank, London
Ensuring mortgages being sold to the public were correctly valued by the bank.

What are the pros and cons of working in the family business?
Pros:
1. You can be a little less formal.

2. You know your family very well, so it's easier to deal with them.

Cons:
1. I can't think of any.

What are the things you most like about your job, and the things you don't like?
Like:
1. The business analyst role. I was creating something, and I got a lot of freedom to do it.

Don't like:
1. The lack of career progression.
2. The salary.
3. I would have liked to work with more people my own age, as in the bank a lot of my team were a lot older.

Which would you prefer to work for: a small company or a big company, and why?
A small private company would be my preference.

Would you advocate going straight into a family business?
No, go work for someone who is not your parents. You will get more rounded experience and a different perspective which is important.

Have you worked long hours over the years?
Yes, during that IT project, there were some long hours. When you know that there is an end, I don't mind doing long hours when you are working towards a goal as you get a real sense of achievement when you achieve it.

Have you had much fun over the years?
Yes, I'm still mates with a lot of the people I've worked with. At the regulatory body, I worked for; there were loads of people the same age,

it was great, those big companies that have big graduate schemes are a lot of fun!

If you could start over and you were 22, but you know all you know now, would you do anything differently career-wise?

I would do different A levels and do architecture even though it takes seven years. I'd try and work as an architect in London for a good few years. Then I would go back and work in my family property business. However, hindsight is great; it is very hard to know when you are 15/16 years old.

Did you do work experience when you were younger?

My summers were spent in financial jobs. I worked for JP Morgan when I was 16, and Barclays the year after that. Maybe if I'd have worked in property instead of banks, I would have realised I was interested in architecture.

What career advice would you give a young person now?

I would say find out exactly what you like, ask yourself what's the thing that you like most? If it doesn't lend itself to making money, do you like it enough to be able to make money out of it? For the really successful people, work for them is not work, it is their hobby. They are so interested in their work, they always think about it, and it becomes easy for them. If you can find whatever that is for you, then you will do very well.

COMMERCE AND INDUSTRY

What I knew before the interviews:

- There are lots of different career paths within commerce and industry.
- The hours are good when compared to other industries.
- You get up close to the business whether it's sales, manufacturing, etc.

What I learned from the interviews:

- It's a lot easier to switch from science to finance than I thought!
- Holland has great work-life balance.
- Just because there are not that many job prospects in something, i.e. sports science, doesn't mean you can't make a successful career out of it.
- Young people should be encouraged to do their own thing. Don't fear failure. You will learn from your mistakes, and it will make you stronger.

ANDREW, 35

16. Finance Director, Media Company, London

What is your degree in?
Bachelor of Commerce (Accounting)

Why did you do the degree you did?
I was struggling with picking what I wanted to do. I was considering doing something a bit more creative or interesting, but I realised I probably would not be very good at it. I did quite well at accounting in school; it was the safe choice.

Did you know what you wanted to do career-wise?
- A lot of it was more circumstance. I felt comfortable doing accounting, I could do it. When I moved to London from South Africa, I got temporary jobs in London and realised this was something where I could apply myself.
- My career never really gained traction until about three years ago. Before that I was just screwing around.

Did you know what your day-to-day role entailed starting off in your career?
I had a rough idea, as my dad was a finance director, but in terms of the day-to-day grind, I don't think I had much of a clue.

When you came out of university did you seek advice from anyone?
In high-school I did. I didn't really enjoy my degree, so I didn't engage much with anyone at university. It was very much a reluctant career path. I was just interested in having a good time and did accounting to pay the bills.

What percentage of what you learned in university have you used in your day-to-day roles?
Doing the ACCA qualification while I was working was very relevant. I found the subject matter a lot easier to study while I was working as

opposed to when I was doing it at university for finance and accounting. I think it's easier to engage with the material because you can relate it more to what you're doing in your job.

With the benefit of hindsight, if you were 18 again now would you do anything differently degree-wise?

I might have done something like economics. Actually no, I don't think I'd do anything differently.

What are the jobs you've done since graduating? And what have they entailed?

2016 – 2018

Finance Director, Media Company, London

Responsible for entire finance function; from paying invoices to budgeting, forecasting, people management, etc.

2013 – 2016

Assistant Controller, International Media Company, London

Responsible for everything finance related for a division of the company, with more responsibility re: people management.

2011 – 2013

Area Controller, International Media Company, London

Responsible for everything finance related for a division of the company.

2009 – 2010

Corporate Accounting Supervisor, Transport Company, London

Responsible for ensuring monthly accounting cycle and processes run smoothly.

2008 – 2009

SAP Implementation Super User, Transport Company, London

Designing finance processes for the rollout of a new company-wide computer system.

2006 – 2008

Accounts assistant, Transport Company, London

Learning basic accounting, i.e. balance sheet reconciliations, posting journals, analysing monthly accounts, budgeting, etc.

What are the things you most like about your job, and the things you don't like?

Like:

1. Recognition and getting promoted.
2. The opportunity to learn lots of different types of roles.
3. Learning how to manage people.

Don't like:

1. Managing people is really challenging.
2. The repetitive nature of finance is tough – you do the same thing every month, looking at the monthly accounts.

Which would you prefer to work for: a small company or a big company, and why?

- They both have pros and cons. In a big company, you learn a level of professionalism, but you get pigeonholed into doing one role. If you want broader experience, you literally have to look for a new job.
- I started off in a big company, learned how things should work, sophisticated processes, etc. Then I moved to a smaller company where you get more varied experience, and it's a lot more stimulating. I now can apply what I've learned in the bigger companies to the smaller companies I'm working with now.

Have you worked long hours over the years?

It's peaks and troughs; at month end when you are finalising the months accounts it's busy, 8:30am – 7pm usually.

Have you had much fun over the years?

Yes, I've had lots of fun. In big companies, there are always people your own age, good fun, etc. As you get older and senior, you want to go out with work less and it's not as much fun.

If you could start over and you were 22, but you know all you know now, would you do anything differently career-wise?

I would have tried to get qualified sooner and try to have applied myself a bit more. I'm relatively happy with the way I did it, I would have tried to push to get different roles when I was more junior. In hindsight, I should have tried to move roles every year, so that I'd have more varied experience. It's very difficult to move between roles when you get more senior.

What career advice would you give a young person now?

- Be open to different roles, try and diversify yourself as much as possible.
- Get a mentor who can bring you up through the organisation.
- Having a strong work ethic can get you far.
- When you are chatting with more senior staff take that opportunity to ask them for advice, it may prove invaluable.

What advice would you give a young person who wanted to do what you do?

I'd recommend doing an ACA qualification as opposed to ACCA, as you get that practice experience. In general, I think the better accountants are ACA. Also, try and move into the industry as soon as possible, network and get as broad experience as you can.

Are you jealous of any of your friends' jobs?

Not really. I quite like the idea of being a contractor, getting some good cash, might try and do it in a few years.

***

ASAF, 32

17. Reporting Analyst, Pharma Company, London

What is your degree in?

Bachelor of Marketing

Why did you do the degree you did?

I did business in my A levels, and I was good at marketing, so I applied for a university course in marketing.

Why did you embark on the career you did?
As I was good at marketing in school, I thought I'd be good at it for a career, but it doesn't necessarily work that way.

Did you know what your day-to-day role entailed starting off in your career?
I did a two-week internship in marketing, and I hated it. They had me doing some data stuff and trend spotting that made me realise I don't want to do this, if this is what marketing is all about. I started applying for jobs. One company said they'd give me a finance graduate placement, I said why not and took it!

When you came out of university did you seek advice from anyone?
I didn't know anyone who worked in marketing. The only thing I knew about it was that two-week work experience in marketing.

What percentage of what you learned in university have you used in your day-to-day roles?
15%, if that. Everything that I do now I had to learn.

With the benefit of hindsight, if you were 18 again now would you do anything differently degree-wise?
- Honestly, I probably wouldn't go to university if I was to go back and do it all over again. In hindsight, I think it limits you to one skill set when possibly you could get broader experience in other ways.
- I would have liked to shadow someone who was working in the music industry for a long time and learn lots from them.
- I was interested in marketing, but I didn't talk to people who worked in marketing. I didn't find out about jobs in marketing.
- You need money to do anything in life. I'm quite creative, I'd like to run my own business, I have ideas but I don't have the financial backing. You get sucked into a 9-5 job to earn money, it then can be hard to get out of that world. You have bills to pay and enjoy having nice things. It becomes a vicious cycle!

What are the jobs you've done since graduating? And what have they entailed?

2016 – 2018

Reporting Analyst, Pharma Firm, London

Consolidating data that support financial reports for senior management

2013 – 2016

Pricing Analyst, Global Pharma Firm, London

Ensuring that all the goods the company manufactured were priced correctly.

2009 – 2012

Trading Partner, Global Pharma Firm, London

Ensuring that all the company's stock was correctly accounted for.

2006 – 2008

Accountant, Global Pharma Firm, London

Filing Tax returns, reconciling receipts and payments to the system, helping to close the accounts at month and year-end.

What are the things you most like about your job, and the things you don't like?

Like:

1. The people – my work colleagues were great. We got on great inside and outside of work, they were all my best friends! (Sometimes the role mightn't be right, but the people will make it).
2. The money is good.
3. Working for a big well-known company is nice.

Don't like:

1. I don't not like anything!

Which would you prefer to work for: a small company or a big company, and why?

A big company is good because you can move around easily. It's good for networking, and there are lots of different people with different backgrounds who can help you move roles too. While you don't get the experience, you would get in a small company, I think there are far more advantages to working in a big company.

Have you worked long hours over the years?
I've done a standard 9-5. I've even had some good bosses in the past that have let me go home when I have all my work done. Like I said, if you are working with good people, your job can be great!

Have you had much fun over the years?
Yes, lots of fun. In the early years in this company, we are all young and worked and socialised together. They are all my friends for life now.

If you could start over and you were 22, but you know all you know now, would you do anything differently career-wise?
- I'd probably focus on something I would have enjoyed more when I was younger, as I'm finding out it's a bit late to do that now.
- From 21 to 28 it's all good - you're earning money, you're having fun, you don't think about where this path will lead you.
- From 28 to 35 you start re-evaluating what you want to do, what you are good at, versus what you are doing now.
- I wouldn't wait until I was 28 to evaluate what I'm good at etc.

What advice would you give to a young person who couldn't decide whether to follow their passion or get a job to pay the bills?
- Don't force yourself to do 9-5; it's not for everyone.
- What we fail to do in society, is show people you should live to work, instead of vice versa. You are in a big company for 5 years, then 10 years then 30 years and you get really pigeonholed. If you are mad to get into a big corporate job, I would say take your time and have a think about it. If you are good at something you think you can excel in, then do that. Happiness, money, and security will come after.

Did you ever try and get into a big music company?

I thought it would be next to impossible to get into a big music company, so I didn't even try. I should have tried to reach out to people working in the industry in hindsight.

Did you ever try and get a mentor?
No, I suppose when you are young you don't think about getting a mentor. All you're concerned about is exams, and getting your first job.

What career advice would you give a young person now?
- If studying is your thing, make sure you pick a subject that you're really going to enjoy and then go find out about what jobs there are available. To do that speak to people who have done it before, speak to lecturers.
- A lot of people do finance because it pays a lot of money, but if you don't really like it, it can make you miserable. Try to stay in line with things that make you happy.
- At 18 you are young enough to fail and pick yourself back up again. Take a risk don't be scared to fail, you family will be there to support you. Don't be worried about what anyone says - just do your thing!
- Find someone to model your ideas on, find someone successful and copy them. If you want to do something, chances are someone has done it before. Try to shadow people, speak to people in the industry, (speak to the right people though! if you speak to the wrong people you will be discouraged straight away). Don't be scared to approach people, some people might say go away but it's a numbers game!

***

CHRIS, 28

18. Finance Business Partner, Pharma Company, London

What is your degree in?
Bachelor of Science (Chemistry)
Master of Chemistry

Why did you do the degree you did?

I looked at subjects I liked most – chemistry and economics. I thought I should pursue chemistry first, as it is more real world, and I could always fall back on economics if I wanted to.

What percentage of what you learned in university have you used in your day-to-day roles?

Probably 40%, as there is lots of overlap when you look at chemistry problems and finance problems.

Did you know what you wanted to do career-wise?

As part of my chemistry Masters, there was a one-year industrial placement. This then led to a permanent job as an analytical research chemist when I graduated, so there was a pretty defined path. After two years in this role, my options were to stay with that company, to do a Ph.D., or do something else, like finance! So yes, my degree gave me an idea of what I wanted to do.

Why did you embark on the career you did?

- I got offered a job after my industrial placement with a Dutch mining company. I spent first year doing what I wanted to do, travelled to loads of different offices, I was paid great, got 42 days' holidays, and got flexible working hours. I really enjoyed it, but still wasn't sure whether to stay and work there, do a Ph.D., or look for something else.
- I enjoyed working in R&D, having to defend my work and implement it. However, it was very linear. You had little control over where you worked, how you worked, etc. I wanted more flexibility and variety in my life. That ruled out the Ph.D., as I didn't want to go further down the academia route. Working in R&D, I realised finance were the key people in the company, they were behind all the decisions. As much as I loved being in R&D, I realised I didn't have the same influence as I would have working in finance, so I was drawn to finance.

With the benefit of hindsight, if you were 18 again now would you do anything differently degree-wise?

I would study something to do with IT - software programming - as using data and programming is so prevalent now.

Could you have done a different degree and still do something completely different?

Comparing chemistry to finance – the objectivity, the process, the rigour is all very similar. There are no physical barriers, however there is a skill barrier. You need to have developed your skills outside of your degree to be able to switch over, i.e. you need to know finance basics and be interested in finance to switch into it. A management accounting (CIMA) qualification is a good way of doing this.

Did you know what your day-to-day role entailed starting off in your career?

Chemistry – 100% from my work placement.

Finance – I had no clue really.

What are the jobs you've done since graduating? And what have they entailed?

2016 – 2018

Finance Business Partner, Pharma Company, London

Optimising the strategy of all the manufacturing sites to reduce costs.

2015 – 2016

Finance Business Partner, Pharma Company, London

Supporting sales and marketing business units, answering any finance questions they had.

2014 – 2015

Financial Accountant, Pharma Company, London

Preparing financial statements for one of the business units.

2011 – 2014

Associate Research Scientist, Eindhoven

Focused on troubleshooting issues and protecting intellectual property. Looking to improve output/yield of the factory, helping to fix any issues that came up. Ensuring other companies didn't rip off our patented products.

What are the things you most like about your job, and the things you don't like?

Like:

1. Intellectual challenge.
2. Collaboration/teamwork, when you achieve, you achieve as a team.
3. Adding value – helping non-finance people by upskilling them in finance stuff.

Don't like:

1. Hierarchical management structures.
2. Complacency – people who don't listen to reasoned arguments. Scientists recognise reasoned arguments, people in finance not so much.
3. Ignorance.

Have you worked long hours over the years?

- Chemistry was short hours, finance seems to be becoming longer and longer hours.
- In R&D in Holland, it was very much 9am - 5pm, get your work done and then go home. In the UK, I used to do my work and then leave; people were amazed!

Have you had much fun over the years?

In R&D it was fun to discover new things, but it was tough as there was lots of failure, and you had to take that on the chin.

Would you be an advocate of a graduate programme?

It depends. I know other companies throw you in at the deep end, but they can be light on education, and the rotation of the different roles. If it's with a big company I would recommend it.

If you could start over and you were 22, but you know all you know now, would you do anything differently career-wise?

I would have gone into the software programming side, but I think I'd still do something finance-related. I'm a data-led person. I want to go into management, through working my way up within a finance function.

What career advice would you give a young person now?
Step out of your comfort zone. You are going to regret things less if you have tried them. what is the worst that can happen? What you imagine may happen is usually going to be worse than the reality.

What advice would you give a young person who wanted to do what you do?
Be bold, do what you want to do, don't be a sheep and do what your friends are doing, do what makes you happy. I didn't know what I wanted to do back then, I still don't really. I may do a start-up, I may continue with a traditional career. Who knows?

***

CHRISTIAN, 38

19. Finance Business Partner, Financial Services Firm, London

What is your degree in?
Bachelor of Engineering (Aerospace Materials)

Why did you do the degree you did?
I enjoyed chemistry, making planes sounded interesting, so I did aeronautical engineering. The degree was very abstract, it was pages and pages of equations. After the first year, I knew it was going to get worse, so I tried to swap to chemistry, but my tutor mentioned aerospace materials; I said 'yes why not'.

Did you know what you wanted to do career-wise?
No, coming out of that degree, the ideal job would have been working in a Formula One team.

When you came out of university did you seek advice from anyone?

No, not really, the careers advice wasn't very good at my university.

With the benefit of hindsight, if you were 18 again now would you do anything differently degree-wise?

Immediately after my degree, a lot of the jobs were in computers. I sometimes wish I'd done computer science. I don't think I'd have wanted to do accounting and finance, as doing something different for your degree gives you a different perspective on things.

What are the jobs you've done since graduating? And what have they entailed?

2013 – 2018

Finance Business Partner, Financial Services Firm, London

Responsible for all finance matters relating to specific products that the company sells, and supporting the departments that sell them.

2012 – 2013

Trading Finance Manager, Retail Company, London

Responsible for reporting, analysing and forecasting sales and stock for all products sold.

2009 – 2011

Commercial Finance Manager, Music Retailer, London

Supporting the product team, stock projects, forecasting sales and stock.

2007 – 2009

Financial Reporting Manager (Qualified), Music Retailer, London

Responsible for all internal financial reporting for the company – from board reports to adjusting the monthly accounts.

2005 – 2007

Supply Chain Analyst (Part-Qualified Accountant), London

Analysing supply chain costs i.e. warehouse/distribution costs, etc.

2002 – 2005

Accounts Payable Clerk, Music Retailer, London

Managing supplier relationships, paying invoices, etc.

What are the things you most like about your job, and the things you don't like?

Like:
1. Finance is quite interesting.
2. The more senior you get, the more interesting it gets, as it's more varied.
3. Building complicated spreadsheets (that makes me sound like a nerd).
4. Learning how the business operates and helping management improve.
5. When you get more senior you learn how the business is performing. In non-finance departments, you never know that stuff.

Don't like:
1. It can be stressful.
2. You always have a budget or a forecast to put together, so you're always busy.
3. If you work in a retailer, people are always looking for sales and stock forecasts.

Which would you prefer to work for: a small company or a big company, and why?
A small company purely because it's more personal, and you can have a much bigger impact. In a big company, you can get lost and it can be a lot colder.

Have you worked long hours over the years?
- It's long hours during month end (finalising the company accounts every month), but it very much depends on the role.
- The company I work for now is very good at having a good work-life balance. I've never had to work stupid hours, like until 10-11 at night.

Have you had much fun over the years?
- The typical finance stereotype is boring, but I've had good fun at the places I've worked.
- Let's put it this way, at one of my companies, everyone ended up at the finance Christmas party, and that was a really fun well-known company.
- I have worked in quite fun industries, so I think it depends more on the industries than the companies you are in.

If you could start over and you were 22, but you know all you know now, would you do anything differently career-wise?
I've ended up in a good position. I could have done things quicker or could have studied other things but it's all made me the person I am today.

What career advice would you give a young person now?
- I've got friends who didn't make it through their professional exams while working. Don't beat yourself up about it. It's hard work to study and work at the same time, it mightn't be for you.
- My cousin did accounting and went to work for a practice and hated it. I tried to explain to him there is much more to accounting than just financial accounts and auditing. I wouldn't even know one accounting standard. I see myself as much more of an interface between the business and finance.

What advice would you give a young person who wanted to do what you do?
I would say you've got to do a management accounting role relatively early in your career. You need to be able to explain the profit and loss accounts to non-finance people who don't have a clue about finance. If you can simplify info and communicate it easily, you will make a great business partner.

***

KEVIN, 34

20. Financial Consultant, Consulting Firm, Dublin

What is your degree in?
Bachelor of Commerce
Master of Accounting
Bachelor of Science (Sports & Exercise Science)

Why did you do the degree you did?

It was the safe option. I didn't really know what I wanted to do. I liked business, but had no massive desire to do it. I started off doing engineering and dropped out as it wasn't for me.

Did you know what you wanted to do career-wise?
Yes, the big accounting firms came to my university and did interviews with the accounting students. They liked me, and offered me a job, so the career decision was really in my second year. I picked to specialise in accounting because it had better job prospects.

Did you know what your day-to-day role entailed starting off in your career?
I didn't really know what we'd be doing starting off. They train you up over the three-year training contract.

When you came out of university did you seek advice from anyone?
- Not really. Lecturers wouldn't really open themselves up to talking to you.
- I knew lots of accountants from the golf club back home, but strangely didn't look to speak to any of them. I should have.

What percentage of what you learned in university have you used in your day-to-day roles?
30%. A lot of what I do now is financial modelling in Microsoft Excel. I did none of that in university; I was rubbish in excel at university.

With the benefit of hindsight, if you were 18 again now would you do anything differently degree-wise?
One thing I wanted to do was sports science, but I didn't do it as I thought job prospects were not good. I thought getting a good job out of sports science would be too difficult. However, after going to university the second time, I learned if you are good enough at something you can make it work. It's a hard one, would I go back and do sports science? I'm not sure.

What are the jobs you've done since graduating? And what have they entailed?

2016 – 2018

Financial Consultant, Consulting Firm, Dublin

Modelling different financial scenarios and outcomes for big companies.

2007 – 2016

Audit Junior to Senior Manager, Big 4 Accounting Firm, Dublin

Valuing companies, assisting companies being valued for sale.

What are the things you most like about your job, and the things you don't like?

Like:

1. People – you make so many friends and have such fun in a big 4 firm, it's kind of like university in a way.
2. The sense of validation you get working for a big prestigious company.
3. Variety of the work that I was doing.
4. Interacting with more senior people, learning from them.

Don't like:

1. The greed side of things, when all people care about is more money, insatiable need for profit.
2. The routine. I didn't like going to same place every day, parking in same spot, etc.
3. Things getting a bit stale, senior people not stepping out of their comfort zone.

Have you worked long hours over the years?

No, not really. Some of my friends in the big 4 got hammered, but I was always not too bad.

Have you had much fun over the years?

Yes, I've enjoyed the people side of things, and always had lots of fun. In my graduate programme intake, there were 300 people, so there were lots of nights out, lots of people the same age. It was great fun!

Which would you prefer to work for: a small company or a big company, and why?
I'd prefer to work for a big company, as there is less pressure, better support structures, etc.

If you could start over and you were 22, but you know all you know now, would you do anything differently career-wise?
I would have left the big 4 firm a year earlier, as I stopped learning and was getting a bit stale.

What career advice would you give a young person now?
Don't underestimate the value of your personality getting you places. The technical side is important, but if you are sound and easy to get on with that will really get you far.

What advice would you give a young person who wanted to do what you do?
Get as much varied experience as you can, early on. Don't stay doing the one thing for too long as that's not good when you are young.

What is your advice on how to get involved in start-ups?
If you want to do it, do it, don't think too much about it. 'Paralysis by analysis,' 'done is better than perfect,' just get it done - it doesn't have to be perfect! You will always find a million reasons not to do something.

Which gets you further in a career – knowing people or being good at your job?
Knowing people – one million percent. The two do overlap as you are not going to go anywhere if you know people and are very bad at your job. I still believe that the more people you know, the better jobs you will get, it's a numbers game.
- Being connected opens so many doors in every walk of life, not just your career. If you know lots of people, you will get offered tickets, deals, discounts, favours, etc.

Would you be an advocate of doing postgraduate study straight after undergraduate?

- In a way, it'd be great to go back to university now, knowing all you know now, as a lot of it is irrelevant, and you could have a great time.
- Would it be good to work for a while before you do the postgrad? The way accounting is, you get exemptions with your postgrad so I personally think you are better off doing it straight away.

***

SAM, 34

21. Account Manager, Software Company, London

What is your degree in?

Bachelor of Arts (Media Writing and Journalism)

Why did you do the degree you did?

I always wanted to be a football journalist growing up. When you have to make your decisions at 17, that was all I knew. I was young.

Did you know what you wanted to do career-wise?

- I hated my degree. I thought it was a waste of time. It qualified me for nothing. It wasn't even an NCJ qualified journalism course.
- I didn't know what I wanted to do career-wise, I had debt, I applied for a load of jobs. I got most of them. A friend of mine said come work with me, so I did. In my mind at the time, this job had nothing to do with my future - I just had an immediate need to pay off debt.
- I'm still close with my friends who did journalism courses, and only one of them has made a success of it. He works really hard at it. Writing and English were always something that came naturally to me, but I'm not sure in hindsight I would have been cut out for a career in journalism.

Did you know what your day-to-day role entailed starting off in your career?

I had no idea about what fraud or risk management entailed. I planned to do this for a couple of years, pay off some debt and then do something else, but life gets in the way. I tried to get apprenticeships, I applied to the BBC but nothing came of it.

What percentage of what you learned in university have you used in your day-to-day roles?
5%

What are the jobs you've done since graduating? And what have they entailed?
2012 – 2018
Account Manager, Software Company, London
Working for a company which sells fraud solutions to other companies.
2006 – 2012
Senior Fraud Analyst, Online Travel Company, London
Looking for suspected fraud for a big online travel company.

What are the things you most like about your job, and the things you don't like?
Like:
1. The temporary nature of some of the early projects. You would fix something and move on.
2. Owning a part of the company I work for.
3. Being part of a small company, working with people I genuinely like.

Don't like:
1. Feeling underappreciated.
2. Fraud roles can be quite monotonous.
3. My small company trying to be more corporate, implementing reporting structures, etc.

Have you worked long hours over the years?
It's not too bad now. However, in my first seven or eight years working, I would have to work 12-15hr shifts and one weekend a month to monitor bookings traffic. Those shifts were horrible.

Have you had much fun over the years?

Yes, my company is 5-10 people, we all get on. It's been great fun.

Which would you prefer to work for: a small company or a big company, and why?

- In a big company, everything is easier.
- Most people start big and then go small. You should try to get to know what big business is like.
- In a small company, there is more opportunity to gain experience outside of your role.
- Big companies pay the most, I could earn more elsewhere but I've got equity in my company.

What career advice would you give a young person now?

- I would tell them to treat university as a learning experience for what they want to learn about, not what they want to do. Commit yourself to something that you love. You will come out of university richer and more knowledgeable than you can imagine.
- I felt from an early age you must decide what you want to do, and that was wrong. Education is not about what you do afterwards. My brother did languages because he loved them, and he was headhunted for how good he was!

Which gets you further in a career – knowing people or being good at your job?

It's not one or the other – I know people who are good at their job and have gone far. I also know people who are thick and have gone far, so it's a combination.

***

STUART, 31

22. Finance Business Partner, Pharma Company, London

What is your degree in?

Bachelor of Arts (Politics and Economics)

Why did you do the degree you did?
I was interested in both, thought they were quite broad. I didn't specifically have a career in mind. I thought I'd determine what I wanted to do job-wise later.

What percentage of what you learned in university have you used in your day-to-day roles?
Very low, but politics gave me presentation skills, debating skills, i.e. you must defend your point of view, it's made me a more confident person. Economics gave me exemptions in terms of accountancy degrees.

Did you know what you wanted to do career-wise?
Initially, I wanted to get into politics, I wanted to support MP's, then I decided civil service. I thought going through university, I'd have an epiphany as to what I wanted to do, but it never really happened. In my last year, I realised I needed to figure it out. Being from Wales, I wanted to move to London, and to pay bills I got a temp logistics/finance role. I landed in a finance job by accident.

With the benefit of hindsight, if you were 18 again now would you do anything differently degree-wise?
Degree-wise I'd do the same, but I would have done more finance modules - I did more humanities modules. Now I work in finance I would have done something to give me more of a base knowledge.

What are the jobs you've done since graduating? And what have they entailed?
2015 – 2018
Finance Partnering, Pharma Company, London
Helping the business set budgets, tracking the spend, assisting with any finance related problems.
2013 – 2015
Finance Reporting, Global Consumer Goods Firm, London

Consolidating the different financial reports from around the world into one to show senior management how the company is doing.

2010 – 2013

Business Analyst, Global Consumer Goods Firm, London

Integrating third-party suppliers to my company's ways of working.

2007 – 2013

Transfer Price Analyst, Global Consumer Goods Firm, London

Ensuring that products are priced correctly before they are shipped off to different countries.

What are the things you most like about your job, and the things you don't like?

Like:

1. The interaction with the business.
2. Challenging people. Is this the right thing to do? Is it the best way to spend money?
3. Working with third party companies all over the world.
4. Getting different roles in the one company, you can plot out your career path in one company.

Don't like:

1. To change things can be difficult in such a big company, they are not as agile as a small company.
2. When the business doesn't check and consult with finance as much as they should and just go and do their own thing.

Have you worked long hours over the years?

The reporting role was long hours, and sometimes my current role can be long hours. I try to find the right balance.

Have you had much fun over the years?

- Great fun, I've met people that have become life-long friends.
- I have been able to train through the company, get a qualification through the company.

Which would you prefer to work for: a small company or a big company, and why?
I wouldn't be able to work for a small company now. Some of the numbers and costs being tiny compared to a bigger company.

If you could start over and you were 22, but you know all you know now, would you do anything differently career-wise?
I would have looked at some graduate programmes, and I would have liked to settle on a career path earlier on.

Would you be an advocate of a graduate programme?
It's great exposure to lots of senior people and different areas. However, some people aren't suited to assessment days. The louder brasher people stand out, and I think that it's a flaw in the process.

What career advice would you give a young person now?
Do a work placement role. The people who have done them here, they are a changed person at the end of it. They even approach the last year of university differently. Also, don't get downhearted with rejections, as it will all work out.

What advice would you give a young person who wanted to do what you do?
- Consider an accountancy qualification and how do you want to do it? Does studying part-time suit you?
- You need to be unafraid to challenge people. If you don't mind asking different questions, then I think you will make a good finance business partner. A finance business partner usually has a finance background. They help the business with business matters, governance, spend, budgets, risk, and opportunities.

***

TONY, 33

23. Process Lead, Hotel Group, London

What is your degree in?
Bachelor of Business Studies

Why did you do the degree you did?
I started a computer engineering degree, did an internship as part of it and realised it wasn't for me. I switched to business mid-way through university as I felt I'd do better in business.

Did you know what your day-to-day role entailed starting off in your career?
No, when I got my graduate role in finance, I'd already done two and half years in IT. I knew that my finance graduate programme would be four rotations in three years but knew nothing about finance.

Why did you embark on the career you did?
I was always interested in economics, and with business, I thought I'd be employable everywhere in the world.

What percentage of what you learned in university have you used in your day-to-day roles?
Less than 10%. We were told when we started the finance graduate programme to put our degrees in the bin!

What are the jobs you've done since graduating? And what have they entailed?
2017 – 2018
Finance Process Lead, Hotel Group, London
Developing and implementing a new way of working for the finance team.
2015 – 2016
Finance Manager, International Media Company, London
Providing process improvement and monitoring key performance indicators (KPI's) for the financial operations team.
2013 – 2015
Manager/Process Lead, Global Pharma Company, London

Implementing a new finance system and new operation model.

2012 – 2013

Revenue Analyst, Transport Company, London

Investigating costs charged to old revenue accounts.

2008 – 2011

Graduate Programme, Bank, Australia

Finance analyst/business partner for the marketing and commercial banking department. Supporting budget processes and assisting with stock market and board of directors' updates.

2005 – 2007

Network Analyst, IT Company, Australia

IT bugs, network issues, etc.

What are the things you most like about your job, and the things you don't like?

Like:

1. The commercial side of it.

Dealing with people who bring money into the business.

2. The high performing culture in one of the banks.

3. Having very good mentors throughout my career. Formal and informal mentors have helped me quite a lot in my career.

Don't like:

1. When people hide behind the process, and it's unclear as to who owns the process - it happens in every organisation.

2. Doing lots of detail, i.e. balance sheet reconciliations

3. Audit; As you couldn't drive a solution to a problem, you could only flag the solution.

Which would you prefer to work for: a small company or a big company, and why?

I prefer big – there is more opportunity, better processes, and more to learn.

Have you worked long hours over the years?

No, I've always done a standard 9-5. You do shorter hours working in industry (media, telecoms companies) than you do in financial services.

If you could start over and you were 22, but you know all you know now, would you do anything differently career-wise?

I would have qualified as an accountant earlier and moved overseas earlier.

What career advice would you give a young person now?

- Just be open to learning, be open to the fact that someone might have a better way of doing something. Be adaptable, especially these days with technology improving all the time.
- Identify the people who can give you honest mentoring and learn from them.
- Don't be afraid to step out of your comfort zone, the best learning is under pressure.

COMPLIANCE

What I knew before the interviews:

- That it paid well.
- There was a great social side to working in financial regulatory bodies.

What I learned from the interviews:

- One of the reasons why regulatory bodies can be such good places to work is they are not trying to make money.
- Depending on the industry you are regulating it can be very long hours, i.e. investment banking.
- You can get to work on insider dealing cases with the police investigating fraud!
- The benefit of trying out lots of different things and being a jack of all trades. If you are agile and try lots of things the bigger chance you have of finding something you love.

CLAIRE, 32

24. Regulatory Manager, Financial Regulatory Body, London

What is your degree in?
Bachelor of Arts (English Literature and History)

Why did you do the degree you did?
Humanities degrees get a bad reputation. However, they teach you how to assimilate information and then repurpose it, which is a good skill to have. I thought I might go on and do law after, but I graduated in 2007 when the recession hit so I didn't bother.

Did you know what you wanted to do career-wise?
No, not at all. I wasn't really worried about it. I always found people who had a clear idea in school and were executing it kind of creepy. How can you be so convinced what you want to do at that age?

When you came out of university did you seek advice from anyone?
No, after I graduated I moved to France with a friend, but after a couple of years I got fed up with that and moved to London.

Why did you embark on the career you did?
When I arrived in London, I put my name down with a temp agency because I needed money, I worked for three months for the debt collection arm of a university. It was a horrible job. I also was in recruitment for an online gambling company, another horrible job. My friend Katherine was on a graduate programme, and she said that there were lots of entry-level jobs in her company. So, I got a job as a secretary and loved it. My manager had been on the graduate programme, and after a few months, she said that I was too clever not to be on the graduate programme. I was happy there and the company had a social value, so I started on the graduate programme!

What percentage of what you learned in university have you used in your day-to-day roles?

Very little of the content but some of the skills I would still use a lot, i.e. report writing, researching.

With the benefit of hindsight, if you were 18 again now would you do anything differently degree-wise?
I would study a more specific degree. I think I would study law if I went back now. However, if I picked law to do as a 17-year-old, I think it would have been too much for me. I'm not sure I would have been able to do it.

Did you know what your day-to-day role entailed starting off in your career?
No, I had no idea, it was a leap of faith, based on me liking the people, and there being some scope for progression.

What are the jobs you've done since graduating? And what have they entailed?
2016 – 2018
Regulatory Manager, Financial Regulatory Body, London
Supervising an investment bank, ensuring they adhere to financial regulation.
2015 – 2016
Executive Assistant, Financial Regulatory Body, London
Assistant to one of the heads of department in the regulatory body I work in.
2013 – 2015
Forensic Investigator, Financial Regulatory Body, London
Worked on an insider dealing case, helping police searching houses, etc.
2010 – 2012
Graduate Programme, Financial Regulatory Body, London
Read debt companies prospectus for companies listing on stock exchange.
2008 – 2009
Secretary, Financial Regulatory Body, London

Did all the admin for the team, filed evidence, ensured it was all in a sensible order.

What are the things you most like about your job, and the things you don't like?

Like:

1. Supervising a firm, understanding their problems, and helping them to address them.
2. The people, everyone is from a very different background.

Don't like:

1. It can be very bureaucratic.
2. Working in an investment bank, it was 15 hours a day. It was awful, don't ever work for one.
3. People complaining to you about regulation as it's making their job and life harder.

Which would you prefer to work for: a small company or a big company, and why?

I think 3,000 is a nice size company – it needs to be bigger than a school and shouldn't be too big.

Have you worked long hours over the years?

Generally, it's quite a good work-life balance; there are peaks and troughs. It attracts a lot of people who used to work in industry, people who have had kids and want more regular hours. My usual day is 8:30am - 6pm.

Have you had much fun over the years?

Yes, brilliant fun, you are encouraged to be yourself, everyone is very nice. There are lots of young people the same age. The regulator is not trying to make money, so there is less pressure, you can think about how to do things.

What career advice would you give a young person now?

- Don't put too much pressure on yourself.

- At the start, you want to be as senior as possible and make a lot of money as quickly as you can. However, after a couple of years, you realise you are going to be doing your job for 45 years. It's important to have a depth of experience and confidence you get by just being good at the job. You come across so many people that rush to be promoted, they get out of their depth, and they feel stressed and unhappy. I think it's a bit of a false economy to try and get very senior as quick as you can.
- Speak to as many people as possible and ask them practical questions as to what the day-to-day entails. Sometimes there is a real chasm between the job description, and what you will actually be doing.
- You should also think what's important to you, money, work-life balance, etc.? Do you get bored easily? If so maybe you should look at project work, as that will have a lot of variety.

What advice would you give a young person who wanted to do what you do?
I'm the only person with a humanities degree, I think you'd have to have some sort of business degree to get in. You just need to get your CV to a place where people will take you seriously. If you did a humanities degree you need something else, either a conversion course or work experience.

Would you be an advocate of going and working abroad?
Yes, 100% - everything is so hard to do in a different country, so if you can get a job, set up a life abroad, it seems easy to do the same back home. You also get a different perspective from living and working abroad. I think you might end up a bit weird if you end up working down the road from where you went to school.

***

CONOR, 34

25. Head of Risk, Construction Company, Dublin

What is your degree in?
Bachelor of Accounting

Why did you do the degree you did?

My dad was an accountant, I liked it, and just the lack of anything else I wanted to do. I applied for law too, but didn't get the grades, and was relieved to be honest.

Why did you embark on the career you did?

I worked for a summer in a big 4 firm, and I hated it, but I didn't want to waste three years of accounting studies starting something else. So, I applied for a role in the risk management department in the big 4 firm as it was something different than straight audit.

With the benefit of hindsight, if you were 18 again now would you do anything differently degree-wise?

My biggest regret is that I didn't do an MBA after my degree, I think it would have set me apart and set me on my way to be a senior leader in a top company.

What percentage of what you learned in university have you used in your day-to-day roles?

Probably zero, as I'm now in risk, but you learn all the basics of economics, strategy, etc., it was a good base foundation. For example, in my role now I can converse with an accountant about regulations, talk about business development with a strategy person, etc.

What are the jobs you've done since graduating? And what have they entailed?

2015 – 2018

Head of Risk Management, Construction Company, Dublin

Sitting with management teams around the world. Ascertaining what the potential obstacles are that prevent them meeting their 2-5 year objectives.

2013 - 2015

Head of Risk, Global Consumer Goods Company, Dublin

The focus was on the insurance side, looking at how much we spend on insurance every year, seeing if we can save on those sums, by self-insuring ourselves.

2010 – 2012

Internal Audit, Global Consumer Goods Company, Dublin

Strengthening the internal processes to ensure auditors don't find any weaknesses

2006 – 2010

Manager, Risk Management, Big 4 Firm, Dublin

Auditing and testing companies processes to see whether they were operating in adherence with accounting standards

What are the things you most like about your job, and the things you don't like?

Like:

1. Working in global roles

I gain a real understanding of how my company works and how we really make money.

2. The travel aspect

Dealing with different cultures, running risk workshops in China, Ukraine, etc.

Don't like:

1. The egos of the senior management in one of the places I worked.

2. In audit, a lot of the work was pointless work that was completed because it was done last year.

Have you worked long hours over the years?

I think I've been lucky in audit, as I didn't really do long hours. In my current role, I tend to do very long hours when I'm travelling.

Have you had much fun over the years?

I would recommend the big 4 as nearly an extension of university; there is a great social element to it. My jobs after the big 4 have been less fun but I think that's just natural as you get older.

Are you a fan of internships?

- Internships are very useful. In my company, a lot of people have got their jobs through internships, as they worked hard, and people liked them. I'm not sure they would have got the jobs if they came in via a recruiter.
- I think grades are overrated. Personality plays a huge role in the workplace. If you have a good personality and are a good fit with teams, then that goes a hell of a long way.

If you could start over and you were 22, but you know all you know now, would you do anything differently career-wise?

I've had some hard times in my career, but I wouldn't change anything. One of my roles, I really hated it, but in hindsight, I learned a hell of a lot. I wouldn't be in the role I'm in now if it wasn't for that experience. In that role that I hated I spent two years researching everything I could about enterprise risk management, so it helped me a lot.

What career advice would you give a young person now?

- Unless you specifically know what you want to do when you grow up, accounting will get you very far.
- All my intake in the big 4, got the same three-year training, but we are all doing very different roles now. Accounting allows you to get your foot in the door of a big company.
- I have three guys working for me that are all the same age as me. They have different backgrounds than me, but their earning potential is a lot lower simply because they are not chartered accountants. The chartered accountancy (ACA) qualification really does set you apart from others. For example, I was looking at job specs when I came out of my big 4 role, and they were all looking for ACA qualified accountants.

What advice would you give a young person who wanted to do what you do?

It's a tough one, as not a whole lot of companies do what I do, but if someone wants to get involved in risk then strategy would be a good route in.

***

KATIE, 31

26. Business Systems Owner, Financial Regulatory Body, London

What is your degree in?
Bachelor of Arts (Political, Economic and Social Sciences)

Why did you do the degree you did?
I had no idea what I wanted to do. I was interested in how humans behaved and law, but I didn't want to do a law degree.

Did you know what you wanted to do career-wise?
I had no idea, I still have no idea! When I was at university, I worked in a hospital during the summer. After graduating I was also working there, I just got fed up and booked a one-way ticket from Australia to London. I needed to make a dramatic change and thought if I did something so different it would help me figure out what I wanted to do. It turns out it didn't help in a career sense, but it helped in a life sense.

What percentage of what you learned in university have you used in your day-to-day roles?
My degree didn't teach me a qualification, it taught me how to think, how to broaden my imagination. I've ended up in a job where I think more broadly, I'm not limiting myself. I'll do this for a couple of years, work hard, then see what comes up.

With the benefit of hindsight, if you were 18 again now would you do anything differently degree-wise?
- No, because I don't know what I would have done.
- I'm not sure, I'm a late bloomer, but I think too much about too many things, so it's hard for me to settle on one thing, I get bored very quickly.

My main aim in my career is to learn loads of different skills and be a generalist.

What are the jobs you've done since graduating? And what have they entailed?

2015 – 2018

Business Systems Owner, Financial Regulatory Body, London

Improving processes, figuring out the best way to do something and building that into the system.

2013 – 2015

Junior Associate, Financial Regulatory Body, London

Worked in the operations team, learning how the company works.

2011 – 2012

Administrative Assistant, Healthcare Start-Up, London

Daily administration for the office and more senior staff.

What are the things you most like about your job, and the things you don't like?

Like:

1. People – I love figuring out how people do things.
2. New ideas.

Don't like:

1. People – they can be really difficult to work with, especially if the culture is bad in a company.

Have you worked long hours over the years?

Not particularly no, I will work when I need to, but generally, my hours are 9-5.

Have you had much fun over the years?

Yes, lots of fun. I work for a semi-state company where there are lots of young people my age.

If you could start over and you were 22, but you know all you know now, would you do anything differently career-wise?
I'm not sure I'd do anything differently. Every decision I made when I was younger has got me to where I am today.

Are you going to keep on being a generalist?
How can you ask that question to a generalist - of course!

What career advice would you give a young person now?
Try everything, unless you grow up knowing what you want to do. I think there are so many people confused about what they want to do. Try it quickly, fail fast, be agile. The more you try the bigger chance you have of finding something you love.

What are the pros and cons of living and working abroad?
- You realise quickly who you are; there is less pressure to conform.
- Being as far away from the people you are comfortable with has lots of advantages. However, it might not work for some people. For me being uncomfortable is where I'm at my most comfortable. Changing jobs every two years works really well for me. I need to not know what I'm doing to get better at what I'm doing.

***

KIM, 32

27. Senior Tax Director, Media Company, London

What is your degree in?
Bachelor of Business (Accounting and Management)

Why did you do the degree you did?
I applied for a few different degrees and couldn't decide between sports science or accounting. The reason I picked accounting was the qualification that I'd get out of it. I was still undecided as to what I wanted to do but said that I would get the qualification first and then re-assess how I felt.

Did you know what you wanted to do career-wise?
No, not really, I was still very unsure when I was 18-20, I wanted to go travelling to figure it out. I ended up getting a job before I went travelling as I needed some cash, then I thought I may as well give the accounting role a go. I did it for a year, then I took a sabbatical, and had a great time!

What percentage of what you learned in university have you used in your day-to-day roles?
A very small percentage, probably less than 20%.

When you came out of university did you seek advice from anyone?
- No, it was more my own research, my three interests were art, PE, and maths.
- I did some work experience in an advertising firm during the summers, so I talked to different people there.

With the benefit of hindsight, if you were 18 again now would you do anything differently degree-wise?
- No, I don't think I'd be in the position I'm in today without that degree.
- I think it would be very interesting to do the degree a couple of years after working as I think you'd get way more out of it.
- Now, I do the sports stuff as my hobbies, not as my career.

What are the jobs you've done since graduating? And what have they entailed?
2016 – 2018
Senior Tax Director, Media Company, London
Responsible for the firm's global indirect tax strategy.
2012 – 2015
Financial Controller, International Media Company, London
Responsible for all finance-related matters one of the entities (countries) within the firm i.e. tax, reporting, payments.
2010 – 2012
Compliance Analyst, International Media Company, London

Responsible for ensuring that all the accounts were completed on time and correctly.

2006 – 2010

Accounts/Audit Senior, Accounting Firm, London

I dealt with everything from sole traders' accounts to auditing bigger companies. I think this was more valuable than going into a big 4 firm, where you get pigeon-holed into doing the same thing for three years.

What are the things you most like about your job, and the things you don't like?

Like:

1. Being put in the deep end, steep learning curves, taking on roles where I've been out of my depth as I have learned so much.
2. The opportunities for progression that you get in a big company.
3. Flexible working hours.

Don't like:

1. I haven't really had a good manager in my working life, I have had to look elsewhere for direction and support.
2. It can be tough to get things done in a big corporate firm.
3. Timesheets – when I was an auditor, they were a real pain!

Which would you prefer to work for: a small company or a big company, and why?

A big company would be my preference, as there is better training, money, processes, and chances to progress. (Although a small company is more enjoyable to work for, and you have better relationships with your co-workers).

Have you worked long hours over the years?

Yes, I've worked long hours over the years.

Have you had much fun over the years?

Yes, I've lived in a foreign country with work, and had a great time with people that I've worked with however the work has been tough.

If you could start over and you were 22, but you know all you know now, would you do anything differently career-wise?

- I would have liked to get into an industry that I'm passionate about. I'd still work in finance, but I would be more interested in what the company does. Also, it would be nice to work in a faster-paced environment, i.e. a start-up, or a smaller more dynamic company.
- It's harder the more senior you get to change careers/roles. If you can jump around in your 20s and get more broad experience, then I think that may be more valuable than trying to get very high up in one company.

What career advice would you give a young person now?

- Are you after money? Or job satisfaction? If you are after money, be sensible about what industry you want to get into as some of them pay more than others. If it's passion, then get lots of varied experience in the industry you are passionate about. Then see if you are passionate enough to pursue it as a career and be ok with not making so much cash.
- There are roles that pay well in cool industries you may be passionate about, but it might take you longer to get these roles. There will also be a lot of competition for them.

What advice would you give a young person who wanted to do what you do?

- Do some relevant work experience and see whether you want to work in that area before you embark on doing loads of exams.
- Try and get into that area, make connections and use those people to open doors.
- It's only in the last few years that I've realised the importance of knowing people, and the opportunities this opens up.

Which gets you further in a career – knowing people or being good at your job?

Being good at your job, as if you are good you will get to know more people.

***

MICHAEL, 34

28. Regulatory Manager, Financial Regulatory Body, London

What is your degree in?
Bachelor of Commerce
Law Conversion Course (two years)

Why did you do the degree you did?
The commerce degree had a lot of choice in it, and I wanted to do something business related. I did the law course because I didn't want to leave university!

Did you know what your day-to-day role entailed starting off in your career?
Very little. In my first interview, I was asked 'do you know what the job is about?'. I gave a big long answer to which the interviewer replied 'it is absolutely nothing like that'!

Why did you embark on the career you did?
It was the second interview I did, and it was the first job I got offered.

What percentage of what you learned in university have you used in your day-to-day roles?
Very little, all I use now from my degree is report writing.

With the benefit of hindsight, if you were 18 again now would you do anything differently degree-wise?
I would have done the same, but I would have done a Masters after the law course. You will never get the fun you had at university back again!

What are the jobs you've done since graduating? And what have they entailed?
2014 – 2018
Lead Associate, Financial Regulatory Body, London

Driving the regulatory relationship with market infrastructure providers.

2011 – 2014

Senior Associate, Financial Regulatory Body, London

Gatekeeper to the stock exchange, deciding and advising on what companies should be admitted.

2007 – 2011

Company Listing Advisor, Stock Exchange, Dublin

Providing advice to investment banks and trading firms, on EU directives, company law and stock exchange listing rules.

What are the things you most like about your job, and the things you don't like?

Like:

1. Getting access to lots of confidential information before anyone knows it.
2. Meeting very senior CEO's of companies and asking them difficult questions.
3. Meeting different regulators across Europe and getting different perspectives.

Don't like:

1. The companies that you review can be quite complex.
2. Lots of administration work – testing whether various procedures are in place, audit work, etc.

Which would you prefer to work for: a small company or a big company, and why?

I'd prefer a smaller company; it's much more fun. You get to know the people you are working with a lot better.

Have you worked long hours over the years?

Starting off it can be long hours, it eases off when you get more senior and you realise long hours get you nowhere.

Have you had much fun over the years?

Great fun! I've had much more fun working for a commercial organisation versus semi-state body. I'd much prefer working for a private company, they take you out for drinks, nights out etc.

If you could start over and you were 22, but you know all you know now, would you do anything differently career-wise?
I'd probably go down the human resources route, it seems to be a nice career path from what I can see.

What career advice would you give a young person now?
People say promotions aren't political, don't believe them, it really is all political - getting promoted is all about sucking up to people. Latch yourself onto someone more senior who is going places, and you'll be dragged along on their coat tails.

What advice would you give a young person who wanted to do what you do?
The easiest route is via a graduate programme, be confident and show eagerness.

CREATIVE

What I knew before the interviews:

I didn't know a whole lot about creative industries, what I did know:

- There were lots of drinks and boozy lunches, and team trips away.
- It was very competitive to get good roles.
- There seemed to be a lot of politics compared to other professions.

What I learned from the interviews:

- There are lots of roles in creative industries
that aren't 100% creative, i.e. planning, account management, etc.
- It's long hours; you are never off the clock.
- Clients can be quite demanding.
- Working as a personal assistant can be quite a good route into the industry.

AMY, 31,

29. Senior Account Director, Creative Agency, London

What is your degree in?
Bachelor of Arts (Graphic Design for Communication)

Why did you do the degree you did?
I studied A level art and then took the usual route to do the Art Foundation course. After that, I decided to specialise in design for communication because I liked the intellectual aspect; the ability to respond in any mix of media, with wit and humour.

Why did you embark on the career you did?
My mother worked in advertising in the 80s (the glory days!), so I guess I'd always had an impression of what a fun, glamorous career it was. I had a natural interest in the people side of things and the psychology of 'selling' ideas. So, when a friend-turned-recruiter told me about a job as an account executive as a digital ad agency, I went for it.

When you came out of university did you seek advice from anyone?
I'd very little knowledge about the types of jobs available in the working world, so my finding the job I did was somewhat serendipitous.

Did you know what your day-to-day role entailed starting off in your career?
When I was in my second year of university, I was lucky enough to do an exchange program to New York where I took advertising classes in an agency. So, I had some experience of what it was like to work on an advertising brief. However, starting out all I knew about my job to be was written on a recruiter's job spec!

What percentage of what you learned in university have you used in your day-to-day roles?
Design for communication as a discipline has absolutely helped me in my day-to-day job. While I'm no longer coming up with ideas myself, an

understanding of the creative process and being able to spot good ideas is what makes a good account director.

With the benefit of hindsight, if you were 18 again now would you do anything differently degree-wise?
On reflection, no. I loved every bit of my degree. It gave me great joy. However, I do wish I'd had more information on the full gamut of industry jobs available to me, to make an informed career choice.

What are the jobs you've done since graduating? And what have they entailed?
2010 – 2018
Senior Account Director, Creative Agency, London
Responsible for different campaigns, managing client expectations, budgets, etc.
2008 – 2010
Account Manager, Advertising Agency, London
Starting to manage campaigns, interacting with clients.
2006 – 2008
Account Executive, Advertising Agency, London
Admin and helping the account managers/directors.

What are the things you most like about your job, and the things you don't like?
Like:
1. Managing a team through a process start to finish (the highs and lows) is very rewarding.
2. Spending my day surrounded by creativity, making work that people talk about.
3. A heavy amount of fun and socialising.
Don't like:
1. Starting out as an account executive is tough. There's a lot of 'admin' involved.
2. Long hours. You're expected to put in hard graft and often some late nights to earn your stripes.

3. The lines between work and play become more blurred in advertising, which is both in my good and bad list!

Which would you prefer to work for: a small company or a big company, and why?
For me, it's not about the size of the company, so much as the attitude and the people that work around you. I currently work in a fair-sized agency, but everyone knows each other very well and it has an intimate feeling. I'd hate to work in a faceless organisation where I didn't feel valued.

Have you worked long hours over the years?
Yes! It's somewhat par for the course. Less so now, but when the time requires (a pitch, for example), everyone is expected to put the hours in.

Have you had much fun over the years?
Absolutely. There is a real sense of team and camaraderie. We all face the trials and tribulations together, so there's plenty of celebrating our successes when a campaign goes live. Not to mention a regular stream of industry parties offering up free-flowing booze. Socialising is very much part of the job.

If you could start over and you were 22, but you know all you know now, would you do anything differently career-wise?
If I were starting again, I'd consider doing the Bucks or Watford course that specifically trains advertising creatives post-university. But that said, I'm pretty happy with where I am now.

What career advice would you give a young person now?
Focus on what you're good at, work hard at it and the right opportunity will present itself. Whatever you do, don't follow someone else's path. If you stick to what you love doing, you won't go wrong.

What advice would you give a young person who wanted to do what you do?

Be cheeky. I'm sure if I applied for a graduate scheme of thousands of applicants, I probably wouldn't have made the cut. If you can go another way in using your own guile and tenacity, do it. Fortune favours the brave.

***

GARETH, 33,

30. Senior Account Director, Advertising Agency, London

What is your degree in?
Bachelor of Business Studies (Marketing)

Why did you do the degree you did?
I did economics as an A level, and found it very interesting; demand and supply, how that applies to people making decisions. There were modules in my economics course about marketing, brands and creating a want and need for a product, which I really liked. There was a course in Brighton that was business studies with marketing, so there was a bit of a balance. I wasn't doing just marketing and putting all my eggs in one basket.

Why did you embark on the career you did?
My degree was a sandwich course, for the third year I did work experience with a famous luxury goods company in London. I worked in the marketing department; my boss told me if I managed to get all my work done, then I could go and get involved with the really cool stuff. So, I used to get all my work done by Tuesday, and then spend the rest of the week speaking to the new product development guys, hanging out with the PR girls, seeing how the adverts are made. That work experience was amazing. I asked the advertising guys and account managers what their roles were like, and what their jobs entailed. I got such great insight into the world of advertising. I couldn't recommend work experience enough to young people these days.

What percentage of what you learned in university have you used in your day-to-day roles?

50% or 60%, I picked my modules to align with what I wanted to do after university. I was quite lucky I figured out quite early what I wanted to do.

With the benefit of hindsight, if you were 18 again now would you do anything differently degree-wise?
I always liked drama and acting. Where I grew up, it was quite poor. I always thought you had to be from a wealthier background to be an actor or performer, as you wouldn't always have money coming in, etc. I was a bit risk averse and didn't want to take a chance. If I could go back now, I'd maybe follow my passion a bit more. That would be the one regret I have.

What are the jobs you've done since graduating? And what have they entailed?
2011 – 2017
Senior Account Director, Advertising Agency, London
Delivering several different campaigns, keeping the wheels moving on all accounts.
2009 – 2010
Account Manager, Advertising Agency, London
Starting to manage campaigns and getting my own clients to manage.
2007 – 2009
Account Executive, Advertising Agency, London
Entry-level position, helping the account managers and directors with admin.

What are the things you most like about your job, and the things you don't like?
Like:
1. The variety. I've worked on 6/7 accounts in 10 years. Every time you get a new account, it feels like you've got a new job.
2. Working in a young creative environment - advertising is young and vibrant.
3. The money – you get paid quite well.

4. You get a lot of responsibility at a young age. When you are 24/25 years of age, you are responsible for budgets of £1m.

Don't like:
1. It's very long hours. Very rarely can you meet a friend on a Tuesday or a Wednesday evening as you are working. It's 9am - 7/8pm, it can be 10-11 hour days.
2. The client fatigue – some clients change things so much that it's not even the idea anymore. On the agency side*, you are constantly selling, trying to please people rather than being the decision maker.
(*A marketing brand manager will tell the advertising agency what they want the advert to look like. The agency then must meet their expectations.)

3. The career progression. On the agency side, the 40-year-olds still do the long hours and stressful days, whereas on the client side the big bosses just do 9-5. It's always a treadmill in advertising - I'm not sure it ever slows down much on the agency side.

Which would you prefer to work for: a small company or a big company, and why?
I started off with a small independent, and it was great. Then I moved to a bigger agency and found it was tough to get things done.

Have you worked long hours over the years?
Yes, most people would say it's a lot of fun, it's the people you meet. Also, clients would stab each other in the back as there is only one brand manager role in their company for that brand/product. In advertising agencies, it's much more of a family that tries and help each other. If someone wins a pitch, we all go out for drinks; there is a nice feel to working in an agency.

If you could start over and you were 22, but you know all you know now, would you do anything differently career-wise?
I might have tried to get into the creative side. When creatives start off, they must do a lot of interning, and create a portfolio of their work. It's

a lot tougher than getting a planning or account manager role. So, I might have tried to go more creative, but it's not easy!

What career advice would you give a young person now?

- Think about what you like. You don't want to end up studying something that you are not interested in. Think about what you might enjoy doing and go get work experience to test and see whether you do like it.
- A lot of the young ones we take in are A level students, who are on their fifth work placement in five weeks! When I was their age I was spending my summers in Ibiza; they are way more on the ball than I was!
- Some of the interns that work for us are not very good. I encourage them to go on holiday and enjoy themselves!!

What gets you further in your career - knowing people or being good at your job?

You must be good at your job. Look at me I didn't know anyone; I was a scumbag working-class boy from Wales! I went to those graduate assessment days, they were all really posh kids. I remember thinking I'm not going to get far here. I went knocking on doors and started in a small agency and worked my ass off, and I've done pretty well!

***

GEORGIE, 31

31. Business Director, Advertising Firm, London

What is your degree in?

Bachelor of Arts (Sociology)

Why did you do the degree you did?

I wanted to do arts, but my mum wouldn't let me, she wanted me to do a more academic degree.

Did you know what you wanted to do career-wise?

I wanted to do something creative, was interested in doing something in music, something creative. Advertising was quite a good mix of commerce and creative, so that's the direction I headed in.

Did you know what your day-to-day role entailed starting off in your career?

- I was completely blind as to what an advertising person does. The last six months of university was very stressful as for the first time I didn't have a path to follow. I felt like I was free falling.
- My dad could get me an in with a few creative industries, I was lucky and ended up getting on a prestigious graduate programme. Graduate programmes aren't everything though; they are few and far between. There are lots of entry-level jobs out there; you must be persistent, show a little bit of intuition.

Out of the people you work with, what kind of degrees have they done?

The people doing the account manager and planning roles would usually have English, psychology, sociology, languages, business management as degrees. They aren't that necessary for the work you go on to do, but they unlock doors and get you to the interview table. Also, most people will be from a certain university as it is very competitive to get into top advertising firms.

Could you have got the job you did without your degree?

I think I could have. I don't think you need a degree to get into advertising. However, the reason I would recommend a university path is because it unlocks doors. My CEO doesn't have a degree, but he is very well connected. Pick a subject that you find fascinating so that you can demonstrate rigour, hard work, and intelligence.

With the benefit of hindsight, if you were 18 again now would you do anything differently degree-wise?

- I wouldn't criticise my mum for pushing me the way that she did.

- I wish I did something a little bit more creative, like art or history of art. However, I did enjoy sociology, and it has helped me in my career!

What are the jobs you've done since graduating? And what have they entailed?

2015 – 2018

Business Director, Advertising Agency, London

Overseeing multiple accounts, responsible for budgets, people, clients.

2011 – 2015

Account Manager/Account Director, Advertising Agency, London

Starting to talk to the client, doing much more strategic work.

2009 – 2011

Account Executive, Advertising Agency, London

Created advertising for that brand. I didn't have much client contact; I was there to support the team.

2007 – 2008

Graduate Programme, Advertising Agency, London

Shadowing people in different departments, it was amazing, I did fake pitches. I was looked after really well.

What are the things you most like about your job, and the things you don't like?

Like:

1. Every single day is completely different.
2. I work with bright, creative people some of whom have gone onto be my best friends.
3. Being proud of my work, making a product that you think is boring fun and exciting.

Don't like:

1. I've really struggled with the admin side of it.
2. Being contactable all the time, never being off the clock.
3. Clients have lost respect for agencies, 24-hour turnarounds, etc.

Have you worked long hours over the years?

Yes, long hours, and you are always contactable, so it can be tough that way.

Have you had much fun over the years?
Yes, it's not a corporate industry, there are nice lunches, flexible working, boozy nights, you get to go on shoots, I've been all around the world, etc.

Which would you prefer to work for: a small company or a big company, and why?
Small agencies tend to be quite dynamic, but often they are quite hard work. They don't always have the roles that big companies have, so you might have to be more of a jack of all trades in a small company. It can be tougher work but more rewarding.

If you could start over and you were 22, but you know all you know now, would you do anything differently career-wise?
- I would have been a bit braver in some of my decisions. If you have lots of different types of experience that stands to you a bit more. It's no longer a career ladder; it's more like a career jungle gym. Variety isn't just about building your skill set; it's also about enjoyment.
- I would have believed in myself a bit more, even though I have done well. Don't presume that everyone who went to a better university than you are smarter than you, find your voice and be confident!

What career advice would you give a young person now?
Don't worry. You will find your path. Try different things out, a lot of people I know who have become very successful have changed paths through hard work.

What advice would you give a young person who wanted to do what you do?
- This is a competitive industry. Show some initiative, make yourself stand out, if I see five different CVs, we're in a creative industry, what will make me pick yours, be different!

- Be persistent, don't give up! Show that you are smart and a grafter. I wouldn't hold out for graduate programmes. There are entry level jobs. I recently hired a team PA/receptionist, they will be doing the same kind of thing as a person on graduate programmes. Get in there, show what you can do, make your own opportunities.

What type of people are more suited to working in advertising?
Creatives need to be leftfield thinkers, whereas to be an account director, you need a high level of emotional intelligence. You need to understand people, how they think, how they make decisions. You can be very academically intelligent and be a flop in advertising. You must be socially intelligent.

Which gets you further in a career – knowing people or being good at your job?
Knowing people gets your foot in the door, but it won't get you to the top, you must be good at your job.

***

ISLA, 31

32. Group Pastry Chef, Food Company, London

What is your degree in?
Diploma in Pastry

Why did you do the degree you did?
After doing my chef diploma in savoury, I decided to further specialise in pastry.

Why did you embark on the career you did?
I have always had an interest in cooking and thought pastry would be a unique challenge.

When you came out of university did you seek advice from anyone?

I did not know anyone particularly well before embarking as a chef. I had great mentors while I was studying who gave me ample advice on my career going forward.

Did you know what your day-to-day role entailed starting off in your career?

To be honest, I had little idea as to what it entailed before studying but my university had an on-site restaurant, so I learned very quickly.

What percentage of what you learned in university have you used in your day-to-day roles?

It's hard to put a percentage on it, but some of the skills I learned at university have benefitted me now, i.e. work ethic and being a team-player,

With the benefit of hindsight, if you were 18 again now would you do anything differently degree-wise?

I am in the right position currently and all my actions have culminated to this point, so probably not.

What are the things you most like about your job, and the things you don't like?

Like:

1. Developing new recipes.
2. Training new pastry chefs and getting them inspired.
3. Meeting an array of fantastic people in the industry.

Don't like:

1. Early morning winter starts for the morning bake.
2. Difficult customers when I ran my own business back in South Africa.
3. Necessary but gruelling kitchen scrub downs.

Which would you prefer to work for: a small company or a big company, and why?

I think both have their merits. A kitchen becomes a family so as long as I am surrounded by good people; that is more important.

Have you worked long hours over the years?
Long hours are part and parcel of being a chef, so yes.

Have you had much fun over the years?
Being a chef has been huge fun. You create great food and bond with fantastic people from all over the world.

If you could start over and you were 22, but you know all you know now, would you do anything differently career-wise?
Honestly, I would not change a thing.

What career advice would you give a young person now?
Find a career that you love and you will never work a day in your life.

What advice would you give a young person who wanted to do what you do?
My biggest advice is to be passionate, have a good work ethic as well as listen to your superior chefs. You can learn a huge amount from others around you. There is no space in the kitchen for big egos.

***

NATALIE, 32

33. Senior TV Producer, Creative Agency, London

What is your degree in?
Art Foundation course (one year)
Bachelor of Fine Art

Why did you do the degree you did?
Art was my best subject at school.

Did you know what you wanted to do career-wise?

- In the art foundation course, you try out lots of things: architecture, jewellery, fashion design, furniture-making. (You couldn't do an art degree without doing the art foundation course). I was good at fine art, so that's what I did.
- It was sad; there was no career advice at my university.
- I did a year at Melbourne university, where I did sculpture. During that year, I did copyright law, and photoshop, but we didn't have any of that in my degree in the UK, I came back not knowing at all what to do.
- I went and worked for an art dealer because I didn't want to be an artist and struggle for money for the rest of my life. Both my parents worked very hard to get to where they did in life. I think I'd have felt guilty if I was the first person in my family to go to university, and just become an artist with no money for the rest of my life.

When you came out of university did you seek advice from anyone?
No, but I did lots of work in galleries, there were no work placements when I went to university. One of my big regrets is not doing some proper work experience as it would have really helped me.

What percentage of what you learned in university have you used in your day-to-day roles?
30% - the degree didn't prepare me for working life. However, you learn a very abstract way of thinking. You objectify everything, you work through problems to get to an outcome; it helps in what I do now.

With the benefit of hindsight, if you were 18 again now would you do anything differently degree-wise?
I would have done something more specific. Fine art was very broad. For example, one of my friends is a knitwear designer, she is Head of Knitwear and doing very well for herself, as it's such a niche genre. If you like pottery, go and do three years of pottery, you will become a master very quickly, as the degree will give you have a very good base.

What are the jobs you've done since graduating? And what have they entailed?

2008 – 2018

Senior TV Producer, Various Creative Agencies, London

Making commercials – being given a budget and a script and making that into a commercial.

What are the things you most like about your job, and the things you don't like?

Like:

1. Advertising is exciting; it's fast-paced.
2. You get to meet so many people, get to go to lots of gigs, events, etc.
3. Everyone is all working together towards the one goal.

Don't like:

1. The long hours.
2. If you don't know what you want to do, advertising can be a tough place to be. If you want to get into the industry, you need to know what you want to do within advertising, as you can spend a lot of time on the fringes not really getting anywhere.
3. It can be stressful. There is not as much money as there used to be, and there is a lot of money at stake. When I make a TV advert it usually costs £1m, that's the equivalent of a 10-part TV mini-series, so there is a lot of pressure to get things right.

Which would you prefer to work for: a small company or a big company, and why?

- It depends on the ethos/vibe of the company; you'll get that from talking to the people who work there.
- Big companies have a lot of rules, and are harder to get into, harder to do things in general.
- Smaller companies are a lot more open and friendly.
- My company is very open; I sit next to four partners who own the company.

Have you worked long hours over the years?

I do a good 60-hour week, sometimes 80.

Have you had much fun over the years?

Yes, you get to go to a lot of gigs, you get to meet famous people, you are continually meeting new interesting people. A lot of talented people bang on your door and want to collaborate with you.

If you could start over and you were 22, but you know all you know now, would you do anything differently career-wise?

- I'd be a radio DJ. I'd be so good. I could talk for hours!
- I feel like I didn't talk to enough people in my 20s, now you've got email and LinkedIn, you can seek advice from anyone.

What career advice would you give a young person now?

I always say be as open and friendly as possible, never be afraid to ask for anything. People love talking about themselves. Work is such a huge part of our lives, when you are young you are afraid to ask people about their jobs. Email is very easy to ignore, so call people, it's tough to say no over the phone.

What advice would you give a young person who wanted to do what you do?

- Get as much knowledge as you can when you are doing that art foundation course. I didn't have anyone artsy to talk to in my family. They were all scientists or carpenters. Contact the heads of every advertising agency and ask to come in and do work experience.
- If you want to start in production, then get a job as a runner, everyone needs a runner.

Within advertising, how do you know if you want to be on the planning side or the creative side?

- Go and chat with planners, account managers, creative people, producers, etc. see what kind of people they are, what are their backgrounds? What are their skillsets? Which of them are you more like?
- At my agency, we have eight runners, and they get to choose after a year which department they want to go into, so that's a good option.

***

SHAUN, 34

34. Branded Content Manager, Football Club, London

What is your degree in?
Bachelor of Science (Media Technology)

Why did you do the degree you did?
I did that because I got fired from the job I took after my A levels and was attracted by the glamour of working in media.

Did you know what your day-to-day role entailed starting off in your career?
I had a rough idea, just what your average movie buff, music video connoisseur, TV addict would know.

What percentage of what you learned in university have you used in your day-to-day roles?
The industry has progressed a lot, so very little. However, my degree taught me a lot about the representation of minorities and women in the media, so it prepared me well. It was a very practical degree; it made me not be fearful of a TV studio.

When you came out of university did you seek advice from anyone?
No, I went into it blind, barring what I knew from the media A level.

With the benefit of hindsight, if you were 18 again now would you do anything differently degree-wise?
I have been as successful as I could hope to be from that degree. If I could go back now with the power of hindsight, I would have chosen to do something more academic. I would have done something that was a bit more solid, instead of media which was bells and whistles, and full of promise.

What are the jobs you've done since graduating? And what have they entailed?

2016 – 2018

Branded Content Manager, Football Club, London

Producing media content, for the club and commercial partners.

2007 – 2016

TV Producer, Advertising Agency, London

Making commercials – being given a budget and a script and making that into a commercial.

2006 – 2007

Intern, Advertising Agency, London

Admin work, learning about the industry.

What are the things you most like about your job, and the things you don't like?

Like:

1. The creative side of my job.
2. The varied, interesting and intelligent personalities you work with.

Don't like:

1. The money is not great to start with – it's a struggle.
2. The hours in advertising, they are awful especially for what it is.
3. Advertising's effect in the world.

Which would you prefer to work for: a small company or a big company, and why?

I prefer working with smaller less process-driven organisations, which suits my personality. It allows you to learn more when you work for a small organisation.

Have you worked long hours over the years?

I do long hours – 50-hour weeks.

Have you had much fun over the years?

Yes, lots of fun.

If you could start over and you were 22, but you know all you know now, would you do anything differently career-wise?
There is a difference between what you want to do, and what you are capable of doing. I'd like to have done something a bit more academic, be the expert in one field, i.e. History – Rome, North Korea, etc.

What career advice would you give a young person now?
- Prepare to a) not do what you're expecting, and b) adapt, your jobs will change drastically over the next 20 years.
- Listen as much as you can in your early years because if you don't, you won't go anywhere.

What advice would you give a young person who wanted to do what you do?
- Nepotism helps!
- Do lots of internships; they are way more important than your degree.
- There are loads of applications, so make sure yours is an enthusiastic application that stands out from the crowd. I have received applications where people send me action figures of themselves to get my attention - stand out, be different!

Which will get you further - graduate programmes or internships?
- Graduate programmes are good, but they are super difficult to get on, they last a year, and you are not guaranteed a job out of it.
- Internships, yes you can be treated like crap, and you can be unpaid, but they are only for a few weeks. Do five or six of them, but if you do well and you are enthusiastic, then you will have an in, instead of having to wait a year. I would favour internships every time.

***

SUZANNE, 31

35. Account Director, Media Company, Dublin

What is your degree in?

Bachelor of Science (Zoology)

Why did you do the degree you did?
I wanted to study zoology when I was a child.

Did you know what you wanted to do career-wise?
Zoology is very specialised. I would have had to do a Ph.D. for another four or five years and then specialise in something very specific. There was an animal care course in the UK which would get you a job working in a zoo, but that wasn't for me. I did look at postgrads, working with fisheries and environmental agencies, but Ireland is quite limited in that area. The UK would have had more opportunities, but I was young, I had confidence issues, I wasn't sure what I was capable of doing. I signed up to a couple of job alerts, but they were all in different countries, I knew I needed a break, so I went travelling.

What did you do when you realised there was no future for you in a zoology career?
- I always wanted to go travelling, after university, but I needed money. My sister worked in finance in a hotel. She got me an accounts assistant job. I worked there for a year, and then went travelling.
- When I came home, there was a recession. For someone with a general degree in a non-distinct field it was a terrible time. I was unemployed for six months which was not a nice experience. A sales job was the only job I could get. The commission was two and a half times my salary, so I ended up being on great money for a 23-year-old!

With the benefit of hindsight, if you were 18 again now would you do anything differently degree-wise?
- I wouldn't have changed my degree, I was interested in it, and it was a well-regarded university. Science is also highly regarded as it's more analytical and not one of the softer degrees.
- Academic universities lack career direction. There is no conversation around career development. We didn't even discuss jobs until the fourth year when they sit down and tell you that you won't get a job out of this

degree. Other universities were a lot more industry-focused, there were work placements, focus on career paths, etc. So, keep that in mind when you are picking universities.

What are the jobs you've done since graduating? And what have they entailed?

2016 – 2017

Account Director, Media Company, Dublin

Managing a set of client accounts, ensuring that they are profitable, and growing.

2013 – 2016

Business Analyst/Finance, Media Company, Dublin

Designing, building and owning finance processes.

2011 – 2013

Accounts Assistant, Hotel Group, Dublin

Supporting the finance team in ensuring all costs and revenues are correctly accounted for.

2009 – 2011

Sales Consultant, Telecom Company, Dublin

Selling and fixing phones in a phone shop.

What are the things you most like about your job, and the things you don't like?

Like:

1. The variety, I get bored easily.
2. Interacting with people, customer/client facing roles.
3. Creativity, even in my finance role, I was designing processes, so I could create and not just conform.
4. Autonomy, being able to do what I want in my role.

Don't like:

1. Monotony, doing the same thing day in day out.
2. Roles that are too rigid – hate companies that time you in and out.
3. Roles that you are just on your own stuck at a computer or in a lab.

Which would you prefer to work for: a small company or a big company, and why?

The company was very small when I joined. There were 30 people now there is 200. I like the small to mid-sized companies. Small companies are easy to progress in, and they are lot more fun.

Have you had much fun over the years?

The most fun jobs I had would be the non-finance roles. Having fun at work is important to me. One of the core values of this company is having fun. Media is also a young fun industry.

If you could start over and you were 22, but you know all you know now, would you do anything differently career-wise?

- I wouldn't change my degree, as I did enjoy it. I'd spend more time researching roles, and what jobs there are, what people do for a living, and what they earn. I didn't even think about money when I was younger.
- I would have focused on the interests that I have, and sought career advice a little bit earlier. I went in lots of different directions, I eventually got here, but I would have liked to get here sooner.

What career advice would you give a young person now?

- You must strike a balance between what you enjoy and what you can earn a decent living doing. Lots of people do something that will pay a lot of money, i.e. law, accounting, but then mightn't really enjoy it. Other people do something in university that is fun and interesting, but you can't get any good jobs out of it.
- Look at job websites, what are the type of roles? What industries are out there? What skills do these jobs look for? Don't just do accounting because it is what everyone else is doing, or go to university because that's the norm. Don't be afraid to take a year out and try and figure things out. Don't rush into something you mightn't necessarily like. Do your research, the more you know, the more informed decisions you will be able to make.
- Also, if you are in a company you do like, but you don't like the role; how can you upskill yourself to get those roles so you are happy?

What gets you further in a career – knowing people or being good at your job?

- You must be good at your job. If you are not, then you will eventually get found out. I got at least two roles by knowing people, it's incredibly important, but people won't recommend you if you are rubbish.
- Even in an organisation, it's important to know the right people, being in the right circles, and to be well respected by the right people, just play the game a bit.
- If I was a kid who didn't have a clue, I would say don't worry about it. It will all work out, just look at my career path!

Questions:

If you have any career questions, please do email them to me and I will try to answer them as best I can.

careeradviceforyoungpeople@gmail.com

Blog Newsletter:

If you liked the book and want to get more exclusive content, please do sign up to my newsletter. You'll find the sign-up form at the end of all my blog posts.

www.1000yearsofcareeradvice.com

ENGINEERING

What I knew before the interviews:

- It can be long hours.
- There was great scope to work and travel with it.
- Jobs can be quite dependent on how the economy is performing.
- There is a good social side to it.
- Some engineering can be very lucrative, i.e. oil and gas, highways, pipelines etc.

What I learned from the interviews:

- There is great satisfaction from seeing something built.
- Not all engineers are good at communicating what needs to be done, the ones who can are the really good ones.
- You can move from different types of engineering quite easily, i.e. water, rail, road, etc.
- The difference between design and site, and civil and structural engineering.
- That you can go into project management very early on in your engineering career.
- Nearly all the engineers who have worked abroad wish they had done even more.
- A lot of engineering is updating reports, and spreadsheets, it's not as exciting as you may think.

DARRAGH, 30

36. Infrastructure Specialist, Water Utility Company, Dublin

What is your degree in?
Bachelor of Engineering (Civil)

Why did you do the degree you did?
I was good at maths and metalwork in school, they were my two best subjects. I would have been poor in English.

Did you know what you wanted to do career-wise?
- No, I still don't. I'm 30, and I still don't know what I want to do with my career!
- There were no engineering jobs in Ireland when I came out of university due to the recession. People with 2.1* degrees couldn't even get a job; there were no jobs as it was the height of the recession. I did an internship with an engineering company, and they offered me a six-month role when I graduated, which was rare at that time.

(*This is an upper second class honours.)

Did your civil engineering degree prepare you for the working world?
You learn more doing the actual work. Doing a work placement gives you an understanding of things. My degree was four years with the third year as a work placement, if your degree was three years in university with no placement I don't think you'd be prepared.

Did you ever think of any other careers?
At 18, I didn't fully know all the different paths you could do, I knew about commerce and business. I thought engineering would be more hands-on and not be so office based. In reality, I'm in the office on excel five days a week, updating spreadsheets.

When you came out of university did you seek advice from anyone?

No, I did a part-time postgraduate degree two years after university, purely because there were no jobs.

With the benefit of hindsight, if you were 18 again now would you do anything differently degree-wise?
I wouldn't do engineering, but don't know what I would do, maybe something in business? Engineering is a lot slower-paced than you think. You must go through a lot of red tape, approvals, government regulations, specifications; it takes a long while for a project to really get going.

What are the jobs you've done since graduating? And what have they entailed?
2017 – 2018
Infrastructure Specialist, Water Utility Company, Dublin
Working on approvals for water infrastructure projects.
2014 – 2017
Project Manager, Engineering Firm, Malawi
Designing water projects in Ireland and Africa.
2011 – 2013
Graduate Engineer, Engineering Firm, Dublin
Assisting senior engineers on jobs.

What are the things you most like about your job, and the things you don't like?
Like:
1. Travelling with my job.
2. The versatility.
I've lots of different types of work in my previous roles, project management, etc.
3. The people.

Don't like:
1. The frustration of trying to get approvals.
It can be quite difficult to get projects off the ground.

2. Boredom – it's not the most stimulating work, it sounds like it is, but a lot of the time its entering data into excel. (I spend an awful lot of time re-writing reports over tiny things).

Which would you prefer to work for: a small company or a big company, and why?
I'd prefer a smaller company as it's more collaborative. In a big company, it can be harder to get other teams or divisions to work with you.

Have you worked long hours over the years?
9-5 but sometimes I do the odd late night.

Have you had much fun over the years?
Yes, I spent one year in Malawi, Africa. It was one of the best things I've ever done, expanding your mind, meeting new people. You see how different countries build things which is very interesting.

If you could start over and you were 22, but you know all you know now, would you do anything differently career-wise?
Tough question, had I not started in the firm I did I wouldn't have got the Malawi opportunity. In hindsight, I would have gone abroad earlier, should have gone at 22 or 23. Going abroad as a professional gets harder once you hit 30, so I definitely would have tried to get international experience in my 20s.

What career advice would you give a young person now?
- Jump at any experience you can get.
- Don't be afraid to have gaps on your CV by going travelling. I have zero gaps in my CV seven years out from university, but I have found the people who have gaps on their CV are at the exact same point as me in their career. I think people are too cautious, and I'm one of them!

What advice would you give a young person who wanted to do what you do?

Work on your maths and physics, and network as much as you can. It's not all about your degree, try and get your foot in the door of a top company and build your network as wide as possible starting out. Make a good impression on everyone you meet, and you'll be surprised how many opportunities will open up.

***

FEIDHLIM, 34

37. Project Engineer, Construction Firm, London

What is your degree in?
Bachelor of Engineering (Civil)

Why did you do the degree you did?
It seemed interesting, and it was more maths and science which were my preferred subjects.

With the benefit of hindsight, if you were 18 again now would you do anything differently degree-wise?
I wouldn't change, it's not the most lucrative, but it's interesting work, which I'm happy enough with.

Did you know what your day-to-day role entailed starting off in your career?
- Yes, I had a fair idea of the consultancy side, not so much the contracting side. I spoke to a couple of engineers and got good job descriptions from them.
- When I finished university, I wanted to go into the design side of engineering, but then the financial crash happened. I didn't really know what the role entailed, but I knew the work that the company did.

What percentage of what you learned in university have you used in your day-to-day roles?
20%

What are the jobs you've done since graduating? And what have they entailed?

2015 – 2017

Project Engineer, Construction Firm, London

Responsible for all engineering deliverables, planning, procurement, technical docs, health and safety, etc.

2014 – 2015

Project Engineer, Residential Construction Company, London

Management and supervision of basement construction projects from site set up through to structural completion.

2012 – 2014

Project Engineering, Renewable Energy Company, London

Co-ordinating various wind farm projects.

2006 – 2010

Civil Engineer, Engineering Consulting Company, Dublin

Developing civil infrastructure design on major multi-million euro civil and structural projects.

What are the things you most like about your job, and the things you don't like?

Like:

1. The variety of work without changing field dramatically – wind farms to basements to traditional buildings.
2. The autonomy, when your boss lets you get on with things.
3. It's interesting, projects are always short term less than two years and then it's something very new.

Don't like:

1. In smaller companies you are dependent on the whim of the boss.
2. Generally, you are dependent on a lot of different people for you to be successful in your role.

Have you worked long hours over the years?

It can be quite long hours, it's the nature of the industry, 10-12 hour days.

Have you had much fun over the years?

Yes, there is always a few guys around that are sound and willing to go out for pints, etc.

Which would you prefer to work for: a small company or a big company, and why?

A big company, as better processes, more support, they are more reliable.

If you could start over and you were 22, but you know all you know now, would you do anything differently career-wise?

It's hard to tell, as I tend not to plan things out. I probably should have left a job I was in too long sooner. However, it was during the recession so that had an effect.

What career advice would you give a young person now?

Come out of university and get stuck into site work, and then get some design experience in an office to see which you prefer. Temporary works* can be quite good experience, as you get nice mix of site and design exposure.

(*Temporary works are props to support structures before they are fully constructed)

Do you prefer consultancy over contracting?

I personally favour contracting as there is more action, but there are pros and cons, as contracting can be day-to-day firefighting.

What advice would you give a young person who wanted to do what you do?

It's all talking to people, go to lots of project managers, talk to them, tell them what you want to do. Target other engineers on-site and they will spread the work you are looking for work/experience.

***

LORCAN, 35

38. Project Engineer, Engineering Company, Australia

What is your degree in?
Bachelor of Engineering (Civil)

Why did you do the degree you did?
I was interested in becoming a marine biologist, but it's very hard to get good jobs in that area.

Did you know what your day-to-day role entailed starting off in your career?
I knew a good bit about engineering. I came from a family of civil engineers. I had an uncle who was a civil engineer that worked in Africa, and I thought that was cool. I also had similar characteristics to those guys, good at maths, etc.

When you came out of university did you seek advice from anyone?
I wanted to get paid but didn't want to try my hardest to find a job, and then just end up working in insurance. I went for a guaranteed profession that would pay money and let me travel around the world.

What percentage of what you learned in university have you used in your day-to-day roles?
20%

What are the jobs you've done since graduating? And what have they entailed?
2013 – 2018
Project Engineer (Pipelines), Australia
Managing all technical aspects of a gas pipeline.
2010 – 2012
Engineer (Highway), Tanzania
Supervision of the construction of a $100m upgrade to a Tanzanian Highway.
2007 – 2009
Junior Civil/Design Engineer, Dublin
Developing detailed designs for major road, rail, drainage projects.

What are the things you most like about your job, and the things you don't like?

Like:

1. The satisfaction of seeing something built.
2. The challenging aspect of the work.
3. The camaraderie of working in construction teams.
4. Travel.

Don't like:

1. The hours.
2. The stress.

Which would you prefer to work for: a small company or a big company, and why?

When you come out of university, I'd advise working for a big company. There is more room for advancement, better training, you are exposed to higher standards, etc. Then when you have some experience, go to a small company. You can wear a lot of different hats, and it will keep it interesting. You will get a richer experience in a big company, but a much broader experience in a small company.

Have you worked long hours over the years?

Some jobs are long hours; this job is 50-60 hours a week. I'd like to do less.

Have you had much fun over the years?

- Brilliant fun, I've had the time of my life.
- I've spent two years in Tanzania, saw lots of Africa during that time. I've spent five years in Australia, during which I've seen lots of Asia.

If you could start over and you were 22, but you know all you know now, would you do anything differently career-wise?

I would have travelled more with my job, even though I have travelled quite a bit already. The pros of travelling with your work are you get to experience different cultures and varied techniques. The cons would be not settling down, missing out on birthdays, weddings, etc., and living a normal life.

Who has a better CV, the Civil Engineer who has worked in one city for ten years, or you who has worked all around the world?

- I would have broader engineering experience than the guy who has stayed in Dublin for ten years. However, he would know that local industry/market inside out, e.g. knowledge of people, and local specs and standards, but I feel I could pick up that stuff quickly.
- Personally, I like the variety; I get bored easily. I've done design for two years, roads for two years, oil and gas for two years, now I'm doing smaller projects like sewerage. After this I might go and do rail for two years, then marine for two years, keep my roles interesting.

What career advice would you give a young person now?

Never get stressed about anything, because it doesn't do you any good. It's a pointless short-term waste of energy. If you are working weekends then you are not effectively managing your time, you are burning yourself out and not doing anyone any favours. If you over work yourself, you are going to underperform. Nobody will thank you for putting in long hours.

What advice would you give a young person who wanted to do what you do?

There is a lot of people who can study engineering, but a lot of engineers can't communicate. The engineers that really do well are the ones that can talk and get across what is required, what the issues are etc.

What gets you further in a career – knowing people or being good at your job?

Being good at your job. In engineering, you'll get found out very quickly; it can be ruthless. I worked with a project manager who fired somebody for forgetting to bring a boot! It didn't matter who that guy knew!

How do you know which stream of engineering is for you?

If you are more academic, or not outgoing, stick to design. If you are more outgoing, i.e. you can talk, negotiate, and lead, go into construction.

***

MARK, 31

39. Senior Quantity Surveyor, Construction Company, London

What is your degree in?
Bachelor of Engineering (Quantity Surveying and Commercial Management)

Why did you do the degree you did?
I was offered money to do it. A quantity surveying company put up half of my fees if I went to work for them upon graduating. I got a government grant for the other half, so I came out of university debt free.

Did you know what your day-to-day role entailed starting off in your career?
I knew elements of what the day job entailed. The degree was tailored, they were very good at identifying what you could expect in the role. The degree course had 16 main contractors involved; one student is sponsored by one of the contractors.

Were there any cons to that company sponsoring your degree?
I know a lot of people were tied to the company for two to three years after graduating or they would have to pay back the funding, but not me. Others had to get a 2.1*, and if they didn't, they'd have to re-pay the bursary.
(*This is an upper second class honours.)

What percentage of what you learned in university have you used in your day-to-day roles?
My course was very specifically tailored to the role that I took after graduating so I'd say 60%.

With the benefit of hindsight, if you were 18 again now would you do anything differently degree-wise?

No! However, I personally wouldn't recommend people going into construction, unless you own your own business. Money-wise there is a very low ceiling, and it's quite a taxing area of work, they tend to run you into the ground. However, I do quite enjoy what I do and find it interesting. I'm not sitting here lamenting every day at work.

What are the jobs you've done since graduating? And what have they entailed?

2014 – 2017

Senior Quantity Surveyor, Construction Company, London

Now part of a change team, if a client wants a change, we price it and tell them how much it costs.

2011 – 2014

Assistant Quantity Surveyor, Construction Company, Haiti

This role was much more office based, I had to manage a much larger contractor, and was responsible for the whole project on my own.

2008 – 2011

Graduate Quantity Surveyor, Construction Company, Dubai/UK

Looking after three smaller construction sites, doing a lot more of the manual stuff. Taking measurements on-site as senior people wouldn't want to do it.

What are the things you most like about your job, and the things you don't like?

Like:

1. Working with contracts is very interesting. It's all about the interpretation of the wording (it can become like a game of chess with a contractor, establishing what you/they are entitled too).
2. Negotiation of the contracts.

Don't like:

1. Taking measurements, it's very dull, very repetitive.

Which would you prefer to work for: a small company or a big company, and why?
I prefer big companies. They have a lot more to offer and have more interesting work.

Have you worked long hours over the years?
- Long hours, when I was working in the Caribbean, I was doing 70-90 hours a week without fail.
- In my current role in London, I do 40 hours and no more. If I work any longer I get overtime, so it's a lot nicer!

Have you had much fun over the years?
It depends on the site, if you are on an isolated site, there can be great camaraderie. People have travelled a long way, might be away from their family, they go out for drinks and meals. Construction is a fairly good-natured industry; socially it's quite good.

If you could start over and you were 22, but you know all you know now, would you do anything differently career-wise?
I'm quite happy with my path, I have always used this job as a passport. I always wanted to work abroad; if I'd stayed in the UK, I'd probably be in a more senior role.

Would you be an advocate of going and working abroad?
It looks very good on your CV. I went abroad very early. Ideally, I'd do five years working at home and then go abroad. I stayed for three and think I'd have benefitted from staying a couple of years more and then going abroad.

What career advice would you give a young person now?
Identify your goal early, know where you want to go, otherwise, you will end up floating about. I never had a goal, I just wanted to go abroad and I did. If I had an end goal, I think I'd be a bit further along.

What advice would you give a young person who wanted to do what you do?

There are two ways:

1. Do a traditional three or four-year course at university.
2. Do a day release course.

A lot of the main contractors will offer four days a week working and then Fridays off to do university. You do your degree over five years instead of three, and you get paid while you are studying.

Which route/type of experience would you favour? Contracting or design?

- For quantity surveying, I'd always advise going contracting first.
- Some people who started off in an office doing design lack an understanding of how things work on a site, and how the works are carried out. They can be difficult to deal with, miss glaring things, and ask the wrong questions. They might say the same about me though!
- I'd advise getting an understanding of the fundamentals of contracting first and then going into the other side but not leaving it too late.

What are the pros and cons of living and working abroad?

For me, working abroad was about the experience of going to different countries and just generally living a bit of an adventure. I met all sorts of others who had different reasons for working internationally. The pros and cons differ depending on location as well:

1. Money

- Working in Haiti, I got paid a lot more than I otherwise would have. Working in less desirable countries as an expat tends to bring hefty financial benefits, tax breaks, perks, more holiday, etc.
- You obviously have a trade-off there re: quality of life. The hours were much longer, often working 70-90 hour weeks. Your freedom was restricted due to safety concerns, and your friends and family are thousands of miles away.
- In contrast, New Zealand didn't bring any financial difference, but the quality of life was exceptional.

2. Career progression
- Moving to an international division within a company you work for gets you noticed, which is obviously good.
- However, there is a lot less of a support structure for people earlier in their career than in the UK, so doing it too early on can be detrimental, as any training essentially stops.
- In my experience the staff hierarchy tends to be a lot flatter, so you have more exposure to seniority and gain a much wider set of skills. You're expected to chip in everywhere, rather than sticking to your job description.

3. Perspective
- I think it also gives you a more well-rounded way of looking at things as well. You have to adapt to the culture you're in.

***

NIALL, 34

40. Chartered Engineer, Rail Company, Ireland

What is your degree in?
Bachelor of Engineering (Civil)

Why did you do the degree you did?
I did it mainly because I was good at maths, engineering was more the practical application of maths. With engineering, you do the maths behind something, and then you build it. Whereas financial maths is all spreadsheets, and theoretical maths is not practical.

Did you know what your day-to-day role entailed starting off in your career?
Going into my degree I didn’t know what it entailed, I possibly should have worked for a few years and then done my degree, but that’s easy to say now! Coming out of my degree I had an idea because I did a work placement as part of the third year of my course. The placement taught

me one thing that I did not want to work on-site. So, I did the opposite; and I went into design.

Would you be an advocate of work experience?
Yes, the work placement was invaluable. You don't need to work on-site long to get a good idea of how it works. In the six months working on-site for my work placement, I learned a lot. I learned that it wasn't for me, 12-hour days for five or six days a week. That might be ok in a nicer climate, but not in Ireland.

What percentage of what you learned in university have you used in your day-to-day roles?
30% - I would have learned a good basis of knowledge, like AutoCAD which I use a lot.

With the benefit of hindsight, if you were 18 again now would you do anything differently degree-wise?
- I probably would have done a Masters straight after university because it's very hard to go back once you start working - Life takes over.
- I think I would have been equally good at accounting or anything else, but I liked the practical side of things.

What are the jobs you've done since graduating? And what have they entailed?
2012 – 2018
Chartered Engineer, Rail Company, Ireland
Inspection of infrastructure assets, i.e. bridges.
2008 – 2011
Structural Engineer, Structural Company, Ireland
Assessing road structures.
2007 – 2008
Graduate Engineer, Ireland
Design of residential, and commercial units and some site supervision.

What are the things you most like about your job, and the things you don't like?

Like:

1. Seeing the work you have done, and be proud of it, there is something tangible.
2. The variety of the roles.
3. The people I work with.
4. Not being in the office all the time – my role is a mix of being outdoors and in the office.

Don't like:

1. Money can be a problem this side of the world. (If you want good cash you must go to Asia/Middle East)
2. Hours can be crazy - in some jobs 12-13 hour days
3. Jobs in engineering can be very based on how the economy is going. Engineering jobs are the first to be hit in a recession.

If you could start over and you were 22, but you know all you know now, would you do anything differently career-wise?

- If I could start over, I would have done a Masters straight after university, maybe structural design. I didn't really know I was interested in it until I'd worked in structural design for a while.
- I would also have mapped out my career a bit better and tried to move around more into different roles. However, the recession messed everything up, you kind of had to take what you were given.

What career advice would you give a young person now?

If you are interested in a particular area, then try and get some exposure to it before or during university before you take the plunge and embark on it as a career.

What advice would you give a young person who wanted to do what you do?

I would advise a lot of engineers to spend a few years working abroad, go abroad and make some good cash, get a nest egg together - engineers aren't paid that well.

***

PADRAIC, 33

41. Project Engineer, Construction Company, Oman

What is your degree in?
Bachelor of Engineering (Civil)

Why did you do the degree you did?
I originally was going to do commerce; it was a last-minute decision to change to engineering. I was always interested in buildings, bridges; I was reasonably good at maths, so that's why really. I did civil as opposed to mechanical because I did technical drawing in school and the civil stuff was what I enjoyed the most.

Did you know what you wanted to do career-wise?
- No, not really during university. I did work experience with a contracting company, re-surfacing roads. Construction companies came to my university looking for graduates, and I went for interviews with them.
- There are two ways you can go, 1. design, or 2. contracting (doing the work that the design team has specified).
- I took a job working as a contractor and enjoyed it. It worked out well because I think if you start off in design, it becomes more difficult to get a job contracting.

Did you know what your day-to-day role entailed starting off in your career?
I was 90% blind starting off in my career. In university, you learn the theory and the technical stuff, i.e. design; it gives you a good foundation. However, it doesn't give you the practical knowledge, i.e. how things work in reality.

What percentage of what you learned in university have you used in your day-to-day roles?
10-20%. If I worked in a design office, I'd use a lot more.

With the benefit of hindsight, if you were 18 again now would you do anything differently degree-wise?
No, I enjoy what I'm doing. It has worked out well for me.

What are the jobs you've done since graduating? And what have they entailed?
2016 – 2018
Project Engineer, Pipeline Construction Project, Oman
The site-based stuff is all pretty similar, but as you get more senior, you start to look after costs and clients more.
2013 – 2015
Construction Manager, Pipeline Construction Project, Australia
Same as below, with more responsibility and more emphasis on people management.
2009 – 2012
Project Engineer, Pipeline Construction Project, Australia
Managing all aspects of a construction project from start to finish within timelines, budget, etc.
2006 – 2008
Site Engineer, Dublin
Helping senior engineers on-site.

What are the things you most like about your job, and the things you don't like?
Like:
1. Responsibility.
2. Dealing with and managing people.
3. Doing something I enjoy for a living.

Don't like:

1. The expectation for engineers to work long hours – to be there from the start of the day to the end.
2. Lots of travel, i.e. there is a five-hour bus journey from the airport to the site in Oman for my current job.
3. Working outside in the weather in Ireland.

Have you worked long hours over the years?

- Yes, you are talking minimum 10-hour days, it can be 12-hour days. You might have to work Saturday mornings if the project is under pressure. You are always dealing with deadlines, the expectation that you will be there and won't look for holidays at busy times.
- If you do fall into some jobs where you work five weeks on and then get three weeks off it's good, but these types of job would be rare.

Would you be an advocate of going and working abroad?

I would advise to wait two years before going abroad, get some good experience at home and then go abroad with experience. Some of my friends came out to Australia with no experience, and they struggled with getting their first job.

Have you had much fun over the years?

Yes, I've worked in Asia and the Middle East, civil engineering is the same around the world. It travels very well, and you get great experience.

If you could start over and you were 22, but you know all you know now, would you do anything differently career-wise?

I think I'd follow a very similar path. I would recommend taking some time deciding on whether to take a job. I usually rush into the next job, and always regret not taking my time. Do a few more interviews, and make sure that the job is right for you, and is the best one you can get.

What career advice would you give a young person now?

- Nothing is forever, you can change. If you go to university and don't like what you did, you can change and it's not the end of the world.

- Try and do something you enjoy doing. You will be working long enough so you might as well enjoy it.

What advice would you give a young person who wanted to do what you do?
Get some experience at home in either design or contracting, go abroad, then build your contacts and see where it takes you.

What are the pros and cons of living and working abroad?
Pros:
1. The time off.
2. Better wages.
3. Seeing new cultures, new people, new ways of working.

Cons:
1. Being away from family and friends, missing weddings, etc.

Is it tough to move around in engineering? i.e. into, rail, road, water etc.
- If you can understand the basics you should be fine, most places have specialists who you can ask and discuss things with.
- Once you are higher up, a lot of the work in engineering is as a project manager, so you can move from rail to road, to gas, etc. easy enough.
- Having said that, if I was go do a fit out of a hotel, I'd probably make a complete mess of it.

***

SHANE, 31

42. Mechanical Engineer, Engineering Company, Dublin

What is your degree in?
Bachelor of Engineering (Mechanical)
Master of Engineering (Mechanical)

Why did you do the degree you did?

I did an aptitude test when I was 16. It said I was good at maths and spatial reasoning and recommended becoming an engineer!

With the benefit of hindsight, if you were 18 again now would you do anything differently degree-wise?
I think I would have done engineering, but I would have done a Masters in a different university, not the same university. I specialised in mechanical very early. In hindsight, I would have been better off getting a better grounding in the other types of engineering.

Did you know what your day-to-day role entailed starting off in your career?
I knew a little bit but there were no jobs available at the time due to the recession, so I had to do a Masters, then go to the UK to look for work. Looking back now I was clueless. The degrees didn't prepare me for the nitty-gritty day-to-day of engineering.

When you came out of university did you seek advice from anyone?
Companies would come out and give presentations to my university class, but no I didn't talk to anyone else.

What percentage of what you learned in university have you used in your day-to-day roles?
Less than 20%.

What are the jobs you've done since graduating? And what have they entailed?
2017 – 2018
Mechanical Design Engineer, Dublin
Mapping out designs for two big student accommodation blocks.
2016 – 2017
Mechanical Project Engineer, Dublin
Co-ordinating drawings, ensure that all the fittings are the right size for building projects.
2010 – 2016

Mechanical Engineer, London

Reviewed consultants' designs, checked them and then put together tenders on why we should win the work. I was the go-to guy for electricians on-site, what to do and where to do it.

What are the things you most like about your job, and the things you don't like?

Like:

1. The interaction with people, learning about what their roles.
2. The responsibility on-site.
3. It's never boring, something different is happening every day.
4. You can see progress, seeing something built is very rewarding.

Don't like:

1. Being stuck at a desk all day.
2. Working in isolation.
3. The client changing their mind, and you must re-do everything.

Have you had much fun over the years?

Yes, lots of fun working in the construction industry, there is a real sense of camaraderie, and everyone is usually up for going out/socialising, etc.

Have you worked long hours over the years?

It can be long hours. The consultancy side is a bit more regular as opposed to contracting work, as your office is not site based.

Which would you prefer to work for: a small company or a big company, and why?

Smaller companies are good experience, but I want to go back to a bigger company as the projects are better.

If you could start over and you were 22, but you know all you know now, would you do anything differently career-wise?

I would have pushed to be a project engineer on a site a bit more, as I would have got better experience.

What career advice would you give a young person now?

- Speak to as many engineers as you can to get an idea of what the day-to-day is like. The degree doesn't prepare you at all.
- Try and get summer internships/work experience. Even if you get a job as a document controller it will give you a good insight into how a site works. Sites are very different to office environments.

What advice would you give a young person who wanted to do what you do?

Try and research as much as you can about the different types of engineering, as a lot of engineers just fall into what they do.

HEALTH/CHARITY

What I knew before the interviews:

- Health professionals worked long and unsociable hours.

What I learned from the interviews:

- Seeing a patient recovering can be very rewarding.
- There are lots of nights and weekend working.
- Some specialisms within medicine take 15 years of studying and working before you are a qualified consultant.

AYA, 32

43. Occupational Therapist, Healthcare Organisation, London

What is your degree in?
Bachelor of Science (Occupational Therapy)
Master of Cognitive Behavioural Therapy

Why did you do the degree you did?
I always wanted to work in mental health. Growing up in Saudi Arabia I saw how bad the mental health care system was.

What percentage of what you learned in university have you used in your day-to-day roles?
30% - because I branched off into cognitive behavioural therapy (CBT).

Did you know what your day-to-day role entailed starting off in your career?
Yes, because I'd done work placements in mental health and shadowed senior people in hospitals.

With the benefit of hindsight, if you were 18 again now would you do anything differently degree-wise?
I would do the same degree to get a core profession, but I would have done a Masters in psychology afterwards. I think it's important to get a core profession path out of your degree, i.e. accounting, medicine, etc.

Would you be an advocate of doing postgraduate study straight after undergraduate?
Yes, I'd say to do it straight after, to get it over and done with. It's just easier that way.

Could you get the job you have now without having your Masters?
No, you would need the CBT training.

What are the jobs you've done since graduating? And what have they entailed?

2017 – 2018

Cognitive Behavioural Therapist, Healthcare Organisation, London

Helping people with personality disorders fight anxiety and depression.

2012 – 2017

Occupational Therapist, Healthcare Organisation, Birmingham

Working as an occupational therapist in an eating disorder service. Helping people with body image, helping them with diet, etc.

What are the things you most like about your job, and the things you don't like?

Like:

1. Working with multi-disciplinary teams.
2. Working with patients.
3. Seeing improvements in peoples' recovery. You can get great satisfaction watching your patients' health improve.

Don't like:

1. Budget restrictions - I think it gets in the way of patient care.
2. Paperwork. I understand why I must do it, but it takes so much time away from seeing patients.

Have you worked long hours over the years?

Yes, I always put in long hours, but that is probably just the way I am.

Have you had much fun over the years?

- Yes, it's interesting, as your patients tell you things that they wouldn't normally tell people. One of my patients once said that I was very nosey!
- There is also a great sense of collaboration and teamwork with the different doctors etc.
- On the flip side, it can be sad as people with personality disorders sometimes can be very draining and hard on you emotionally.

If you could start over and you were 22, but you know all you know now, would you do anything differently career-wise?
I wouldn't have stayed so long in my first role. I should have moved on, and progressed quicker. I should have only stayed two years instead of five.

What career advice would you give a young person now?
Work hard, know what you want, take a year out, don't rush into stuff, try and figure out as best you can what you want. If you can't do that, if you are not sure, do something you are passionate about. If I didn't do mental health, I would have studied English, as I loved to write - do something you enjoy.

What advice would you give a young person who wanted to do what you do?
Have a core progression of some sort, i.e. do your degree, do something that gives you a title or a profession, and then go and build on that.

How did your Masters compare to your undergrad, i.e. hours and fun etc.?
In my postgrad, we were working three days and studying two days. There was not that much drinking but everyone got along so well, we all had a common bond as we have worked in mental health for so long. I'm very close to my postgrad university mates.

***

EMMA, 32,

44. Senior Policy Advisor, Charity, Dublin

What is your degree in?
Bachelor of Arts (Politics and Philosophy)
Masters of Sustainable development
Ph.D. in Human Geography

Why did you do the degree you did?

I was always very interested in politics growing up in Northern Ireland; the philosophy taught me to think in different ways. I knew from a young age I wanted to work in international development. Being a kid in Belfast, it was tough to know how to do that. It seemed like an arts degree was a good way. I got a scholarship to do my Masters.

Did you know what your day-to-day role entailed starting off in your career?
Probably not, the jobs are all really different - working in the field is very different to working in an office in a big city. While doing my degree, I had no idea of the extent of the different opportunities. There are a lot of different areas in an NGO - marketing, fundraising, policy and research, and programs.

What percentage of what you learned in university have you used in your day-to-day roles?
Not a huge amount. I haven't used much of the content, but I have used some of the other skills, i.e. writing, debating, etc.

With the benefit of hindsight, if you were 18 again now would you do anything differently degree-wise?
It's hard to say. I've had very different jobs, which have given me a broad skillset.

What are the jobs you've done since graduating? And what have they entailed?
2017 – 2018
Senior Policy Advisor, International Charity, Dublin
Policy lead on the charity's humanitarian campaign.
2015 – 2017
Senior Research and Policy Advisor, International Charity, London
Produced research on broad range of issues relating to international development.
2013 – 2015
Research Fellow, University, UK

Producing research on humanitarian and development issues for department of foreign affairs.

2009 – 2012

Ph.D. Researcher, University, Ireland

Researching labour rights and abuses in Chinese owned copper mines in Zambia.

2007 – 2009

Programme Officer, Development Charity, South Africa

Working in a South African national park. Helping indigenous people to sell their local traditional plant products to international markets.

What are the things you most like about your job, and the things you don't like?

Like:

1. Subject Matter – you are dealing with something that you feel inspired about.

While there are many negatives in working with an NGO, you feel like you are making a difference even if you don't know the people you are helping.

2. You work on a range of issues from domestic, to EU and global.

3. People you are working with are also very passionate about what they are doing.

Don't like:

1. NGO work can be precarious; you don't have full-time permanent contracts.

2. The pay is a lot less than private companies or even governments.

3. It's very competitive, for not having great pay comparatively.

If you aren't living in London or a big city, it can be very hard to get involved in development.

Which would you prefer to work for: a small company or a big company, and why?

I think a small company. In the big development organisations, the opportunities are brilliant. For example, I presented at the United

Nations, and you can specialise more into your area. With smaller development organisations, you are much more involved, but they have less money and you have to do more multi-tasking.

Have you worked long hours over the years?
It can be, but it's manageable. For me personally I've had standard 8:30am to 5pm.

Have you had much fun over the years?
Yes, as you are working with people who are also inspired. It can be stressful but overall, you're working on something you are really interested in.

As an NGO worker, what have you preferred? Working abroad or at home?
- The experiences of working abroad for an NGO can be very different. You can be isolated and lonely in a rural part of a country, but equally, you can be a big city staying in a hotel with a swimming pool. It can be tough moving around from country to country, difficult to keep relationships going - I lived in 5 countries in 10 years in my 20's. You see your friends settling down, buying houses, etc. That can be a negative depending on your outlook on life.
- I think when people get into their 30's, they tend to start looking for desk jobs, but others love it and work abroad for NGO's for years.

If you could start over and you were 22, but you know all you know now, would you do anything differently career-wise?
I'm happy now, so probably wouldn't change. I'm thinking now about doing something practical, maybe a law diploma part-time. I've done three degrees now and I think I've got better at the same set of skills instead of trying to get new skills.

What advice would you give a young person who wanted to do what you do?

- A lot of people working in development come from different professions such as media and communications, politics, international NGOs, and governments.
- If I were talking to someone who wanted to work in development, I'd say make your first degree a really practical degree, as that's what is missing in this sector. You have a lot of people like me with arts degrees, who can string an argument together, but not many qualified professionals with a craft. i.e. nursing, pharmacy, law, engineering - those people are so useful in development.
- I'm 32 years old and this is my first permanent contract, working in development you are very dependent on funding cycles, and you have to be very mobile. So, I think it's important to get that base qualification to fall back on if you lose your job or want to do something different.
- Also, you'd have to have at least two years abroad to get into middle management.
- It's often knowing the right people that help you get a start in NGOs, as it's very competitive.
- One of the reasons I picked the masters I did was it had four small internships. Even though I worked for small NGOs, it made the difference when I was applying for bigger NGOs.
- I'd advise contacting someone you know who works in that area. People are very approachable and very keen to give young people advice. Get a professional qualification and then get some fieldwork experience. (People automatically think you need experience working in the field abroad, but do charity work in your own community. It will show that you are passionate about development in all contexts, not just overseas).

***

HAWWA, 30

45. General Practitioner, GP Clinic, London

What is your degree in?

Bachelor of Medicine
Bachelor of Surgery

Why did you do the degree you did?

A few reasons. I was good at science at school, and as I went to an international school in the Middle East, this equated to either doing medicine, pharmacy or engineering. I also used to feel very emotional when I would see news reports of famine or health crises around the world and I wanted to help.

Why did you embark on the career you did?

After medical school, I worked in the hospital for a couple of years. During this time, I realised that I didn't like the haphazard working schedule including nightshifts and lots of weekends. I decided on GP because this would allow me to continue working as a doctor but have some routine to my working life.

When you came out of university did you seek advice from anyone?

I shadowed many doctors at medical school. However, I didn't know many doctors growing up. One of my mother's friends was a doctor, and she helped me find work experience. This was during my A level years.

Did you know what your day-to-day role entailed starting off in your career?

Yes, I did. Luckily medicine is quite a practical degree. Before qualifying, you do different placements at medical school. So, during my time at medical school, I shadowed many specialities and had a feel for what I liked and didn't like. For instance, I knew from very early on I didn't like surgery.

What percentage of what you learned in university have you used in your day-to-day roles?

I think what I learned at university provided a good background knowledge of what I need to know on a day-to-day basis. Having said that, it's my post-medical school experience that provides the main source for everyday practice. A simple example would be that at medical school you'll learn how to spot an infection and whether you need antibiotics to treat it. However, you don't necessarily know which antibiotic and what dose to use until you start practicing.

With the benefit of hindsight, if you were 18 again now would you do anything differently degree-wise?
Although I do enjoy being a doctor, I've also always enjoyed writing fiction. I don't know if I were to do it again, I might have gone down the humanities route.

What are the jobs you've done since graduating? And what have they entailed?
2017 – 2018
General Practitioner, GP Clinic, London
Attending to patients at a local GP clinic
2014 – 2016
Junior Doctor, Hospital, London
Three different rotations in different hospitals (geriatrics, psychiatric, A&E).

What are the things you most like about your job, and the things you don't like?
Like:
1. Making a difference - It sounds a bit corny but sometimes feeling like something I did saved a life. Believe it or not, this doesn't happen that often. Also, people generally show a lot of gratitude, even when I do a very small thing for them and I realise that this is a privilege.
2. Regular hours - Currently working as a GP it means that I have fixed hours, with no night shifts and very little weekend work. Working as a GP also provides the opportunity to pick my own hours in the future.
3. Medicine is a very rewarding career. If it's something you really want to do, it's worth pursuing. I've been at it for almost ten years since starting medical school, and I still enjoy it. Almost every day I hear of an obscure symptom, disease or drug I've never heard of before. So, if you're someone who likes surprises, it might be the right fit for you.

Don't like:
1. Irregular hours - As I mentioned before, I didn't enjoy working nights when I worked in the hospital. This is because it was difficult to flip my sleep pattern and I found it could be very physically draining.
2. Staff shortages - All the hospitals I worked at were always understaffed, and this could lead to very pressurised working conditions. This was difficult as I would find myself juggling more responsibilities than I could handle and leaving late on most days.
3. A&E - One of the things I really struggled with is the lack of resources in many hospitals. This led to many patients receiving delayed care, something I particularly noticed working in A&E.

Which would you prefer to work for: a small company or a big company, and why?
No hospital is my answer. I much prefer working in a community setting and having continuity with my patients.

Have you worked long hours over the years?
Yes. While in hospital, on-call shifts were generally between 12 and 13 hours. And even on a normal working day of eight or nine hours, I'd leave late as there would be so much to do.

Have you had much fun over the years?
I think there has been. When you work on a big team in a hospital, there is usually a sense of community and comradery. Patients all have their own stories and personalities. This can lead to very interesting conversations and new outlooks on life.

If you could start over and you were 22, but you know all you know now, would you do anything differently career-wise?
I'm generally happy with the choices I made. I decided early on in my training that I would be a GP and I think it's the right choice for me. I'm glad I didn't go down a long hospital training route only to realise years later that it wasn't right for me and have to retrain.

What career advice would you give a young person now?
Medical school admission can be quite competitive. Grades are very important but remember there are other things they are looking for on an application too. I think it's very important to showcase your skills and interests on your application, whether they be in sport or art, it all counts. You should also try to show an interest in medicine by doing placements in a healthcare setting. Contact your local hospital or GP surgery and see if they will allow you to shadow them for a day or two.

What advice would you give a young person who wanted to do what you do?
After getting into medical school, the path to becoming a GP is quite straightforward. You only have to do a couple of years of hospital work before you can apply. However, what I'd say is that almost everyone I knew changed their mind during medical school. So, it's likely if you start out wanting to be a GP, you'll end up a Surgeon or vice versa! So just take your time, enjoy the experience, and you'll get to where you're meant to be.

***

JULIA, 32

46. Senior Policy Adviser, Charity, London

What is your degree in?
Bachelor of Science (Natural Sciences)

Why did you do the degree you did?
I failed to get the grades I needed to get into medical school!

Why did you embark on the career you did?
During my degree, I discovered that I was much better at, and enjoyed much more, thinking about how science and society interact rather than mixing things in a test tube.

When you came out of university did you seek advice from anyone?

I had one lecturer who was really encouraging. I asked him for some general advice about what I should do with my life.

Did you know what your day-to-day role entailed starting off in your career?
I was totally blind. My career decisions were also heavily influenced by the fact I was trying to move to London. Job searches were predominately influenced by geography rather than trying to find my dream job.

What percentage of what you learned in university have you used in your day-to-day roles?
About 10%. The policy work I did in my last term of university is still helpful in a very general sense. I have not made a molar solution in over two decades.

With the benefit of hindsight, if you were 18 again now would you do anything differently degree-wise?
Knowing how much I enjoy my current job, I would study development and languages.

What are the things you most like about your job, and the things you don't like?
Like:
1. I've been lucky in that many of my jobs involve meetings with very smart people and (attempting) to ask them smart questions. This is especially true of my time in Westminster.
2. I have learned a huge amount and developed expertise in new areas.
3. I have met some brilliant, inspiring people who are a genuine source of motivation.

Don't like:
1. Meetings – so, so many meetings. Sometimes pre-meetings for meetings. It can be hard not to get meetings fatigue.
2. Changing organisational priorities. I understand why this happens but it can be frustrating.

3. The never-ending stream of admin.

Which would you prefer to work for: a small company or a big company, and why?

I have done both. Think there are pros/cons to each. I currently work for a large organisation, and I really enjoy being part of a global effort.

Have you worked long hours over the years?

Yes – to the extent that sometimes I think it would be expedient just to bring a sleeping bag to the office to save myself the commute.

Have you had much fun over the years?

It's been a huge amount of fun. Largely because of the people I have worked with. Also, because things can change very quickly and I enjoy having to think on my feet. It's a weird combination of exhilarating and exhausting.

If you could start over and you were 22, but you know all you know now, would you do anything differently career-wise?

I wish I had more experience in development – particularly in the field. However, I have taken valuable lessons and experience from all my previous roles, so it's hard to feel too regretful.

What career advice would you give a young person now?

When you're looking for a job, think to yourself 'am I going to get to have interesting conversations every day if I do this?' If the answer is no, it's probably not the job for you.

What advice would you give a young person who wanted to do what you do?

Be persistent and try and amass as much experience as you can. Demonstrable passion is a very valuable commodity. Don't undervalue it.

***

NASIR, 28

47. Urology Surgeon, Hospital, UK

What is your degree in?
Bachelor of Medicine

Why did you do the degree you did?
- I knew from a young age that I wanted to go into medicine. My mum was a doctor. One evening she left me in the canteen to finish my homework. It was clean and there was some chilled music playing. I thought that it would be a nice place to work!
- My sister who was also a doctor tried to put me off. 'You will have to spend all your time studying and working; it will ruin your life.' She took me to a dissecting room and opened this bucket of half dissected heads, but it had the reverse effect. I thought it was cool!

Did you know what your day-to-day role entailed starting off in your career?
No, I was blind as to what a doctor did, all I knew is that it wasn't a desk job, it involved different random things, some patients can be unwell. I didn't know how much paperwork, and documenting of everything you did there was, which is a real pain!

When you came out of university did you seek advice from anyone?
I didn't really ask anyone; I just went for it! I asked some doctors at the end of medical school about coming to work in the UK, but that was it.

How different is the medical degree from working as a doctor?
- In Sudan, our clinical time was different to the UK where you are on placements in the hospital all the time. We got two hour-long slots every day, so consultants would send us to see rare cases.
- My degree didn't show us what working as a doctor would be like. It taught me a lot about medicine, but it wasn't really that practical in terms of skills you would need daily.

How did you settle on what you wanted to specialise in?

- I ruled out what I didn't want to do, i.e. orthopaedics, paediatrics, it was either general medicine or surgery for me.
- At the end of the fifth year, I went on an exchange programme to Holland for a month. I couldn't speak Dutch, so they put me in theatre all the time. It was really an eye-opening experience. The surgeons, nurses and anaesthetists on one team all working together. Nice music would be playing; it was very relaxing. That's when I decided I think surgery is the way for me.
- When I first moved to the UK, urology was my very first rotation. In the exchange programme in Holland, I saw one surgery done by a robot, which I thought was so cool. Urology departments use diverse methods; it is the main surgical speciality that uses robots. From a surgical point of view, you are really the jack of all trades.
- Then I started to think about work-life balance. I started looking at it from the consultants' perspective. They almost never have to come in at night, so they have quite a good work-life balance. It's probably one of the best specialities in surgery from a work-life balance point of view.

Would you be an advocate of taking a year out?

Work experience is valuable if you are undecided, if you know what you want to do, I would say just go for it. I didn't know what I wanted to specialise in starting off in my degree, you will have time to figure it out before you graduate.

What are the jobs you've done since graduating? And what have they entailed?

2017 – 2018

Urology Surgeon, Hospital, UK

Operating on people with urinary tract diseases.

2014 – 2016

Junior Doctor, Hospital, UK

Three different rotations in different hospitals (A&E, psychiatric, paediatric).

What are the things you most like about your job, and the things you don't like?

Like:

1. Always being part of a team.
2. Doing practical things with my hands/being in theatre.
3. When you do something for a patient, and they feel better, it's very rewarding (but you don't get it very often).

Don't like:

1. You end up staying late as there are staffing shortages. You get feelings of guilt because you want to go home, which you wouldn't get in other jobs, it's just because its people's health
2. Getting paged - you can get paged repeatedly. For the person on the other side, if you don't answer within ten minutes, they will want to call you. Sometimes it's very hard if you are with a patient who is unwell as you can't talk.
3. The number of people who come to A&E that do not need to be seen by A&E, which creates problems with waiting times.

Have you worked long hours over the years?

It's tough, some shifts are 13 hours, and you must do seven or eight night shifts in a month.

Have you had much fun over the years?

Yes, you get to travel a lot. You get put on different interesting rotations. I've lived in three different towns/cities in my three years as a doctor, all of them great!

If you could start over and you were 22, but you know all you know now, would you do anything differently career-wise?

I'm quite happy with where I am, don't think I'd want to change anything.

What advice would you give a young person who wanted to do what you do?

Work hard, see if they can join surgical societies. Surgery is a very competitive speciality, so you need to aim to be the best.

Does it matter what country you study medicine in?
I used to think it did, but then I realised we were all equally lost little puppies in the hospital starting out. It's the same textbooks around the world; it is just how you apply your knowledge.

Does it matter which university you study medicine in?
They are all equally good in the UK, there's no difference really.

HR/RECRUITMENT

What I knew before the interviews:

- HR is often underappreciated by people who don't know the value that it can add.
- Dealing with difficult people is tough.

What I learned from the interviews:

- Psychology and human resources are quite closely related.
- Recruitment can be very lucrative if you are good at it.
- In-house recruitment is a very good way of getting into human resources.
- Offering to work for free can be a great way to get your foot in the door of a company.

DAVID, 33

48. HR Business Partner, Financial Trading Firm, Dublin

What is your degree in?
Bachelor of Business Studies
Master of Human Resource Management

Why did you do the degree you did?
- It was a straight business degree starting off, and in the fourth year I had to make a choice - HR was the one I was best at.
- I was always interested in business; I always read the business pages of the paper.

Did you know what your day-to-day role entailed starting off in your career?
Very little, I knew they dealt a lot with people, but the nooks and crannies of it I didn't really know.

Did the HR degree prepare you for the working world?
Some of it, a lot of the degree is focused on law, a lot of it is theory, Maslow's hierarchy of needs, etc. Does it allow you to understand motivation in terms of your workforce? Does it help you understand employee engagement day-to-day? I can't say I've ever referred to much of the theory in my daily role.

When you came out of university did you seek advice from anyone?
I knew someone working in HR, so I talked to them, and researched a little bit about HR. At the time, I saw HR as a means to an end; I wasn't necessarily thinking I was going to build a career in HR.

What percentage of what you learned in university have you used in your day-to-day roles?
30%

Would you advise people to do a postgraduate degree?

- At the time, I had no experience, and there were no jobs. You needed something to differentiate your CV.
- I think it would be much more useful to do the Masters now having worked in HR for a few years.
- My advice would be to make sure you do a degree that has work experience in it. That way you have experience before you even leave university.

With the benefit of hindsight, if you were 18 again now would you do anything differently degree-wise?

I would have done something in IT, whether I had the skills or not is another thing! I think IT pays well compared to some other careers.

What are the jobs you've done since graduating? And what have they entailed?

When I finished my degree, I did a Masters, as it was the height of the recession and there were no jobs. I went to a big insurance company and asked them could I work for a month for free. After working like a demon for a month, I asked them for another couple of months. I worked for three months for free, then a maternity contract came up, and they gave me that role.

2015 – 2018

HR Business Partner, Financial Trading Firm, Dublin

Employee disputes, strategic people plans, employee engagement, workforce planning, helping the business.

2011 – 2015

Resourcing Specialist, Multinational Insurance Company, Dublin

Large-scale recruitment, filling over 200 roles a year.

2010 – 2011

L&D Officer, Multinational Insurance Company, Dublin

Induction, exit interviews, planning events, sourcing vendors to do training, etc.

What are the things you most like about your job, and the things you don't like?

Like:

1. Working with people on a daily basis.
2. Helping the business solve problems.
3. Dealing with senior executives.

Don't like:

1. I'm the one who has to say no when the business is trying to do things
2. Paper pushing, HR is a lot of administration.
3. Telling people they don't have a job is not easy to do.

Which would you prefer to work for: a small company or a big company, and why?

If you are trying to grow your career from a HR point of view, I would say a small company is better. You can get stuck into everything. I went to a smaller company, and I set up the whole HR desk, wrote the policies, etc. However, there are a lot more teething issues in a smaller company.

Have you worked long hours over the years?

It's peaks and troughs, one project where I was working on hiring a whole new call centre I worked 9am – 9pm for three months. Now I leave at 6pm, then log on in the evenings and take a quick look at my emails.

If you could start over and you were 22, but you know all you know now, would you do anything differently career-wise?

- I probably wouldn't have stayed in the insurance company as long as I did. They were not really concerned about progressing your career. It wasn't very meritocratic.
- I should have been strategic a little bit earlier and known my own worth a little bit better.

What career advice would you give a young person now?

- I've never really had joy with career guidance counsellors – I was told to do engineering!

- Talk to someone who is already in the role. Reach out to someone in HR on LinkedIn, and they will be happy to tell you what's involved.

What advice would you give a young person who wanted to do what you do?
- The easiest way is to go into recruitment. Everything hinges on recruitment, it's the backbone of every company.
- If you become a recruitment co-ordinator, you set up interviews; you also build relationships with all the managers in the company.

***

GIULIA, 31

49. Anti-Bribery Consultant, Bank, London

What is your degree in?
Bachelor of Law

Why did you do the degree you did?
I always wanted to be a lawyer. I liked what I was studying, the reason I didn't pursue a legal career is mainly because it was a very long path. It would have taken me way too long to become financially independent.

With the benefit of hindsight, if you were 18 again now would you do anything differently degree-wise?
No, I wouldn't change anything, as having a law degree opened a lot of doors for me, it makes you think, and use your mind.

Did you know what your day-to-day role entailed starting off in your career?
- My first job was a random internship screening airport workers. Then I fell into recruitment
- I knew nothing coming out of university, absolutely nothing.

What percentage of what you learned in university have you used in your day-to-day roles?

5%, but the way of thinking I learned in university helps me a lot in my day-to-day job.

Was the internship valuable?
If you do it in the right place and with the right people. The one I did, they just hired us because we were cheap.

What are the jobs you've done since graduating? And what have they entailed?
2015 – 2017
Anti-Bribery Assistant Manager, Bank, London
Making sure there is no bribery in the bank, and that they comply with regulations.
2015 – 2015
Recruitment Consultant, Global Bank, London
Finding suitable candidates to work for the bank.
2011 – 2015
Recruitment Consultant, Various Recruitment Companies, London
Lots of cold calling to see if you can place the candidates into roles.
2010 – 2011
Screening Co-Ordinator/Team Leader, UK
Performed background checks on airport staff.

What are the things you most like about your job, and the things you don't like?
Like:
1. Recruitment – enjoyed having lots of contacts with loads of people.
2. Anti-Bribery – it's interesting.

Don't like:
1. Recruitment – KPI/sales environment, it's all about quantity and not quality, and it's cut throat.
2. That anti-bribery's importance is not yet as well recognised as other areas of compliance, as it's still a fairly new area.

Have you worked long hours over the years?

I always worked long hours, 8-10 hours, banking especially, as there can be tight deadlines.

Have you had much fun over the years?

- Recruitment is work hard, play hard, very long working hours and equally long drinking sessions! This is however very common in an industry like recruitment full of young people!
- Anti-bribery can be good fun, but maybe not the most fun department of the bank.

Which would you prefer to work for: a small company or a big company, and why?

I prefer big corporates, good processes, more stability. With small companies, you get involved more, but there can be poor processes and policies which can be hard to work with.

If you could start over and you were 22, but you know all you know now, would you do anything differently career-wise?

I would skip a couple of jobs, and go straight into the anti-bribery one.

What career advice would you give a young person now?

- Don't put too much pressure on yourself trying to figure out what you want to do right away. It might take you a few years to figure it out. I've gone from one job to the other trying to find out what I like doing, I've finally found it after eight years. I went through a law degree, screening, recruitment and now I'm in compliance.
- Try to go to open days and try small internships and see if you can get a taste of something you might enjoy.

What advice would you give a young person who wanted to do what you do?

Pick the places you would like to work and pick up the phone or send a specific email instead of applying via the website. Try and do something to differentiate yourself from the crowd.

Which gets you further – knowing people or how good you are at your job?
Knowing people, you can be great at your job, but if no-one knows that you are there, they will never come for you!

***

ISABELLA, 31

50. Head of HR, Private Equity Company, Dubai

What is your degree in?
Bachelor of Science (Psychology)
Master of Human Resources Management

Why did you do the degree you did?
It was the first thing that I was really interested in. I would read psychology books outside of school.

Did you know what you wanted to do career-wise?
- I came out of university in a recession.
- My summer jobs in university were in HR, all my friends were in PR as it was a lot cooler, so I battled as to whether to do HR or PR.
- I find the way that people interact and leaders work fascinating.

Did you know what your day-to-day role entailed starting off in your career?
I knew I liked it. I found it challenging and stimulating. My first job was employee relation disputes, finding solutions to things, I liked it.

When you came out of university did you seek advice from anyone?
- No, not at the time, but I did pick up a thing or two about HR in my summer jobs.

- My form tutor at school told my parents that I should do something like HR, something with people.

What percentage of what you learned in university have you used in your day-to-day roles?
Not much, but it gave me a good grounding in how people think and relate to each other. I don't think you need to do a HR degree; I think it's more about the personality. I think you could do HR without doing a HR degree.

Out of the people you work with, what kind of degrees have they done?
A mixture, English, sociology, etc. It's more about your emotional intelligence, understanding people and relationships.

With the benefit of hindsight, if you were 18 again now would you do anything differently degree-wise?
No, I would stick with psychology. Understanding the brain, understanding the way groups relate to each other, I find all that stuff so interesting. My friends from my course have all done clinical psychology.

What are the jobs you've done since graduating? And what have they entailed?
2014 – 2018
Head of HR, Private Equity Company, Dubai
This is a very strategic role, how HR fits into the medium to long-term strategy of the company.
2012 – 2014
Senior HR Adviser, International Media Company, London
A generalist role, doing everything from recruitment, to contracts to disputes, etc.
2009 – 2012
HR Adviser, City Council, London
Employee relations disputes, admin, supporting my boss, etc.

Would you be an advocate of going and working abroad? As you clearly have done well out of moving to Dubai.
Definitely. Our graduate programme has 2-3000 applicants. When they join us, we send them off to Ghana, Mexico to get experience. It's fantastic work and life experience!

What are the pros and cons of living and working in the Middle East?
Pros:
1. The talent pool is a lot smaller. I'd never be able to become a head of HR in a major company in the UK.
2. Growth is arguably accelerated across all roles.

Cons:
1. It's a double-edged sword as the HR people in Middle East are not as talented as they might be in London, New York, etc.
2. You may have to be more of a jack of all trades, but you get great experience.

What are the things you most like about your job, and the things you don't like?
Like:
1. Every day is different.
2. I work hard, but it gives me a very good lifestyle too.

Don't like:
1. I hate being away from home.
2. I hate missing out on things.
3. While I never miss London, I do miss the people.

Have you worked long hours over the years?
Very long hours, I'm always contactable, the hours are ridiculous, I do 10-hour days a lot of the time.

What career advice would you give a young person now?

Build relationships, take the time to invest in relationships, have a good network. If I lost my job tomorrow, I could call on several people and get a new job no problem at all. Write to someone on LinkedIn, ask to meet for a coffee. A lot of them won't reply, but some will and their advice will be invaluable to you.

What advice would you give a young person who wanted to do what you do?
I think if you show drive, ambition, and enthusiasm, you will never fail. Figure out what you want, make a plan and start achieving that plan step by step.

Which gets you further in a career – knowing people or being good at your job?
In the right organisation, being good at your job. My firm is so big on diversity etc., but a lot of graduate programmes are given to people solely due to nepotism.

***

KATHRYN, 38

51. Client Engagement Manager, Pharma Company, London

What is your degree in?
Bachelor of Business Management

Why did you do the degree you did?
I did Business as I wanted to work for a big multinational like Coca-Cola or IBM, and I wanted to travel with my job.

Did you know what you wanted to do career-wise?
No, I didn't know what I wanted to do. My first role wasn't related to my degree as I worked for an auditing company, then I went into recruitment.

Did you know what your day-to-day role entailed starting off in your career?

I knew nothing, I was trained from scratch in my first job, so it didn't really matter what degree I did.

What percentage of what you learned in university have you used in your day-to-day roles?
15%, business management isn't related to recruitment, but it gives you a good foundation.

With the benefit of hindsight, if you were 18 again now would you do anything differently degree-wise?
I would have done something that gave me a specific skill, business management doesn't really give you that. I probably would have concentrated more when I was doing my degree, as I just did the basics to pass.

What are the jobs you've done since graduating? And what have they entailed?
2013 – 2017
Client Engagement Manager, Pharma Company, London
Working in-house for a big firm, handling all their recruitment needs.
2009 – 2012
Senior Recruitment Manager, Recruitment Firm, Australia
Same as below only for multiple clients.
2004 – 2008
Senior Account Manager, Bank, Australia
Handling the account of a big bank, doing all the recruitment for them as an external client.
2001 – 2003
Audit and Compliance Team Leader, Quality Institute, London
Checking auditors' performance to ensure they were competent to go out to external clients.

What are the things you most like about your job, and the things you don't like?
Like:

1. Managing a team, you can achieve your targets more easily.
2. The pay, the better I was at my job, the more I got paid.
3. The lifestyle, I like talking to people, in recruitment you must be friendly and chatty with people, it really helped my personality.

Don't like:
1. The long hours.

Have you worked long hours over the years?
You can do long hours, especially for big companies, when things have to be done, and there are deadlines.

Have you had much fun over the years?
A lot of fun, you spend a lot of time entertaining clients, and vice versa, meet a lot of fun people, it's great.

If you could start over and you were 22, but you know all you know now, would you do anything differently career-wise?
I probably should be a lot more senior than I am. I was quite comfortable in the roles that I was in, and just didn't want the stress. On reflection, I'm not sure I would change much!

What career advice would you give a young person now?
Coming out of school, you just need to do a course that you are going to pass, don't overstretch yourself. I took subjects which I dropped for ones that I knew I would pass. Pick something you like and excel at it, instead of struggling with something because people think it's a better option.

What advice would you give a young person who wanted to do what you do?
In recruitment, you get trained on all you need to know on the job, all the courses in the world are no good to you. Get in with a person that is great at selling, and great at placing people and learn from them! Recruitment is basically selling.

***

KIRSTINE, 34,

52. Resource Manager, Pharma Company, London

What is your degree in?
Bachelor of Science (Psychology)
Master of Organisational Psychology (Part-time)

Why did you do the degree you did?
I wanted to do HR management or marketing, but my mum wouldn't let me do it. My sister had failed that course, so she said we are not having a repeat of that!

What percentage of what you learned in university have you used in your day-to-day roles?
20%

Why did you embark on the career you did?
- Initially, when I was studying, I worked for a recruitment company, telephone interviews, etc., that's how I got my start really.
- I never did any sales recruitment, always did in-house recruitment.
- I did my dissertation for my Masters while working in my first job – 'Why firms pick who they do for jobs?' There was a lot of similarities between what was in the Masters and that role, so that's how I started off in recruitment.

Did you know what you wanted to do career-wise?
I had no idea what I wanted to do. It was all quite daunting.

What are the jobs you've done since graduating? And what have they entailed?
2013 – 2017
Resource Manager, Multinational Pharma Firm, London
Looking at all the projects, ensuring they are adequately staffed.
2010 – 2013

Recruitment Specialist, Global Professional Services Firm, London
Finding high calibre experienced resources for top jobs.
2006 – 2010
In-house Recruitment, Various Firms, London
Sourcing candidates and filling roles.

What are the things you most like about your job, and the things you don't like?
Like:
1. People interaction – working with senior stakeholders.
2. The global aspect of it, i.e. dealing with countries from all around the world.

Don't like:
1. Relying on other people to give me what I need.
2. People not pulling their weight.
3. Not feeling supported when things go wrong.

Do you prefer projects or business as usual (BAU) jobs?
I would say projects. You get more variety project to project. You deal with different people, it's never monotonous. There is always scope for new challenges.

Have you had much fun over the years?
Yes, a lot of fun! Within a big company there is always somebody like minded that you can have fun with.

Which would you prefer to work for: a small company or a big company, and why?
A big company. There are more chances to grow, more support, more opportunities.

If you could start over and you were 22, but you know all you know now, would you do anything differently career-wise?

I always wanted to be a make-up artist, but generally, I think I'm quite happy working in big companies.

What career advice would you give a young person now?
Try and get as much experience as possible. Would I have gone straight into work and skipped university? No, I don't think so, it's all about the social aspect of university, more than the learning of skills you will use working.

What advice would you give a young person who wanted to do what you do?
Get your foot in the door. Working in project management is quite high visibility. You get to deal with a lot of senior people that you usually wouldn't in a BAU role - so you can use that to your advantage.

Which gets you further in a career – knowing people or being good at your job?
It's a bit of both. I've got roles through simply knowing people, but ultimately you must be good at what you are doing!

***

SARAH, 33,

53. HR Business Partner, Utilities Company, Ireland

What is your degree in?
Bachelor of Arts (English and Geography)

Why did you do the degree you did?
I was originally planning to become a secondary school teacher.

Why did you embark on the career you did?
- Following my undergraduate degree, I completed a Graduate Diploma in Business Administration which was a conversion style programme for non-business graduates. As part of this course, I completed multiple

human resources related modules which gave me an insight into this business area.

- Following this course, I applied and was accepted into a Human Resources Management Masters which was a full-time course. The natural progression once I graduated was for me to cut my teeth in the big bad world. I secured a HR administrator position with an insurance company with approx. 1,500 employees.

When you came out of university did you seek advice from anyone?

Yes, I spoke with several HR professionals for my Master's thesis. They provided me with an insight into how HR managers engage with various business units.

Did you know what your day-to-day role entailed starting off in your career?

I had an overview of key roles and responsibilities within HR but not so much on day-to-day activities.

What percentage of what you learned in university have you used in your day-to-day roles?

20% approx.

With the benefit of hindsight, if you were 18 again now would you do anything differently degree-wise?

No, I don't think so.

What are the jobs you've done since graduating? And what have they entailed?

2016 – 2018

HR Business Partner, Utilities Company, Ireland

Supporting the business in all aspects of HR, organisation design, employee engagement, employee relations.

2012 – 2015

HR Specialist, Facilities Company, Ireland

Collaborating with the HR manager in all HR related fields such as compensation and benefits, recruitment, performance management.

2009 – 2012

HR Officer, Insurance Company, Ireland

Management of recruitment, conducting exit interviews, producing reports for senior management.

2007 – 2009

HR Administrator, Insurance Company, Ireland

Providing first line of support to managers in all matters relating to HR.

What are the things you most like about your job, and the things you don't like?

Like:

1. All my roles have been generalist in nature – which I enjoy. I engage with management and the general employee base on talent, succession planning, employee relations, industrial relations, corporate social responsibility and the full suite of HR functions.
2. I love having the opportunity to observe the dynamics between people. While my roles have been generalist, each company I've worked in has had a strong focus on employee relations and industrial relations.
3. I have loved working in different industries, i.e. insurance, facilities, fast moving consumer goods (FMCG) and utilities.

Don't like:

1. The politics in organisations.
2. Mistrust/cynicism towards the HR function in some organisations.

Have you worked long hours over the years?

Not particularly, I usually work 35-40 hours per week and have flexibility in my hours.

Have you had much fun over the years?

I've always had a positive and upbeat approach to tackling issues and trying to do the best thing for the company I work for. I love that because one solution doesn't fit all, you must tailor a specific approach to a situation and see how it plays out. I like having my finger on the pulse of the organisation so to speak.

However, there have been ups and downs. I've dealt with redundancies, dismissals and constructive dismissals and many employee relations issues which have been difficult to navigate and adherence to employment law has been critical.

If you could start over and you were 22, but you know all you know now, would you do anything differently career-wise?

I would have sought out some work experience in HR.

What career advice would you give a young person now?

- Identify your strengths and weaknesses early on.
- Try and do as much research as possible into the course and what career opportunities will open up from the course.
- Work experience is key. I'd suggest a course that incorporated some work experience during the term of the course.

What advice would you give a young person who wanted to do what you do?

- If you thrive working with others, then HR is worth considering. However, it's important to acknowledge that while you will be dealing with people in positive circumstances such as recruitment, compensation, and benefits, work-life balance there is also the more negative slant to the function such as dealing with grievances, disciplinary, redundancies etc.
- Get some work experience in HR.

INFORMATION TECHNOLOGY

What I knew before the interviews:

- There were several types of IT jobs: IT technicians, business analysts, project managers, IT specialists, software developers, etc.
- It paid well and was good fun.

What I learned from the interviews:

- You can easily change from civil to software engineering by doing a Masters, I had no idea it would be that easy.
- That if you are unhappy, it's much better to think of the years ahead where you can be working in a job you like, instead of looking back and not wanting to waste everything you've done so far.
- Don't be afraid to bite the bullet and change careers, it mightn't be easy in the short-term, but you will come out the other side much better off!
- That you don't have to be a coder or very technical person to work in IT. You can be a project manager or a business analyst and a lot of your job will be people management using your softer skills.
- Whatever you do in your 20s, it will all come good if you want it to.
- The well-trodden path of university, graduate programmes etc. is not for everyone, you must find your own way, what works best for you!

DAN, 31,

54. IT Business Partner, Pharma Company, Switzerland

What is your degree in?
Bachelor of Science (Information Systems with Accounting)

Why did you do the degree you did?
I did three years working after my A levels, as I never planned to go to university. My head teacher knew someone who ran a small company (20/30 people), and I got a job in IT through him. I worked there for three years, after that I felt I had to change paths, as I was too comfortable. I was earning £20k a year at the time, which was quite good for where I was living. While it was fun, it wasn't any way ambitious or stretching, so I then decided to go to university - I did IT because I was really into computers.

Did you know what your day-to-day role entailed starting off in your career?
Yes, as I had worked in an IT job for three years.

What percentage of what you learned in university have you used in your day-to-day roles?
- The degree got me inspired to think big in terms of companies and locations. Where I'm from in the English countryside, you would never think I was going to go and work for a company with 90,000 employees.
- The skills I picked up in university, some of them were softer, some of them more technical. After a few years of working, I realised that the technical stuff can generally be outsourced, but the softer skills remain very useful.

Could you have got the job you are in now without a degree?
I think there are other routes, apprenticeship schemes, etc. It's harder nowadays though; there are companies that won't even look at you without a degree. I'm fortunate that IT is one of the areas where graduate jobs are readily available.

What are the jobs you've done since graduating? And what have they entailed?

2015 – 2018

Warehouse and Distribution Lead/Business Partner, Switzerland

Leading all aspects of rolling out new IT system in a major warehouse, testing, documentation, project management.

2014 – 2015

SAP Role Mapping Consultant, London

Ensuring that all users have the correct profiles on a new IT system, training, user acceptance testing, etc.

2013 – 2014

IT Business Process Partner, London

Delivering back-office IT solutions to enable a micro-insurance product to be piloted in Zambia.

2012 – 2013

IT Project Manager, London

Accountable for delivering the project on time and to budget, monitoring, and reporting on project risks.

2011 - 2012

Service Improvement Analyst, Pharma Company, UK

Improving IT service in a manufacturing plant.

2004 – 2007

IT Portfolio Manager, UK

Networks, connectivity, general IT issues, etc.

What are the things you most like about your job, and the things you don't like?

Like:

1. Revisiting my technical past.

Being able to speak to people at a business level about technical stuff and make it simple for them to understand.

2. Moving away from where I'm from. I see it as a very comfortable/non-ambitious area.

It's almost uncool to be clever; I like that in London people encourage ambition.

Don't like:

1. Project Managers.

Good project managers will pretend to care about the work you are doing. Bad project managers will make it apparent that they don't care, they just want to know when you will get the work done by.

2. How slow it can be to progress in big organisations.

Which would you prefer to work for: a small company or a big company, and why?

I have worked for a very small company that was too little. I've also worked for a very large company; I think you need a knack for navigating a very big company. I know people who have progressed very quickly and got promotions fast. They know who to impress and who to talk to, but I find it hard to be false and pretend to be something I'm not.

Have you worked long hours over the years?

The work never goes away. I really don't like how stressed I can get about it. It has taken some very aware managers to realise that I'm pulling my hair out. I realised that things that are meant to be very urgent really aren't and nobody will die if I don't do this.

Have you had much fun over the years?

Working at a manufacturing site was very different. People usually drove to the site and had lots of family commitments, so there was less of a social side. Whereas when you come to a big head office, there are loads of young people, loads of graduates, etc., you could probably go out every night if you wanted to.

If you could start over and you were 22, but you know all you know now, would you do anything differently career-wise?

It's taken me three and a half years to realise that I didn't want to go down the route that I went down. I was encouraged to do one thing, whereas my heart and soul was being a bit of a techie. I spent a lot of time doing totally different things, while that helped me understand what I don't want to do, I feel like I'm four years behind the techies. Would I change the lot? I'm not sure, some of the experiences that I've picked up have really benefitted me. If everything was perfect all the time, you'd never learn anything.

What career advice would you give a young person now?
- Don't be afraid of trying anything when you are younger, when you are not starting families, buying houses. Try as much as you can when you are young without much risk.
- I think you really need to have a network of people in big organisations, who you know will unlock so many doors. Go to the networking events as cringeworthy as they may seem.
- Also, put yourself forward for opportunities, as even if you can't do something, showing the enthusiasm to want to do it is half the battle.

***

EOGHAN, 31

55. Business Analyst, Bank, Dublin

What is your degree in?
Bachelor of Commerce
Master of E-Business

Why did you do the degree you did?
I went back to university as a mature student, even then I didn't have a clue what I wanted to do. It was a very broad course, with a lot of choices.

Did you know what you wanted to do career-wise?
No, I had no job in mind when I went back to university at the age of 25.

Did you know what your day-to-day role entailed starting off in your career?

I did a Masters in e-business so they had some business analysis modules in there. I thought I had an aptitude for it so that's the road I went down. I didn't want to do the coding or very technical stuff, I wanted to use my people skills.

When you came out of university did you seek advice from anyone?
- Not really, once I finished my Masters I started applying for jobs. I applied for anything at all that I thought I could possibly do.
- My university had a careers department, which gave you some interview advice, but they never gave you any career and job advice.

What percentage of what you learned in university have you used in your day-to-day roles?
25%

With the benefit of hindsight, if you were 18 again now would you do anything differently degree-wise?
- I don't think I'd do anything differently, and that's with starting university at 25. It's all worked out great for me.
- The one change I might make was doing a degree without a work experience element to it. It didn't have any value for me later in life. If I could pick a course that was only three years that would enable me to get out of university faster, then maybe I would have done that.

In hindsight, if you could go back now would you have done the Masters straight after your undergraduate?
- I wouldn't have got my job without the postgrad. I needed to do the Masters after getting a 2.2* in my degree.
(*This is a lower second class honours.)

What are the good things and bad things about doing a Masters?
I took my Masters a lot more seriously than my undergraduate. It was very project driven; I was never a good studier, so that worked well for me. There was a lot of coding in it and I never saw myself as a coder, so that wasn't great.

Would you be an advocate of doing a postgraduate course?
I would definitely advise doing a Masters; you will be working long enough. I did enjoy the project work side of it. It was harder work than my day job though – be warned!

What are the jobs you've done since graduating? And what have they entailed?
2017 – 2018
Business Analyst, Bank, Dublin
Same as below.
2015 – 2017
Business Analyst, Multinational Bank, Dublin
Presenting complex information to people who don't have the correct level of understanding. Breaking down processes to help people understand the business and IT requirements.

What are the things you most like about your job, and the things you don't like?
Like:
1. Lots of autonomy.
2. Working with people. Being in meetings and workshops, getting info out of people instead of being at a desk all day long.
3. You are always learning in my job - every project is new and different.

Don't like:
1. I'm left to my own devices a lot, I could do with some more mentoring, coaching.
2. The IT heavy parts of my job i.e. coding, programming.
3. Being put out of your comfort zone a lot – it can be a good thing or a bad thing.

Which would you prefer to work for: a small company or a big company, and why?

- I would much prefer a smaller business. As a business analyst doing a change role, there is a lot of bureaucracy, in a smaller company it's a lot easier to talk to people, to make decisions.
- In a big company, it's manager upon manager and lots of levels of red tape. In the bank, I work for now, I did a presentation to the CFO after about four months. In the bigger bank, I used to work in I barely knew what the guy looked like.

Have you worked long hours over the years?
I do a 34-hour week, with very little overtime.

Have you had much fun over the years?
Fun? I don't think I would describe it as fun! I spent ten years working in bars and nightclubs – that was fun! I wouldn't describe my business analyst job as fun!

If you could start over and you were 22, but you know all you know now, would you do anything differently career-wise?
- I worked in bars until I was 25. I wouldn't change that as I grew up a lot as a person and made some great friends. The way university has gone and my jobs have gone, it's all worked out great.
- A big regret of mine is that I got a 2.2*, but it didn't have an impact on how my life worked out. I was just disappointed I didn't get a 2.1*.
(*2.1 is an upper second class honours, 2.2 is a lower second class honours.)

Are you jealous of any of your friends' jobs?
Of all the roles in IT, I think I found the one that I'm most suited to. I could see that I'd be good in a sales type role because I'm good at bluffing, but no I'm not envious of anyone.

What career advice would you give a young person now?
I messed around in school and had a laugh until my late 20s. Some people rush into things. The fact that I was 25 before I started university was good for me personally. It seems like bad advice to tell people, to do what

I did, but my Leaving Certificate (A levels) results haven't mattered at all to me! It all has worked out really well for me!

***

LINDA, 32

56. Quality Engineer Team Lead, IT Company, London

What is your degree in?
Bachelor of Science (Computer Science)

Why did you do the degree you did?
I honestly didn't know what I wanted to do at the time and was encouraged by my parents into doing computer science because it had jobs.

Why did you embark on the career you did?
- I didn't have a strong interest in pursuing the typical computer science roles. I wanted to get into a career which played to my strengths using my degree as a foundation for working in the IT industry. I started my career in very technical roles, and I actively pursued moving into areas of project and program management where I could play to my strengths a lot more.
- More recently I have taken up a position where I am now directing a team of quality engineers. I have the balance of being able to work with people while also maintaining my knowledge on the latest technologies. This gives me the best of both worlds.

When you came out of university did you seek advice from anyone?
Not really. I know that there were resources available to me but I never fully availed of them and I think that that was a bad idea in retrospect because I didn't get a real sense of the wide range of options available to me.

Did you know what your day-to-day role entailed starting off in your career?

I definitely went in blind. My career evolved as I worked and saw the breadth of things that I could do. Each step I took was a stab in the dark, and as I tried different roles, I got a better sense of where I wanted to be and how to get there.

What percentage of what you learned in university have you used in your day-to-day roles?

Not as much today, but at the start of my career, it was much more. I think your degree essentially gives you a foot in the door of a company, but it doesn't necessarily define where you will be a few years down the line.

With the benefit of hindsight, if you were 18 again now would you do anything differently degree-wise?

I think I would make sure to pursue something that I really liked rather than something that I felt would get me a good job. Jobs and careers are important but having a passion for what you do is so much more rewarding. If you have a passion for it, you will make a fulfilling career out of it no matter what.

What are the things you most like about your job, and the things you don't like?

Like:

1. I have really enjoyed getting to interact with many different and extremely smart people across the world. When I could get a group of very diverse people, both culturally and professionally, to successfully work together in delivering a common goal it has always provided a great sense of job satisfaction for me. Breaking down the communication barriers means having to really understand each and every view point. I have found that I also learn a lot from them in return along the way.
2. The continuous learning opportunities that keep me engaged and challenged. Each new project, or each new role, has come with the opportunity to learn something new and I really enjoy that.
3. As I have progressed in my career, I have really enjoyed being able to get a broader view of the company strategies and seeing things from a

higher-level perspective. It has helped me to get a better understanding of why we do the things we do, and in turn, I'm able to communicate that much better with the people I work with.

Don't like:
1. Sometimes trying to navigate a large company can be hard. There have been some roles which I have done where I have had to accept that I can't necessarily change things overnight. Shifting people's mind-sets to be in sync is a slow and arduous process. Especially at times where I had to be a change agent. I've learned that people don't accept change easily and in a larger company, it's harder to influence direction.
2. The politics of an organisation has sometimes gotten in the way of effectively doing my job. This is something that will happen in every company no matter how large or small it is. Learning to operate in that environment is crucial, but it's not something that I necessarily enjoy.
3. Having to get out of bed on a Monday morning!

Which would you prefer to work for: a small company or a big company, and why?
Both have their merits. Right now, I work for a large company and with that comes the security of knowing that you work at a company where your job is less likely to be at risk. However, it also comes with a lot more boundaries in what you can do. There's less opportunity to put your own spin on things as there will be rules and processes in place that need to be followed. In a small company job security is less guaranteed due to the nature of how they operate and how they get their funding. However, you get to have more of a say in how things should be done and a lot more autonomy in doing it.

Have you worked long hours over the years?
Yes, at various points in my career up until today I have had to work long hours when a project deadline is coming up. It's not ideal, but it does happen, and as long as it doesn't happen often, I don't usually have a problem with it.

Have you had much fun over the years?

- Surprisingly yes. I thought that having not really enjoyed my degree that that would follow on into my career. However, once I started working, I realised that your career is what you make it and you can carve out a path for yourself. I have had an opportunity to apply some of what I learned in university, but my main learnings came after I started working. Those learnings are much more enjoyable because it's about what I experience first-hand and about developing myself both personally and professionally.
- I found that I have enjoyed the challenge of working in an industry that is a foundation of how society operates today. As technology becomes a bigger part of people's lives, I really enjoy being able to be a part of building the foundations of how people interact with each other.

If you could start over and you were 22, but you know all you know now, would you do anything differently career-wise?

I think I would be more assertive earlier on in my career. When I first started out I found that I spent too long doing things which I did not enjoy out of fear of stepping out of my comfort zone. The only person that can influence your career path is yourself and that's something that I learned along the way.

What career advice would you give a young person now?

- Make sure that you pursue something that you have a passion for. Whether that's your university course or a career move. Make sure you are doing what you love because at the end of the day you will end up spending a lot more of your time in work than anywhere else. If you choose a job based on financial gain, the enjoyment will be short lived.
- Be assertive in what you want. Don't be afraid to be yourself and voice your opinions. Honesty and directness will always help you as you navigate your career. If you want to try something new, don't be afraid to ask or take an opportunity that comes your way.

What advice would you give a young person who wanted to do what you do?

- Read up on the career options that are out there in the technology industry. There is a broad and varied spectrum of careers in technology. Find out what you are interested in and develop the skills you need earlier rather than later.
- If you want to ultimately move into a management position, or even try out new projects, make sure that you make that clear to your managers. It takes time and having the discussion early helps management to ensure your career heads in the direction you want.
- Volunteer your time at a smaller company to see if it's something that you might like to do before jumping into a full degree course.
- Don't get overwhelmed by what you don't know. Every new role will have things you don't know, no matter how well you have prepared yourself for them. Be patient with yourself and enjoy the journey along the way.

***

NIALL, 33

57. Software Engineer, Airline Company, Ireland

What is your degree in?
Bachelor of Engineering (Civil)
Master of Engineering (Software)

Why did you do the degree you did?
- I was always interested in big construction projects.
- However, looking back at it, I liked the bigger picture of what went on instead of the nitty-gritty day-to-day engineering side of it.

When you came out of university did you seek advice from anyone?
I talked to my cousin who did engineering, he liked it, and he recommended it.

Did the degree prepare you for working as an engineer?
- The course was as good a course as any other university course. However, when I went back to do my postgrad ten years later in the same

university, I noticed a big difference, they were a lot more modern. In their teaching methods. In my civil undergraduate degree, the lecturers were old guys doing long detailed hand calculations. There was hardly any computer modelling which is what you use all the time when you get out working.

- I'm not sure the civil undergrad course prepared you that well for the real world. Sometimes the university courses are a bit removed from the working world. If you are looking to do something like software, try to look for the most practical courses geared towards jobs/industry.

With the benefit of hindsight, if you were 18 again now would you do anything differently degree-wise?

Both my parents were teachers. I was probably a bit one track minded in thinking I need a job, and this is the degree I need to get to do that job. I liked the idea that a civil degree led to a job in civil engineering. I'd probably do maths as it was what I liked and it would not have narrowed my options down as much as the civil engineering degree did.

What are the jobs you've done since graduating? And what have they entailed?

2017 – 2018

Software Engineer, Airline Company, Ireland

Writing software for a range of applications.

2014 – 2017

Software Engineer, Global Telecom Company, Ireland

Writing software for a range of applications.

2013 – 2014

Software Development Intern, Digital Research Centre, Ireland

Design of the user interface for a cloud-based engineering application.

2006 – 2011

Structural Design Engineer, Construction Company, Dublin

Designing structural elements for large construction projects.

What are the things you most like about your job, and the things you don't like?

Like:
1. The problem-solving aspect of both jobs.
2. Like applying maths to solving practical problems.

Don't like:
1. The boom and bust nature of the construction industry, there is never a middle ground, it's always one or the other.
2. The long hours in the construction industry.

Which would you prefer to work for: a small company or a big company, and why?
- I've worked in both and would prefer working somewhere mid-sized. My first job had 80 people in the company, so management knew you which was good, but you don't have huge security if things go wrong.
- In a bigger company, there are more opportunities, whereas in a smaller company you are nearly waiting for someone to leave to get an opportunity.

Have you worked long hours over the years?
- Civil: It's long hours, there are a lot of Saturdays working in the construction industry in general, it can be stressful and time pressured.
- Software: There is an endless supply of work, projects are broken down into nice planned chunks. You are always busy, but it's very structured compared to engineering. You do your 40-hour week and go home at 5pm and don't worry about your work in evenings and weekends.

Have you had much fun over the years?
- There is a lot more collaboration in software; you are always part of a team, it's always good fun.
- In civil you might be the one representative of your company on-site and it can feel a bit isolated.

How did you know you needed to make a career change?
I found the bigger picture of how construction projects came together more interesting than the day-to-day grind of civil engineering. I liked the

maths and problem solving, but when I worked in civil, I would have found the day dragging so I knew I wanted a change. Working in software, I never find myself looking at the clock.

Would you have been able to make the switch without the postgraduate study?

- The course I did was nine months then an internship for three months which then led to a full-time job.
- I don't think there is any reason you couldn't switch careers without a postgrad, but you'd be up against people with lots of experience. The postgrad gave me some experience and was very related to my coursework, so that was a big advantage.
- Even if you did a four-year degree, companies are reluctant to give graduates a chance. They all want people with four years' experience instead of four years' study. I'd advise doing a course that has an internship in it, that way you will have a great chance to stay with the company if you do well.

If you could start over and you were 22, but you know all you know now, would you do anything differently career-wise?

I like my job now, the one thing I'd do is a broader degree, keep more doors open for myself. I had a six-month on-site placement in the third year. I had no interest in working on-site, all it did was confirm to me that I didn't want to be on a building site.

What career advice would you give a young person now?

- Keep your degree as broad as possible, then try to figure out what you want to do when you are a little bit older, i.e. 21 or 22. It's very hard to know what you want to do at 18, so try and give yourself a few options instead of closing doors on yourself.
- No matter what degree you do you can do a postgrad once you have a few years of work under your belt. That way you are a little bit older and have more of an idea about what you want to do.

What advice would you give a young person who wanted to do what you do?

Do a good degree in computer science, or do maths and then a conversion course into what specific area you want to be working in.

Was it hard to switch careers?

- The postgrad course was tough, but the software engineering work I didn't find hard. The hardest thing was deciding to switch, it was only a one year course but at the time it was a massive decision. I was battling with the fact I had wasted the last five years of my life working as a design engineer. Then I realised it's better to cut my losses if I'm not happy, as I have to spend the next 40 years working!
- I know loads of people on my course who were 40 years old when they switched, and they will probably work for another 30 years in software. It's definitely not one job for life anymore.

Which gets you further in a career – knowing people or being good at your job?

In professions like law it might be about connections, but in software, its black and white about what you can and can't do. So, it would be more being good at your job in software engineering.

***

RICK, 33

58. Software Engineer, IT Company, Dublin

What is your degree in?

Bachelor of Computer Engineering
Higher Diploma in E-Business
Master of Business Analytics

Why did you do the degree you did?

I always liked computers, and felt it was a nice mix of computers and electronics. In the end, I realised I didn't like the electronics side of it, and that I was more into the computers side of it.

With the benefit of hindsight, if you were 18 again now would you do anything differently degree-wise?
I wouldn't be pushed on computers; I'd think more about what you do after your degree.

Did you know what your day-to-day role entailed starting off in your career?
I had a job lined up after graduating; I did interviews, so I had an idea on what was on offer. I looked at graduate programmes, but I'm glad I avoided them, on a scale of 1-10 I knew about a five about what a software developer did.

When you came out of university did you seek advice from anyone?
No.

Why did you embark on the career you did?
It was a mix of finance and technology; I didn't want to go into anything too specific, so stayed broad.

What are the jobs you've done since graduating? And what have they entailed?
2010 – 2017
Senior Software Engineer, IT Firm, Dublin
Started debugging and writing software, am now designing and architecting software.
2006 – 2009
Applications Developer, Spread Betting Company, Dublin
Started off software development for back office and middle office for financial company (spread betting company).

What are the things you most like about your job, and the things you don't like?
Like:
1. Managers that trust you.

2. My team and company – a lot of my friends don't like their teams or companies (I go to the pub with mine all the time).
3. Flexibility – I can work from anywhere i.e. remotely.
4. Hackathons!

Didn't like:
1. Micromanagement/interfering.
2. Businesses that are driven by short-term goals, and not interested in the long term.
3. Separation of sales and technology in companies, prefer if everyone is on same team/page.

Have you worked long hours over the years?
It's very changeable, can work 12-hour days, and weekends. When it comes to release time, it's hectic, but after that the hours are fine. I like a bit of a deadline, and then take it easy after.

Which would you prefer to work for: a small company or a big company, and why?
Small company, you feel more valued, and there is more of a team spirit.

Have you had much fun over the years?
I'm lucky, still meet up with the guys in my old workplace and get on great with people I work with now.

If you could start over and you were 22, but you know all you know now, would you do anything differently career-wise?
When I was 18, I wanted to do computers and that was it. Your preferences and wants will change every few years. Try and keep doors open, as you never know when you might want to go and do something different. For instance, I was adamant in my youth I never wanted to manage people, not I don't feel that way.

What career advice would you give a young person now?

- I wouldn't be so wrapped up in career and corporate ladder, as that is one way to make money, but it's not the only way. There are lots of different ways to make money, don't get so sucked into the rat race and become a follower.
- I'd try and think about how you can make money, pay yourself first!

What advice would you give a young person who wanted to do what you do?
To get a job as a developer in a lot of companies, you'll need a decent degree. If you want to be a programmer, I'd question the validity of a four-year university course, and then coming out of that course in debt. There is so much stuff you can learn online now if you are self-driven. You can do intensive programming courses that are better bang for your buck. If I met someone who wanted to be a programmer, I'd recommend they check these courses out. They are one or two months and are intense, but suddenly you are done and are out earning cash in the real world instead of paying off university loans.

***

TAJ, 34

59. IT PMO Manager, Consulting Firm, London

What is your degree in?
Bachelor of Business Studies

Why did you do the degree you did?
It was a broad degree, with modules you could pick and choose from, marketing to HR to finance.

With the benefit of hindsight, if you were 18 again now would you do anything differently degree-wise?
No, I wouldn't change anything, as the business degree gave me a good varied base of knowledge. However, seeing the industrial placement students working in the company I work in now, I think doing a work placement would have been really beneficial for me.

Did you know what your day-to-day role entailed starting off in your career?
I knew I wanted to do a graduate programme but didn't have an idea about what the day-to-day of a PMO role entailed or any job really!

What percentage of what you learned in university have you used in your day-to-day roles?
Probably very little, as my roles are all project-based, and you don't really do that in university.

Why did you embark on the career you did?
I went into a company as project support then got promoted and moved upwards.

What are the jobs you've done since graduating? And what have they entailed?
2010 – 2017
IT PMO Manager, Various Companies, London
Tracking progress on projects, monitoring KPI's and reporting on projects progress, collating lessons learned.

What are the things you most like about your job, and the things you don't like?
Like:
1. Working with people from other countries, travelling to different sites.
2. Delivering projects, and structured working.
3. Problem-solving, tracking issues to resolution.

Don't like:
1. It can be long hours.

Do you prefer projects or business as usual (BAU) jobs?
I like both, projects can be very rewarding as lots of teamwork, and you learn a lot, as every project is so different.

Have you worked long hours over the years?
It can be long hours but it's varied, there are peaks and troughs.

Which would you prefer to work for: a small company or a big company, and why?
A big company as there are so many different people you can work with, and so many people you can learn from.

If you could start over and you were 22, but you know all you know now, would you do anything differently career-wise?
Nothing I'm really happy with my career!

What career advice would you give a young person now?
Before you come out of university, about a year beforehand try and find out what you are interested in. Try and whittle it down to the areas/direction you want to go. Also, do a work placement, as it gives you an understanding of:
- Corporate culture.
- Where you might want to go.
- What you don't like!

What advice would you give a young person who wanted to do what you do?
Try and get a project support/document controller role and get a feel for the different roles and tasks in a project. Work hard and try and soak up as much knowledge and info as you can, and you will go places!

***

WARREN, 34

60. IT Project Manager, IT Company, London

What is your degree in?
Diploma in IT Engineering

Why did you do the degree you did?
I didn't have time to think, to be honest. I was good with computers, that was the main reason. I started a Computer Science Degree but realised I wasn't too keen on programming, so I changed and got a Diploma in IT Engineering.

Why did you embark on the career you did?
It just seemed like the logical route, I had done the IT course, so it seemed as though I should do an IT Job.

Did you know what your day-to-day role entailed starting off in your career?
I didn't really understand how your IT degree progressed into an IT career. Initially my career was about fixing computers. Only when I moved to the UK from South Africa did I see the variety of IT jobs that you could do.

When you came out of university did you seek advice from anyone?
No advice, in hindsight. I wish I had been given some advice.

What percentage of what you learned in university have you used in your day-to-day roles?
About 10%, what you learn in university, is vastly different to what you have to do in IT jobs in the real world.

With the benefit of hindsight, if you were 18 again now would you do anything differently degree-wise?
Yes, I wouldn't go into my field. At the time, I was good at computers. I didn't think about it in a business way. Now I understand the business knowledge, I'm not sure I'm a fan of the careers you can get out of IT.

Would you have benefitted from a graduate programme/internship?
Yes, you will get a massive understanding of what IT is about. In fact, if you didn't do a degree, and just interned you would pick up all you need

to pick up in six months. A lot of what is in the IT books is irrelevant. It's like maths; you learn stuff you will never use in the real world.

What are the jobs you've done since graduating? And what have they entailed?

2015 – 2017

IT Project Engineer/Manager, IT Company, London

Working on the project management side of things, doing mass migrations of data for companies that are changing computer systems.

2013 - 2015

Senior Engineer, IT Company, London

Network issues, cloud computing, etc.

2010 – 2012

Junior Engineer, IT Company, London

Learning more about servers, etc.

2006 – 2012

Trainee IT Engineer, IT Company, South Africa

Sorting out printers, PCs, etc.

What are the things you most like about your job, and the things you don't like?

Like:

1. Dealing with clients and people that I like.
2. Solving very technical problems.

Don't like:

3. Working for small businesses in IT.
4. Corporate atmospheres.

Which would you prefer to work for: a small company or a big company, and why?

I would go for a bigger company. While it might be soulless, I find smaller IT companies try to be corporate too, and when they do that, they can be horrible places to work.

Have you worked long hours over the years?
It doesn't have to be long hours, again it depends on where you work. Some places there is an expectation that you will work long hours and weekends etc., i.e. 50 hours.

Have you had much fun over the years?
It's hit and miss, depends on the company you work for, the first company I worked for was amazing! So, it depends.

What career advice would you give a young person now?
I would say have a good long think about it, and if you aren't sure, don't rush into a decision. Do a good broad university degree, don't worry about finding your perfect career right away. Start with something that you are comfortable with, and you will add to your knowledge of the working world and then you can build on that.

What advice would you give a young person who wanted to do what you do?
Do they really want to do IT? Ask people who have worked 5-10 years plus in IT, as IT jobs are very different from what you learn in degree courses and university books.

Which gets you further in a career – knowing people or being good at your job?
Unfortunately, in all my jobs, it's putting in long hours that gets you further in your career. To progress you need to hit this set of targets, and to do that you need to put in a lot of hours.

INVESTMENT MANAGEMENT/ BANKING

What I knew before the interviews:

- It can be very corporate, a bit stiff.
- There are long hours and demanding deadlines.
- It's competitive when it comes to getting a good role.
- There are a lot of different departments in the bank.
- You can be limited to living in cities as that's where the jobs are.

What I learned from the interviews:

- There are financial operations jobs outside of the major financial hubs, i.e. London, Dublin.
- Internships are so important if you want a good job in banking.
- A lot of banking is just sales, selling the bank's products.
- Some jobs may well become obsolete in 20 years as the banks are embracing technology.
- If you want it bad enough, you can do a Masters and get a job in investment banking regardless of your degree.

CHARLOTTE, 32

61. Senior Business Strategist, Fund Company, London

What is your degree in?
Bachelor of Arts (Geography)

Why did you do the degree you did?
I enjoyed it and was good at it.

Did you know what you wanted to do career-wise?
No, not at all, I went into recruitment, because it was the easy thing to do. I got a 2.2* at university, so that closed a few doors. I went in thinking I would move out of recruitment quite quickly. However, I really enjoyed recruitment and was very good at it, so I stayed there for ten years.
(*This is a lower second class honours.)

With the benefit of hindsight, if you were 18 again now would you do anything differently degree-wise?
I probably wouldn't do anything differently. I went to Cambridge; it does open doors for you. People will take the time to talk to you, and are interested in you. However, I found university difficult. I went from being a strong student in school to being an average, even below average, student in Cambridge. I went from a mixed comprehensive school to an all-girls university. It was worlds apart; a totally different way of teaching.

When you came out of university did you seek advice from anyone?
- No, I think I just did some researching on what to do if you don't know what to do.
- Recruitment aligned to strengths – interacting with people, etc. It was an easy way to make money quite quickly.

What are the jobs you've done since graduating? And what have they entailed?
2017 – 2018
Senior Business Strategist, Fund Company, London

I make sure the business runs properly, i.e. reporting is done, goals are met etc.

2015 – 2017

Leadership Development Programme, Fund Company, London

Eight-month rotations in various senior leadership roles. 35 of us picked globally in a company of 40,000.

2012 – 2015

Talent Acquisition Consultant, Fund Company, London

Sourcing and placing candidates for roles in-house.

2017 – 2012

Talent Acquisition Consultant, Fund Company, London

Sourcing and placing candidates for roles with various clients.

What are the things you most like about your job, and the things you don't like?

Like:

1. The constant interaction with people.
2. Lots of diversity, and variation in the roles I've done.

Don't like:

1. Peoples' perceptions of recruitment.

Lots of people would ask me why I'm in recruitment if I went to Cambridge.

Have you worked long hours over the years?

Normal hours for the city 8:30am - 6:30pm.

Have you had much fun over the years?

Yes, there are lots of drinks, dinners, and social events in recruitment. It's a sales environment, it is demanding, you have your goals, but you have a good time too.

If you could start over and you were 22, but you know all you know now, would you do anything differently career-wise?

I might have gone in-house (i.e. working in recruitment solely for one firm) a little earlier, as it was less of an aggressive environment.

What career advice would you give a young person now?
Do a lot of research into universities, talk to people about what it's like to be in university, as I don't think schools prepare you for that. I know a lot of people who didn't necessarily enjoy university, so make sure you do your homework on the different ones you can go to, and what they offer, etc.

What advice would you give a young person who wanted to do what you do?
- Be prepared to start at the bottom, shadow somebody, learn the ropes.
- A lot of graduates are very gung-ho when they come out of university and rush into things.
- Ask for and take on constructive criticism as it will really help your development.
- Also, don't be totally set in your ways. I kind of have a career path but am also open to new opportunities. If you leave university, and want to be something that's fine, but don't close other doors on yourself, you may live to regret it.

What did your employers see in you to pick you for that leadership programme?
I think they saw flexibility and willingness. I could wear different hats and communicate with lots of departments and different levels of staff both junior and senior.

***

JENNIFER, 34

62. Investment Banker, Investment Bank, London

What is your degree in?
Bachelor of Science (Industrial and Pharmaceutical Chemistry)
Master of Computational Finance

Why did you do the degree you did?

- A lot of my family work in pharma, they all did chemistry degrees, my dad is a science lecturer.
- I did a year placement in a pharma company and liked the work. However, my boss who was a lab manager, I didn't want to end up like him. Around that time, all the banks were crumbling. I was interested in the how and why, and decided finance was for me. So, I looked at switching from chemistry to finance.
- I then did a Computational Finance Masters which was all about computers and the pricing of financial instruments. The guy who ran the course said your background isn't in finance at all. I said to him that the maths in chemistry and finance was all the same.

Did you know what you wanted to do career-wise?

- I wanted to be a trader, but I didn't have the background to go into the mergers and acquisitions (M&A) side. There were no graduate training programs at the time because of the recession.
- I was very lucky to get a break working in risk. I was incredibly lucky; a lot of your career comes down to timing. I cannot stress how extremely lucky I was. I'm not sure I'd advise taking the path I did, it's a minefield.

When you came out of university did you seek advice from anyone?

- I had a chat with my dad. He said to go for it if it is what you want to do. However, he also said that he knew no-one in finance so he wouldn't be able to help with contacts.
- I talked to a friend of my uncle who was an Investment Banker, but nothing came out of that.

What percentage of what you learned in university have you used in your day-to-day roles?

A lot of it was very relevant, the undergrad was very general, but the postgrad was more specific.

With the benefit of hindsight, if you were 18 again now would you do anything differently degree-wise?
No, I wouldn't change anything. Doing chemistry gave me a different perspective, so I'm happy with the way I did it.

What are the jobs you've done since graduating? And what have they entailed?
2015 – 2018
Investment Banker, Investment Bank, London
Buying and selling government bonds, currency swaps, etc.
2010 – 2015
Risk Analyst, Various Global Banks, London
Modelling the risks that the bank faces on a day-to-day basis.

What are the things you most like about your job, and the things you don't like?
Like:
1. The hands-on, independent work.
2. The buzz is incredible - even if you haven't slept in four days, you are totally engaged, it's so stimulating.

Don't like:
1. The risk stuff wasn't exactly what I wanted to do.
2. The caustic personalities, it's a vicious environment, you've got people telling you to fuck off all the time - I can't stress how vicious it is.

Which would you prefer to work for: a small company or a big company, and why?
A smaller bank is more easy-going and relaxed, in the bigger banks it's frenetic, it's the highest operating speed possible, which I prefer.

Have you worked long hours over the years?
I get up at 5:45am, in for 6:45am, and I'm home for about 8ish. You only really have ten years before you burn out in investment banking, it can be intense.

If you could start over and you were 22, but you know all you know now, would you do anything differently career-wise?
I would have tried to get better grades, so I could go to a more prestigious university, as those things stay with you and they do matter.

What career advice would you give a young person now?
Make sure you get good grades, they open doors, no one can take them away from you. A lecturer told a friend of mine that a high 2.2* is the same as a 2.1*, there is zero truth in that – don't believe that for a second, you need a 2.1*.
(*2.1 is an upper second class honours, 2.2 is a lower second class honours.)

What advice would you give a young person who wanted to do what you do?
- You need to get into the red brick universities. You probably need to go to private school, get your 2.1* or 1.1*.
- In the big investment banks, they have what's called 'spring week.' you need to get referred to it by someone internally. Then you have to get an internship, but you can only get one if you've done the 'spring week.' Then you have to get on the graduate programme; you can't get on the graduate programme unless you've done an internship. Once you are on the graduate programme then you are in. Something like 5% of applicants succeed.
- On the trading side, you will be doing 7am – 7pm, if you are on the M&A side, you could be there all-day long. They have this thing called the 'The Magic Roundabout' where you just go home and shower and then come back to the office. A couple of kids have died doing those kinds of hours. They order food in, they have a gym and dry cleaning at the office. They never leave the office.
(*2.1 is an upper second class honours and 1.1 is a first class honours.)

Which gets you further in a career - knowing people or being good at your job?

Getting into these banks requires a phenomenal amount of effort. You need to be meticulous and strategic in your networking, if you leave it to meeting organically then forget about it.

***

MARCUS, 33

63. Head of Finance, Bank, Dublin

What is your degree in?
Bachelor of Commerce
Master of International Strategy

Why did you do the degree you did?
I wasn't exactly sure what I wanted to do, and it sounded quite general. I liked the idea of working in a business, working with numbers. Basically, it was a good general degree, and it allowed me to specialise after a couple of years.

When you came out of university did you seek advice from anyone?
No, not really. In hindsight, I really should have done, as people would have been only too willing to talk to a young person trying to find out more about a career.

Did the degree prepare you for the working world?
- Working in product development, I do a lot of marketing (approaching your customers) and some accounting and economics (demand and supply, elasticity, pricing). The degree gives you a good base of knowledge on those topics.
- Also, my Masters would have given me confidence in presenting in front of people, messaging, etc. I had a bit of a head-start on people who hadn't done a Masters in that regard.

Would you be an advocate of doing postgraduate study straight after undergraduate?

I think there would be more value doing it after a couple of years working. It's harder to apply what they teach you in the Masters to real life when you don't have that experience. I did a Diploma in Banking after a few years of working and found you can really relate it to what you are doing day-to-day, and you can use what you learn in work.

What percentage of what you learned in university have you used in your day-to-day roles?
Less than 25%, university just gives you the basic framework for you to build on.

With the benefit of hindsight, if you were 18 again now would you do anything differently degree-wise?
I was a bit wary of choosing a specific path. I thought that people who did, would be stuck in that career for life and there would be no way out of it. As I progressed in life, I saw people doing very specific degrees going on to work in something totally unrelated. So, if I was to do anything different, I'd be more open-minded when it came to making some decisions.

What are the jobs you've done since graduating? And what have they entailed?
2015 – 2018
Head of Finance, Bank, Dublin
Ensuring lending targets are met, interacting with sales, marketing and regulatory teams.
2013 – 2015
Product Manager, National Bank, Dublin
I worked on developing new products for the bank. Ensuring business and functional requirements were included in the new products.
2011 – 2013
Product Management Role, International Bank, Dublin
Managing the bank's existing suite of products i.e. deciding if margins/rates would change. Making sure everything was ok regulatory wise.

2007 – 2011
Product Development Specialist, International Bank, Dublin
Developing and managing the bank's products, i.e. investment bonds.

What are the things you most like about your job, and the things you don't like?
Like:
1. The people element – trying to coax people into doing things to ensure targets are met.
2. The sales side of it, even though we don't sell to customers, we sell to our sales team.
3. Getting good exposure to very senior people.

Don't like:
1. Being very dependent on other departments within the bank to get things done. Sometimes you're fighting for your corner and not getting much support.
2. Having to constantly watch and be compliant with regulation.

Which would you prefer to work for: a small company or a big company, and why?
In a small company, you get much more exposure to senior people. You get to work on a variety of projects and roles; that you wouldn't in a bigger bank. In the bigger banks, the work is very siloed. You don't get that chance to work across departments.

Have you worked long hours over the years?
- As I've got more responsibility, the hours have increased. The more 'skin in the game' you have the more prepared to put in the work you are.
- I usually would work 8:30am - 6:30/7pm, hard work doesn't bother me.

Have you had much fun over the years?
- Yes, there is always quite a good social side to it, lots of young people, nights out. etc. The banks I've worked in have always been good socially, I've made a lot of mates through work.

- It's important to be light-hearted as it's only a job at the end of the day!

If you could start over and you were 22, but you know all you know now, would you do anything differently career-wise?

I think in my earlier years, I should have been a bit more ambitious. Looking at some of the young guys here who are pushing for promotions, maybe I should have pushed myself a bit harder. It was the recession at the time and I was happy to have a job. Maybe I should have pushed myself a bit harder? I think you can enjoy your 20s and still try and do well in your career at the same time.

What career advice would you give a young person now?

- Talk to as many people as you can, spend a bit of time seeking out people in different sectors and companies.
- There is too much attention paid to career guidance counsellors, at the end of the day they are just teachers!
- I didn't really try to talk to anyone. People are good with their time. Go and speak to the people who have lived it and done it.

What advice would you give a young person who wanted to do what you do?

A great way is through a graduate programme, but it's not always easy to get on them. Also, spend some time researching the different departments of a bank i.e. marketing, credit, risk, and what a day-to-day role working in them entails. People will tell you to take the first job that you get offered in the bank. I would say the opposite - choose wisely. You don't want to go into a department where you can be pigeon-holed, and it's very hard to get out of.

***

NIALL, 35

64. Trader, Asset Management Firm, London

What is your degree in?

Bachelor of Commerce

Master of Finance

Why did you do the degree you did?
I had a general interest in the topic, particularly economics, it was commercial and practical as well.

Would you be an advocate of doing postgraduate study straight after undergraduate?
I would want to stay in education, instead of working and coming back - I preferred to do it in one shot.

Do you think the Masters was needed in hindsight, could you have done without it?
Yes, I think it was needed, there is such a proliferation and dilution of the value of the degree now. There is a huge amount of generic degrees around, having a postgraduate degree shows a higher level of focus.

Could you have become a Trader if you had a non-business degree?
I think I could have, but it would have made it more difficult. My background was slightly applied, so that helped.

Do all the people you work with have business degrees?
Everyone would have some level of third level education. In trading and portfolio analysis, the main degrees that people would have would be maths, business, economics, engineering. One or two guys have degrees in politics, but they would be in the minority.

Has the Masters helped you in your day-to-day roles?
Yes, none of the concepts are new to you, the Masters gives you a good basic academic understanding. It would give you a bit more confidence.

To work as a Trader do you have to keep up with what's happening in business in general?
Yes, that's a basic requirement, because of the dynamism of the industry, the market is constantly changing, the sands are always shifting.

What percentage of what you learned in university have you used in your day-to-day roles?
40-50%

With the benefit of hindsight, if you were 18 again now would you do anything differently degree-wise?
Would I change anything? Probably not.

In the trading game, does it matter where you go to university?
Yes, I think you must go to a named university, one that people will recognise and know.

What are the jobs you've done since graduating? And what have they entailed?
2016 – 2018
Head of Equity Trading Desk, Asset Management Firm, London
Managing European equity trading for an asset manager worth £3bn.
2011 – 2013
Equity Trader, Investment Management Firm, London
Responsibility for hedging funds to minimise risk.
2009 – 2011
Trader, Investment Management Firm, Dublin
Executing trades on the system for asset managers.
2007 – 2009
Fund Accountant, Investment Management Firm, Dublin
Ensuring financial funds are properly accounted for and reconciled to the system.

What are the things you most like about your job, and the things you don't like?
Like:
1. The challenging environment.
2. The scope to grow in a meritocratic environment.
3. Working with high calibre of people.

Don't like:
1. The hours (6:45am - 6pm).
2. The stress.
3. Arrogant individuals.

Is it tough to switch off?
When things are really rocking, and rolling, it is tough to switch off, other times it's fine.

Which would you prefer to work for: a small company or a big company, and why?
Small, I prefer the camaraderie, I'd rather work in the smaller teams, as opposed to just being another number in a big machine. Generally, people tend to get lost in bigger companies. It's also much easier to get things done in a small company.

Have you had much fun over the years?
Yes, at periods and times it's been great fun, both inside and outside work.

If you could start over and you were 22, but you know all you know now, would you do anything differently career-wise?
I would have moved to London sooner, as there are more opportunities.

What career advice would you give a young person now?
- When you are interviewing try to be yourself, try to be personable. Try to communicate effectively what you can do, what you are good at. Don't overthink it, don't try to be the re-incarnation of Mother Theresa or Bill Gates.
- Remember the person sitting across from you will be working with you for large chunks of the day. Bear in mind there is a huge practical aspect of the interview. People will want to be happy to sit beside you for 10 hours of the day as opposed to sitting beside some sociopath.

What advice would you give a young person who wanted to do what you do?
Embrace technology generally, and always swim with the tide in an ever-evolving industry.

What does that mean?
Try to be innovative and try to stay ahead of changes coming down the road. Be comfortable with technology, be comfortable with an environment where things are being more and more automated. Make sure that you future-proof your job.

Do you reckon in 10 years' time your job will be redundant?
If I was just to stay what I'm doing now; that job will be redundant. That is why you've got to move with the times.

***

NIAMH, 33

65. Head of Client Engagement, Asset Management Firm, US

What is your degree in?
Bachelor of Commerce
Master of Finance

Why did you do the degree you did?
Watching my father working in business, a corporate environment always interested me. As when I looked at possible courses, I thought an open-ended course in business would be a great base degree. During the course, international business and financial services emerged as a strong interest. So, I focused my degree and Masters in that direction.

Why did you embark on the career you did?
- I didn't know much about the asset management industry. So, during my undergrad, I sought out some work experience in the industry to see if it was something I was interested in.

- On leaving my Masters, I had a strong interest in client solutions and investment. I knew portfolio management was not for me, so I researched other roles in the industry. I was fortunate to find an open position in the relationship management team within an international asset management firm. They were willing to take a risk on a new graduate with limited experience.

When you came out of university did you seek advice from anyone?
Yes, I spent some time with an independent career advisor who helped me think about how to market myself as a new graduate seeking employment.

Did you know what your day-to-day role entailed starting off in your career?
I was a bit blind - I think everyone is. I was fortunate to join a team that was willing to work with me, train me and I had the courage to ask questions.

What percentage of what you learned in university have you used in your day-to-day roles?
Very little of the theory, but my degree opened doors for me, and helped my confidence.

With the benefit of hindsight, if you were 18 again now would you do anything differently degree-wise?
No - I loved my degrees, courses and university experience. I would perhaps look for more work experience options as part of my degree to help me prepare for the working world.

What are the jobs you've done since graduating? And what have they entailed?
2017 – 2018
Head of Client Engagement, Asset Management Firm, US
Same as below only with more responsibility.
2006 – 2016

Senior Client Relationship Manager, Various Asset Management Firms, US and London

Leading client relationships for clients with customised liability-driven investment (LDI), fixed income, and index solutions.

What are the things you most like about your job, and the things you don't like?

Like:

1. The mobility - I have worked in Ireland, Australia, London and the US.
2. Providing client solutions and being able to utilise the size, scope, and rigor of an international organisation to partner with our client base.
3. The variability in the role and the people I work with has kept me on my toes and kept things interesting.

Don't like:

1. The lack of empowerment in certain roles to make changes and make decisions.

Which would you prefer to work for: a small company or a big company, and why?

- I have worked in both. I would prefer a bigger organisation.
- I would attribute much of the success in my career to working with strong mentors and the opportunities afforded you in a bigger organisation.
- I've worked in a smaller company where I felt constrained by the founder. I didn't feel I had the autonomy that I was looking for from the smaller organisation. In the end, I left to move back to a larger company.

Have you worked long hours over the years?

Absolutely, I've worked long hours and sometimes still do. However, it is needs based and not a regular occurrence.

Have you had much fun over the years?

Yes, it has been challenging. My job pushed me to grow as a person and I have been afforded the opportunity to work in many different environments and cultures. It's exactly what I was looking for in a career.

If you could start over and you were 22, but you know all you know now, would you do anything differently career-wise?
Yes - I would try to seek out mentors, sponsors more and try to learn from peers and members of senior leadership.

What career advice would you give a young person now?
Don't worry - It will all work out! Stay positive and remember sometimes the right no is better than the wrong yes!

What advice would you give a young person who wanted to do what you do?
There are great entry-level jobs in asset management especially RFP and reporting. You learn an amazing foundation about a company's products, operations, and philosophy. Be patient and learn the ropes, it will benefit you in the long run.

***

NICOLA, 30

66. Funds Manager, Fund Company, Dublin

What is your degree in?
Bachelor of Commerce

Why did you do the degree you did?
It was a broad business degree; you could do marketing, economics, accounting. There was a lot of options.

Did you know what you wanted to do career-wise?
I decided I wanted to move to Dublin, I applied for various jobs. I got one in funds and off I went!

Did you know what your day-to-day role entailed starting off in your career?
I had no idea. I found everything out in the interview.

What percentage of what you learned in university have you used in your day-to-day roles?
15%

With the benefit of hindsight, if you were 18 again now would you do anything differently degree-wise?
Probably not, degree-wise nothing, I'd do more research into what jobs you could do and what jobs you could get out of them.

What are the jobs you've done since graduating? And what have they entailed?
2013 – 2018
Senior Account Manager, Fund Company, Dublin
Regulatory, setting up of funds, more dealing with clients, etc.
2007 – 2012
Senior Fund Administrator, Global Bank, Dublin
Calculating the price of investment funds.

What are the things you most like about your job, and the things you don't like?
Like:
1. The variety.
2. There is a lot of exposure to develop yourself.
3. Increased understanding of the financial markets – it makes more sense when you hear about them on the news.

Don't like:
1. The long hours.
2. It's very easy to get pigeonholed.
Once you get in it's very hard to get out of.
3. The lack of opportunities in Ireland in the funds industry.

Which would you prefer to work for: a small company or a big company, and why?
I prefer smaller companies. You get more exposure, and there is not as much red-tape in getting things done. Working in a big company was very political, you had to be in the right cliques to get good roles. In a small firm, you are rewarded for the work you do, rather than the brown-nosing!

Have you worked long hours over the years?
Yes, it's been long hours, 10-11 hour days.

Have you had much fun over the years?
There is a quite a good social aspect to it. There are a lot of Friday night's spent socialising. The funds industry in Ireland is quite young.

If you could start over and you were 22, but you know all you know now, would you do anything differently career-wise?
I would have done more internships. I'd love to have done a few different stints in different companies instead of just starting in the first job I got.

What career advice would you give a young person now?
Don't be afraid, if you want to change job or go travelling, do it, don't be listening to all the cautious people. Just do it, step out of your comfort zone, don't waste away in the one role stagnating and not learning anything new.

What advice would you give a young person who wanted to do what you do?
Be prepared to work; no one will do it for you. It is a deadline driven industry, be prepared it is a demanding job, don't expect 9-5 with a nice lunch. However, on the flip side, there is a lot to learn from it and you can progress quite quickly.

Which gets you further in a career - knowing people or being good at your job?
Knowing people, networking is a huge part of getting ahead in work.

***

OISIN, 34

67. Second Vice President, Fund Company, Ireland

What is your degree in?
Bachelor of Science (Financial Maths and Economics)

Why did you do the degree you did?
I wanted to do finance and thought doing a maths degree alongside it would look good. I was always interested in finance from a young age; I read the business pages in the newspaper before the sports pages.

Did you know what you wanted to do career-wise?
No, not really, I wanted to go down the investment bank route, but there wasn't much opportunity in Ireland.

Did you know what your day-to-day role entailed starting off in your career?
I got a job with Bear Stearns. I didn't know anything about the job, just knew that they were one of the big 5 investment banks (before they went bankrupt). I took the job on that basis, didn't do a whole lot of research, to be honest. I thought that job would lead to investment banking. However, all they had in Dublin was investment management and operations, which has led me to where I am today.

What percentage of what you learned in university have you used in your day-to-day roles?
I recently used some of the theoretical mathematics I learned at university to solve a problem at work. Up until that point, I hadn't used my degree, as the maths we learned wasn't very practical.

With the benefit of hindsight, if you were 18 again now would you do anything differently degree-wise?

- No, I don't think so, it enabled me to get a 2.1* – that's the most important thing. Your degree is not going to define you; it's what you do in work that will define you. Getting a 2.1* is a must. All your degree does is shows you can commit to something and complete it.
- A lot of people are good talkers but never follow through on what they say they will do.
- I might have been a bit soberer in university if I was to change anything!

(*This is an upper second class honours.)

What are the jobs you've done since graduating? And what have they entailed?

2015 – 2017

Second Vice President, Fund Company, Ireland

Same as below only with more responsibility, and more people management.

2013 – 2015

Team Leader Fund Accounting, Fund Admin Company, Ireland

Working for an administration company managing reconciliation of funds for third parties.

2010 – 2013

Product Control Analyst, Investment Management Firm, Ireland

Working on the investment manager side, doing product control, managing system reconciliations.

2007 – 2009

Senior Operations Specialist, Fund Company, Ireland

Providing day-to-day oversight and management of different funds, ensuring their values reconciled to the values as per the system.

2006 – 2007

Derivative Settlements, Investment Bank, Ireland

Making sure the cash is settled correctly, reconciling amounts as per the system to the actual trades.

What are the things you most like about your job, and the things you don't like?

Like:

1. Problem-solving.

Coming up with solutions to address business challenges.

2. Working with senior people and trying to learn from them.
3. Learning from mistakes.
4. Adapting to change.

Don't like:

1. Managers that are bullies. The best thing is to disengage with them.
2. Financial operations roles are not decision making, they are support roles.
3. The limited opportunities in Ireland – having said that I live in the countryside now back home where I'm from, so there are pros and cons.

Which would you prefer to work for: a small company or a big company, and why?

It doesn't really matter, the most important thing is who you are working with and their skill level, so you can learn from them. It's all about learning and if you aren't learning you should move on.

Have you worked long hours over the years?

No, I've done a standard 9-5.

If you could start over and you were 22, but you know all you know now, would you do anything differently career-wise?

- I don't think I'd change anything. My career path has enabled me to live and work in the countryside in Ireland.
- I didn't specialise, I was more a generalist and didn't back myself into a corner, I stayed flexible, I think there is a lot to be said for that.

What career advice would you give a young person now?

Be open-minded, focus on learning, the more you learn, the more valuable you are. It's how you invest your time that is important - don't do stuff that's going to be redundant in the future. Accumulate as much knowledge as you can, so you are a high-value candidate. If you are not learning, then you are not investing your time well.

What advice would you give a young person who wanted to do what you do?

- Do a few internships, try out different companies, see which one you like best.
- Do a finance degree, and when interviewing, demonstrate a positive can-do attitude.

***

SHANE, 33

68. Fund Structurer, Bank, London

What is your degree in?

Bachelor of Science (Pharmaceutical and Industrial Chemistry)
Master of Economics
Master of Computational Finance

Why did you do the degree you did?

- I studied all science subjects for my A levels, so naturally enough I went on and did a science degree. I didn't do that well in my degree and wasn't that good at it.
- In the third year of my degree, I spent a year working with a pharma company, and realised it wasn't for me.
- I was a bit different as most of my class would have got jobs with big pharma, I think that kind of work would have bored me, I just wasn't interested enough.
- I then did economics as a bit of a conversion course. It was light and fluffy as most economics courses are. After that, I did a Masters in Computational Finance, and that opened up more career opportunities for me.

Did you know what you wanted to do career-wise?

I had an idea once I finished my degree that I wanted to work in finance or banking. When I was picking my postgrads, I looked at ones that would a) get me up to speed with the finance stuff, and b) open some doors for me.

When you came out of university did you seek advice from anyone?
I would have spoken to a few lecturers.

Did you know what your day-to-day role entailed starting off in your career?
I thought I had an idea of what the day-to-day entailed. My Masters course was quite useful It was well funded, so they built a small trading floor to give you an idea. You had all the screens, looking back it did give the graduates good insight and was useful for them at interviews.

What percentage of what you learned in university have you used in your day-to-day roles?
50%, you learn all the financial maths basics.

With the benefit of hindsight, if you were 18 again now would you do anything differently degree-wise?
Yes, I would be more aware of the future. Everything is moving more towards technology, even back then it was obvious it was moving towards technology. These days the banks are full of programmers. You are future proofing your career if you become more of a tech geek.

What are the jobs you've done since graduating? And what have they entailed?
2010 – 2017
Fund Structurer, Bank, London
Structuring specific types of deals for the bank and clients, basically any kind of bespoke deal.

What are the things you most like about your job, and the things you don't like?

Like:
1. A large part of the role is problem-solving which I find quite interesting.
2. It's well paid in terms of industry roles in banking.
3. Every year you get more knowledge, and you become a bit more valuable, it's a bit like consulting.
4. It's a job that's kind of future proofed, as it's very bespoke.

Don't like:
1. Job security at times can be quite low, as there is always restructuring going on in the investment banks.

How did you end up in structuring?
I took the first internship I was offered in corporate finance, but I wanted to move to a more quantitative role. I was brought onto a desk, and not expected to know a huge amount, just expected to learn as much as I could.

Which would you prefer to work for: a small company or a big company, and why?
I've only ever worked with average-sized banks, but it depends team by team in the bank on what kind of environment you have.

Have you worked long hours over the years?
No, 9am - 6pm, a bit longer when you first come into the role.

Have you had much fun over the years?
- Yes, you get to work in cool cities around the world, it's quite a young age group, most people in banking are 25-40 years old.
- Even though it's quite challenging, you are working with smart people, so that's enjoyable.

Is it stressful?
Not overly, but it does have its moments.

If you could start over and you were 22, but you know all you know now, would you do anything differently career-wise?

- I think I'd definitely work abroad somewhere.
- I would have done a few different internships to get a feel for various departments and roles.

What career advice would you give a young person now?

- The door is never closed; most people only realise what they want to do in their mid to late 20s. It's never too late to change your career if you are unhappy. Up until you are 30, there are loads of conversion courses that quickly enable you to change careers.
- There are so many variations of different Masters, if you can't get into one in your home country, that doesn't mean you can't get into just as good a course in Europe. In your 20s you can always pop in and do a one year Masters. 12 months is not a long time. Some of these Dutch universities they have really low fees, pop over there and do a Masters.
- My background is the most unusual one you could find to end up in banking; I did a Masters and I'm in a totally different industry now.
- People should place a high value on getting the right experience, and learning instead of chasing a 5, 10, 20% pay increase, especially early in your career. Once you are getting good experience and you are learning, don't worry about the salary. Peoples' careers are so long; the big wages will be more weighted towards the end of their careers.

What advice would you give a young person who wanted to do what you do?

- Try and build up the relevant background, i.e. quantitative finance. Then I would try and get a range of internships, not just one, so you can compare different roles and departments.
- Teams and managers like it when young people go to them saying they are really interested in an area. Once you get an internship, then you will have your foot in the door.

Which gets you further in a career – knowing people or being good at your job?

Being good at your job by far.

Questions:

If you have any career questions, please do email them to me and I will try to answer them as best I can.

careeradviceforyoungpeople@gmail.com

Blog Newsletter:

If you liked the book and want to get more exclusive content, please do sign up to my newsletter. You'll find the sign-up form at the end of all my blog posts.

www.1000yearsofcareeradvice.com

LAW

What I knew before the interviews:

- A lot of my peers went down the law route.
- It was quite difficult to get apprenticeships but this could have been due to the recession.

What I learned from the interviews:

- It can be difficult dealing with local people that you know in a small practice.
- Being a lawyer for a company is a lot more structured than in a practice.
- Studying law is very different to practicing law.
- Your days can be really varied.

ASHLING, 32

69. Solicitor, Law Firm, New York

What is your degree in?

Bachelor of Arts (Legal Science and Politics)
Law Conversion Course

Why did you do the degree you did?

I always had teaching in the back of my head. I did some teaching subjects in first year but then dropped them for other ones. People told me arts would give you options. I picked legal science, sociology and politics to specialise in, a lot of people were picking the same subjects.

Is what you learned in the law conversion course very different to the day-to-day life of a solicitor?

What you learn is somewhat related, but that can be said about any course. It's completely different when you start in an actual job doing something for real.

Did you know what you wanted to do career-wise?

No, my sister was going down the law route, so I knew bits and pieces, but I hadn't worked a day in an office before going into law.

With the benefit of hindsight, if you were 18 again now would you do anything differently degree-wise?

I'd be quite hesitant about advising people going down the law route, every day I think there must be easier ways to make money. I'm not sure it is the job for me. I fell into law and it takes so long to get qualified before you realise that maybe this wasn't a good choice. It takes nearly as long doing law as it does to do medicine.

What are the jobs you've done since graduating? And what have they entailed?

2016 – 2018

Solicitor, Law Firm, New York

Litigation, white collar crime, insider trading etc.

2012 – 2015

Solicitor, Law Firm, Dublin

Litigation, medical negligence, running my own cases, conducting settlement negotiations.

2009 – 2011

Solicitor, Law Firm, Dublin

Training contract - litigation and conveyancing.

2007 – 2009

Legal Assistant, Law Firm, Dublin

Assisting solicitors to prepare for court, admin, filing legal documents, etc.

What are the things you most like about your job, and the things you don't like?

Like:

1. The money – let's be honest!
2. The variety – no two days are the same.

Don't like:

1. The lack of work-life balance – it kind of takes over your whole life. In the US, they expect you to be on call 24-7, it's pretty intense.
2. The pressure and the stress. A lot of the work is criminal defence work; it takes its toll emotionally and physically. When the case goes your way it's great, but when it goes the other way it's tough.
3. I'm not really a fan of the people working in the law profession. People have some serious notions about themselves.

Which would you prefer to work for: a small company or a big company, and why?

I'd prefer to work for a medium size company, you get the best of both worlds, you are not just a cog in a big machine, and you get paid better than a small company.

Have you worked long hours over the years?

Long hours, you can be working on cases until 3am.

Have you had much fun over the years?
It was fun when I was working in my training contract, lots of nights out. etc., but as you get older it's tough work.

If you could start over and you were 22, but you know all you know now, would you do anything differently career-wise?
Honestly, I'd go down the teaching route. I feel like I'm trapped in law. You start doing exams; then you have to do your traineeship. It becomes hard to walk away from it and feel like you've wasted all that time and effort.

What career advice would you give a young person now?
- I'd advise doing a degree where you have a title/qualification at the end of it. It took me years before I was qualified, and by then it was too late, it was too huge a thing to go back and do something else.
- Getting practical experience is a big thing, the first firm I worked in wasn't until after I got my final exams. Go into a local office for a week/month just to get a feel for what goes on.
- Also, build up your network as much as you can. In Ireland, we are so bad at it, in the US that is how you get ahead, by connecting with other people and making those relationships.

Would you be an advocate of going and working abroad?
The experience you gain is so beneficial, it's the opportunity of a lifetime, especially in a legal office. I got to read evidence out loud in open court in New York, that was incredible.

***

DAVID, 32

70. Solicitor, Law Firm, Dublin

What is your degree in?
Bachelor of Arts (Legal Science and History)

Law Conversion Course

Why did you do the degree you did?
I did some work experience in a solicitor's office and enjoyed attending court and seeing all the different cases involved.

Did you know what your day-to-day role entailed starting off in your career?
I don't think you ever really know about the career you embark on until you're three to four years into it. At the time my knowledge of a career in law was the more exciting bits and pieces that you see in a very short stint in a solicitor's office.

What percentage of what you learned in university have you used in your day-to-day roles?
Very little, less than 20%.

With the benefit of hindsight, if you were 18 again now would you do anything differently degree-wise?
I would do a commerce degree as it's a broader qualification to have, with law you are tied to a legal career either being a solicitor or a barrister.

What are the jobs you've done since graduating? And what have they entailed?
2014 – 2018
Solicitor, Various Law Firms, Dublin
Managing your own file workload, drafting docs and assisting partners in respect of larger commercial property transactions.
2006 – 2009
Trainee Solicitor, Law Firm, Dublin
Assisting qualified solicitors with preparing their briefs for court, closing documents for real estate transactions.

What are the things you most like about your job, and the things you don't like?

Like:
1. Working on larger transactions.
2. Having so many young people your age working alongside you in the big firms.
3. The scope for career progression.

Don't like:
1. Long hours.
2. Stressful situations.
3. Meeting demanding and unrealistic time-frames from clients.

Which would you prefer to work for: a small company or a big company, and why?
It depends on the stage of your career, at the beginning you should start in a small firm as you get broader experience. As you progress in your career, you need to go to a bigger company if you'd like to specialise and work on larger transactions.

If you could start over and you were 22, but you know all you know now, would you do anything differently career-wise?
I'm happy with my career so far, going from a small to a larger firm. I was happy to get hands-on experience in a smaller firm, and then go and see how a big firm operates.

Have you worked long hours over the years?
It's generally long hours, on average 9am – 7pm, sometimes later if you are working on a deal.

What career advice would you give a young person now?
- Pick a broad degree that you can then pick what you want to do at the end of it. It's very difficult to know at 18 what career path you'd like to take.
- Make sure you have a good work-life balance, it's too easy to get sucked into doing long hours, especially in law.

- Take as much advice on board as possible from people working in your chosen area.

***

EOIN, 33

71. Solicitor, Law Firm, Dublin

What is your degree in?
Bachelor of Arts (Legal Science and Economics)
Law Conversion Course

Why did you do the degree you did?
I wanted to do straight law, but I didn't get the results, which happened to a lot of people.

With the benefit of hindsight, if you were 18 again now would you do anything differently degree-wise?
- I decided I wanted to be a lawyer when I was 15. While studying it, I really liked it, however, working as an actual lawyer is very different.
- I probably wouldn't change my degree as I can't think of anything I would prefer to do really. After my degree, I could have moved towards economics. I liked it but didn't see a potential career path that I liked, I didn't fancy academia or working for a big fund company.

Did you know what your day-to-day role entailed starting off in your career?
I knew very little, when you finish a degree, you're far from qualified. You must do another set of exams, 90% of what I learned in university, I don't use.

Why did you embark on the career you did?
I was never keen on being Ally McBeal. I wanted a job that had decent pay and was challenging.

When you came out of university did you seek advice from anyone?

Yes, I spoke to family friends who were in the profession. Ultimately, I was trying to line up an apprenticeship by talking to all these people, as you need to serve with a solicitor. It took me six years to get a traineeship, as the country went down the tubes during the recession.

What are the jobs you've done since graduating? And what have they entailed?

2016 – 2018

Solicitor (Aircraft Finance), Law Firm, Dublin

Advising financial institutions on aircraft acquisitions and sales.

2014 – 2016

Solicitor (Transactional Finance/Banking), Law Firm, Dublin

Advising leading international financial institutions and corporate clients on all aspects of banking and finance transactions.

2011 – 2014

Trainee Solicitor, Law Firm, Ireland

Gaining experience in the following areas: banking law, corporate recovery and insolvency, commercial litigation, commercial and residential property, and immigration.

What are the things you most like about your job, and the things you don't like?

Like:

1. It's challenging.
2. It's quick moving, i.e. lots of deadlines

Don't like:

1. The long hours.
2. It's extremely competitive.
3. It can be repetitive/not the most stimulating.

Have you worked long hours over the years?

Yes, there is a long hour's culture in law.

Which would you prefer to work for: a small company or a big company, and why?

In the past, I would have preferred a big company. However, as I get more senior, I am more interested in smaller companies - it's easier to do things and there is less red tape and clunky processes.

If you could start over and you were 22, but you know all you know now, would you do anything differently career-wise?

- Drink significantly less!
- Taken more time to consider my options.
- Quite a high number of people who qualify as lawyers in their first year realise that their job is totally different than they thought!

What career advice would you give a young person now?

Take time to consider your options. Try not to be too single-minded about what you want to do, as you will shut doors on yourself.

What advice would you give a young person who wanted to do what you do?

- The main thing is to plan every step. What are employers looking for at each level, school, university, apprenticeship, etc. What are the actual skills and experiences you need to differentiate yourself from everybody else? Ultimately every firm will have a certain profile that they look for in candidates. As it's so competitive, they look at things that really aren't relevant i.e. A level results. You need to be clued in from very early on. It's never too early to be gaining the experience that they are looking for.
- Law degrees should include photocopiers, binding machines and wine bars in their curricula!

***

MICHAEL, 32

72. Solicitor, Law Firm, Ireland

What is your degree in?

Bachelor of Arts (Legal Science and Politics)

Law Conversion Course

Why did you do the degree you did?
I did a Bachelor of Arts, as I wasn't sure what I wanted to do. I was unsure, so I felt it was a broad degree that would give me lots of options.

Did you know what your day-to-day role entailed starting off in your career?
Nothing, I was completely blind. I'd never spoken to a practicing solicitor or a barrister until I qualified. I had never stood inside a solicitor's office.

Why did you embark on the career you did?
The subject I was most interested in studying was law. However, the study of law and the practice of law are two completely different things which you don't realise as a student.

What percentage of what you learned in university have you used in your day-to-day roles?
Less than 10%.

With the benefit of hindsight, if you were 18 again now would you do anything differently degree-wise?
With hindsight, before I picked a course, I would have tried to speak to people working in that field i.e. what was it like to be a lawyer, a scientist. I would have considered the end-product of the education more, what jobs my degree might lead me into.

What are the jobs you've done since graduating? And what have they entailed?
2016 – 2018
General Practise Solicitor, Law Firm, Ireland
Conveyancing – the buying and selling of property.
Probate – the drafting and administering of wills.
Litigation – both civil and criminal.
Misc. – all other aspects, employment law etc.

2014 – 2016

Solicitor, Law Firm, Dublin

Full responsibility for corporate transactions, working in areas of corporate employment, insolvency, and investment funds.

2011 – 2013

Trainee Solicitor, Law Firm, Dublin

Assisting solicitors and partners in corporate transactions, working in areas of corporate employment, insolvency, and investment funds.

What are the things you most like about your job, and the things you don't like?

Like:

1. The drafting of documents.

The sense of accomplishment that you get from drafting something well.

2. People interaction.

The sense of satisfaction you get from helping someone out.

4. The job variety - no two days are the same.

Don't like:

1. Pressure to make money for the firm.
2. Dealing with clients can be very difficult at times, especially when they get very defensive.
3. Lack of work-life balance.

Which would you prefer to work for: a small company or a big company, and why?

- I'd prefer a small firm, as you have more control over projects/transactions, you get to be the person in charge faster.
- In a larger company, you might be working 20 years before you get that control over transactions.

Have you worked long hours over the years?

It fluctuates, there is a culture of long hours. The work is never done, you bring the work home with you, both literally and metaphorically.

Have you had much fun over the years?

Yes, training as a lawyer with the Law Society with so many people your own age was great fun. Lots of nights out, lots of black tie balls, etc.

What career advice would you give a young person now?

Think of ten careers that you might like to work in. Speak to someone who works in each of these areas, to get a feel of what each of these jobs entails and then pick one. You really should do this at 18, but the reality is you won't do it until you're 22. Even doing it at 22, it will be a worthwhile exercise, as it can be time-consuming to change roles if you don't like something.

What advice would you give a young person who wanted to do what you do?

To get a job as a solicitor, you need to get some practical work experience. If you are in school, just get unpaid work for a few weeks in the summer. If you are in university, try and get a month working with a law firm. Then when it comes to interviews, you will be a step ahead of the people with no practical experience.

Are you jealous of any of your friends' jobs?

I've been jealous of teachers and their annual leave. I would be jealous of other people's work-life balance, their ability to clock out at 5pm, and then leave the job there at work until 9am the next morning. Being a lawyer, you can't do that.

***

PAUL, 33

73. Solicitor, Law Firm, London

What is your degree in?

Bachelor of Law

Why did you do the degree you did?

- I came from a family where no one had gone to university. I also came from an area where not many people went to university. All the schools were trying to provide career advice; there was no advice based on previous experience. Careers advisors just told you what they had read.
- I wanted to be a lawyer, and mistakenly thought you had to do a degree in law to do that, but that's not the case.

Did you know what you wanted to do career-wise?
Yes, I always fancied becoming a lawyer.

When you came out of university did you seek advice from anyone?
In the summer of my second year in university, I did an internship with one of the big law firms. All the big law firms do summer vacation schemes, for you to get to know what it would be like even though it's only a three-week period. I was going through this process in the boom, law firms were taking on record numbers of solicitors, so it was a lot easier than it is now. I only wanted to do one because I didn't want my whole summer taken up, but now I would advise people to do a few as it's a lot more competitive.

With the benefit of hindsight, if you were 18 again now would you do anything differently degree-wise?
I would have done an English degree and then done a law conversion course.

What percentage of what you learned in university have you used in your day-to-day roles?
Not a great deal, I learned about human rights law in university, I will never use that now. A proper law degree in a proper university is more academic; it's not practical. That's a good thing. Degrees should be there to stretch your mind, you learn how to write, how to think about things, etc. On your legal practice course, you learn the practical elements of working in law.

What are the jobs you've done since graduating? And what have they entailed?

2016 – 2018

Senior Associate, Law Firm, London

Legal advice but you get involved in more complex transactions.

2010 – 2016

Associate, Law Firm, London

Providing legal advice on transactions, dealing with all aspects of advice on property law.

What are the things you most like about your job, and the things you don't like?

Like:

1. The money is good.
2. Law is interesting.
3. The problem-solving nature of it all. Clients come to you with complex issues, and you must find a solution.
4. How varied every deal can be – you are doing a transaction that you think is going to be the same but it's not.

Don't like:

1. The hours – there is an hour's culture in law, late nights etc.
2. The stress – when you are dealing with such complex and high value, there is pressure to not make mistakes.
3. Nature of professional services – negotiating fees with clients can be quite annoying.

Which would you prefer to work for: a small company or a big company, and why?

If I were to move, I'd go to a smaller firm. I'm in a very big company now.

Have you worked long hours over the years?

Yes, long hours, that is just the nature of the law profession.

What career advice would you give a young person now?

- When it comes to applying to firms, focus on quality over quantity. Don't just fire out 50 applications, make sure that they are as good as you can get them. Set yourself apart in some way, you have no idea how many of the same applications are submitted.
- Talk to people in the profession. They will give you a good steer as to what is good and bad. Try to talk to people when they are not being an ambassador for their firm – the drinks events at university are good, but they are selling the firm. If you can talk to a person through a friend of a friend, then they will tell you the truth, and what really goes on.

What advice would you give a young person who wanted to do what you do?

- I would say get a good degree, but it doesn't matter what you do, do whatever you want.
- Law firms will want more classically academic degrees; they are a lot more comfortable with history, classics, English. If you have a music technology degree, it's harder to get accepted.
- Talk to people, see what their route was like, how they did it, what advice they would give. Explore other routes into law, internships, etc.

***

RONAN, 37

74. Solicitor, Large Country Law Practise, Ireland

What is your degree in?

Bachelor of Arts (Legal Science/Politics)
Law Conversion Course

Why did you do the degree you did?

I missed straight law by five points; it was my third or fourth choice.

With the benefit of hindsight, if you were 18 again now would you do anything differently degree-wise?

Happy enough with the degree as it's good and general. I would have liked to do something with IT as it is so prevalent nowadays.

Did you know what your day-to-day role entailed starting off in your career?
I had worked in my father's office over the summers, so I had a lot of exposure to solicitors, so I was well clued in.

If you didn't do a work placement over the summer, do you think it would have changed the way you turned out?
Possibly, it was a different style of practice, we have a large country firm with eight solicitors and support staff. If I didn't do that summer work, I might have ended up in a big corporate law firm. Who knows?

What percentage of what you learned in university have you used in your day-to-day roles?
It's more that university gave you the principles, the degree wouldn't have given you any of the procedures that you use daily.

Why did you embark on the career you did?
I never knew what I wanted to do; it was never expected that I'd go into the family business. I chose to do legal science as it was a good general degree that would keep my options open. It was only at the end of a two-year law conversion course that I decided I wanted to go ahead and work in the family business.

What are the jobs you've done since graduating? And what have they entailed?
2008 - 2018
Solicitor, Law Firm, Ireland
Solicitor in a large country law firm for my whole career.

What are the things you most like about your job, and the things you don't like?
Like:

1. The day-to-day variation of my work.
2. Interaction with all my colleagues and clients.

Don't like:
1. The huge level of pressure – sometimes you are dealing with a lot of clients, and everything needs to be done right and on time.
2. Dealing with people you don't necessarily like, (maybe that is the same with any job!?).
3. Mondays.

Have you worked long hours over the years?
8am – 6pm, it varies, there are some pressure times when you must do more, i.e. an extra 10 hours a week.

Have you had much fun over the years?
Yeah, a lot of fun and camaraderie with colleagues, especially during my training contract where there is a big group of you working and studying.

If you could start over and you were 22, but you know all you know now, would you do anything differently career-wise?
- I wouldn't mind being an in-house solicitor for one of the big tech firms i.e. Facebook or Google.
- I like the idea of having just one client instead of loads of clients and having more of a structured day.

What advice would you give a young person who wanted to do what you do?
Get ready; you must knuckle down and study, and get work experience. Your degree only gives you the principles of law, you've got to learn how it is applied in the real world.

Which gets you further in a career – knowing people or being good at your job?
Knowing people gets your foot in the door but being good at your job will make you stand out!

MANAGEMENT CONSULTING

What I knew before the interviews:

- Provides great exposure to senior leaders in broad range of companies.
- You get to work with very smart people.
- You could be sent anywhere working at the client site.
- It can be long hours, due to client and manager demands.

What I learned from the interviews:

- Your experience can be very dependent on the client/manager you are working for.
- The smaller consulting firms are very different from the big prestigious ones.
- Problem-solving and adding real value for clients can be extremely rewarding.
- There is high turnover as people burn out after years of doing long hours.
- People who make the switch from industry to consulting find the deadline driven nature of it difficult.
- It's a great option if you know you want to work in business but are unsure as to the area.

DENISE, 33,

75. Management Consultant, Consulting Firm, London

What is your Degree in?
Bachelor of Business Studies

Why did you do the degree you did?
I wanted to go into business but wasn't sure what exactly so it was a good general degree to do. A career in consulting seemed interesting to me.

What percentage of what you learned in university have you used in your day-to-day roles?
Probably less than 5%, consulting is very much dealing with people and applying common sense as opposed to what you learn in university.

If you could go back what would you do and why?
With hindsight, I would have done business information systems. It's a great degree, and you get work experience as part of it, which means you are very employable the second you finish it.

What are the jobs you've done since graduating? And what have they entailed?
2012 – Present
Management Consultant, Consulting Firm, London
Working with various clients to identify what's not working in their company, benchmarking processes to best in class, presenting key findings to management and developing action plans to improve the situation.
2009 - 2012
Risk Associate, Consulting Firm, London
Planning audits, finding issues in clients' systems and processes.

What are the things you most like about your job, and the things you don't like?
Like:

1. Working for big multinational companies. You get great exposure to very impressive people and best practice ways of working. I wouldn't have had that chance with a smaller company.
2. My managers and mentors have been great, I've really learned a lot from them.
3. Getting to understand how big businesses work and make profit.

Don't like:
1. Clients can have a negative attitude towards you, thinking you are just a consultant who doesn't care about the company.
2. It can be very difficult to make a change in big organisations, so that can be very frustrating.
3. The amount of re-working documents that you do.

Have you worked long hours over the years?
Yes, it would be long hours, some weeks it's a regular 40-hour week, but some jobs I'm on it can be 50-60 hour weeks. It all depends on the client you are working for.

Have you had much fun over the years?
It can be, but I haven't worked on many teams with young people, so it depends. When you are part of a big firm there are plenty of nights out and a good wider network of people, it is good.

Would you be a fan of graduate programmes?
Yes, however, I've seen people have negative experiences due to the client or the manager they end up with. So, it all depends on who you work for and the client you are working with.

If you could start over and you were 22, but you know all you know now, would you do anything differently career-wise?
I'm not sure I'd do anything different, as I don't really know what I want to do in my career. I'm happy right now, some days aren't great, but other days I like my job, every day is challenging.

What career advice would you give a young person now?

- If I were coming out school, I'd tell them to look at the different university courses, but it's very hard to know what you like and what you don't like when you are young. I paid for a career guidance person. He was completely useless, so it's a bit of trial and error I think.
- If I was coming out of university now, and I wasn't sure what I wanted to do, I wouldn't rush into a Masters. I'd take some time out, go travelling, see what your mates get into, then come back and try and pick peoples' brains as to what you might do.
- Think about what jobs will be needed in 20 years – not what jobs are needed now and tailor your education to that.

What advice would you give a young person who wanted to do what you do?

Get a good base knowledge in business and IT. If you do a business degree, try and do some IT modules. If you don't like it that's fine, at least you know. Also, try and keep your skills and experience relatively broad so you don't get pigeonholed.

Has working for a big company put you off?

I don't want to be working for a big company all my working life. I'm happy I've done it and it's been a great experience. However, I do prefer the personal touch more, and it's easier to get things done and implement change in a smaller firm.

***

FRANK, 33

76. Manager, Consulting Firm, Dublin

What is your degree in?

Bachelor of Electrical Engineering

Why did you do the degree you did?

Around that time mobile phones were becoming popular, I was always into science and maths. It was a toss-up between being an architect or engineer. An electronic engineer came to my school and gave a really engaging presentation, and that piqued my interest.

Did you know what you wanted to do career-wise?

- I had no idea. I only started looking at consulting in the last year of university. I didn't know anything about it and couldn't understand how you could purport to be an expert on a topic when you are straight out of university!
- I went away for the summer working on a student visa in America after graduating. When I came back, I got a great job in the Department of Communications. It was a scheme that took on new graduates for a year, to work on the launch of a digital terrestrial TV network.

When you came out of university did you seek advice from anyone?

I spoke to a couple of former lecturers and went to the head of electronic engineering in my university. By chance, he happened to have the notice about this Department of Communications graduate programme on his desk.

What percentage of what you learned in university have you used in your day-to-day roles?

Approximately 25% of my degree would be relevant to what I'm doing now.

With the benefit of hindsight, if you were 18 again now would you do anything differently degree-wise?

No, I don't think I would.

What kind of jobs have the people out of your class done?

My three best mates out of the university class have gone into academia, and software development for financial companies respectively.

What are the jobs you've done since graduating? And what have they entailed?

2008 – 2018

Manager, Consulting Firm, Dublin
Advising clients on their telecoms strategy – it's management consulting, with a focus on telecoms.
2007 – 2008
Electronic Engineering Graduate Programme, Dublin
Assisting with the pilot scheme for a digital terrestrial TV network.

What are the things you most like about your job, and the things you don't like?
Like:
1. Satisfaction from completing a project and doing it well.
2. Opportunity to go in and talk to the big bosses of big multinational companies, advise them based on what their rivals are doing.

Don't like:
1. When senior staff don't protect you from over-demanding clients.
2. The tedious and repetitive nature of answering parliamentary questions working in the Department of Communications.

Which would you prefer to work for: a small company or a big company, and why?
A small company, as there is too much bureaucracy in working in a large organisation. In a small company, it's a lot easier to get things done.

Have you worked long hours over the years?
Yes, it would be long hours, but that's the nature of management consulting and client deadlines.

Have you had much fun over the years?
Yes, we all get on well, it's a small office, I enjoy the travel component, so yes, it is a lot of fun.

If you could start over and you were 22, but you know all you know now, would you do anything differently career-wise?

- I would insert an extra year in the undergraduate degree, made up entirely of work experience.
- Electronic engineering is full on, you're knee deep in equations during the degree and it's hard to see the wood for the trees. You get a lot of hard theory thrown at you, and you must learn it all and absorb it when there is very little chance to apply it in the real world. I think a year of working in the industry would be invaluable to today's graduates.

What career advice would you give a young person now?
There is a decision to be made when you are in your 20s; you need to figure out if you want to work overseas? If you do want to, do it young, then bring what you've learned back home. If you don't want to do it young, then ask yourself when? Try to plan it into your career, or be aware of when or how you might fit it in. It's a lot harder to do as you get older, you get comfortable. You don't want to move for various reasons.

What advice would you give a young person who wanted to do what you do?
It's specialised, you need to know your electronic engineering. Get a good foundation of knowledge, which will help you pick things up quick.

Do people usually burnout at consulting?
- Yes, people do burnout. I would put it down to poor management and poor leadership.
- In the big firms, there is high turnover with young people. Often clients make unrealistic demands, and junior staff are really stretched.

Do people come into consulting late?
Occasionally they do, but they don't seem to last in my experience. The deadline-driven nature of it all is different to what they are used to; they struggle with the work-life balance.

***

GEMMA, 32

77. Management Consultant, Consulting Firm, London

What is your degree in?
Master of Mathematics, Operational Research, Statistics and Economics

Why did you do the degree you did?
I was good at maths but thought it was a bit boring. Reading about operational research, how it applied maths and logic to operational issues appealed to me. I always quite liked statistics too, so when I was looking through university prospectuses, I found this course and liked the sound of it.

With the benefit of hindsight, if you were 18 again now would you do anything differently degree-wise?
I did maths and statistics, because I was good at it, not because I liked it. In hindsight, I think it would have been interesting to do business studies, but because it was seen as a bit of a cop-out in my school, I didn't do it.

When you came out of university did you seek advice from anyone?
No, I just looked at books and courses and tried to figure it out for myself.

Did you know what your day-to-day role entailed starting off in your career?
In between my third and fourth years of university, everyone was doing internships, I went to an internship fair, and thought I wanted to do finance. I was going to do audit, but someone told me that audit was boring, so I applied for tax. Then I did the eight-week internship, and they offered me the job at the end of it, but it was boring. It was a job offer, but I was reluctant, I said I didn't want to do tax. So, they said have a look at our website and see if there was anything I liked as they really liked me. I had a look and said I wouldn't mind trying management consulting, so I started in that department.

What did you know about management consulting going into it?

- I knew they helped companies do things better, faster, cheaper and more efficiently. I knew people who got grades did it and knew about the company which had a good reputation - so I wasn't totally blind.
- They say you will be dealing with high powered CFO's and CEO's, but in the first few years you will be just be reformatting PowerPoint slides. However, you do get a lot of exposure to lots of different companies. In the first three years, I would have worked in 10 major companies, which is quite cool.
- The downside of that is that it can be quite daunting. You are 23 and put in front of someone very senior who has been doing their job for 20 years, but you learn lots.

What percentage of what you learned in university have you used in your day-to-day roles?
Very little – 5%.

What are the jobs you've done since graduating? And what have they entailed?
2016 – 2018
Managing Consultant, Consulting Firm, London
Responsible for winning new work and attracting new clients.
2007 – 2016
Consultant, Big 4 Consulting Firm, London
Started off meeting clients, flowcharting processes, understanding how clients' businesses work, presenting findings back to senior management. Worked on 20-plus major companies during my time in this job.

What are the things you most like about your job, and the things you don't like?
Like:
1. The people – you're working with the best and brightest people who are all really driven to improve things for clients.
2. Wide exposure to different industries and departments – it's like having a new job every couple of months, you learn loads.

3. The chance to build a business. It's only relevant to my new job in a smaller company, but there's a real sense of entrepreneurialism, growing a business, etc. There is a wide range of things to get involved in, from setting up our new pension scheme to organising the Christmas party!

Don't like:
1. The uncertainty when you're between projects. Your next project could be the other side of the world or worse some random business park in the UK! You never know until very late notice.
2. The hours can be long as you're always working to deadlines, and your clients are paying a lot for you, so they expect lots.
3. The inflexibility – most of the time you must be face-to-face on client site, or back in your base office. Working from home, starting late or finishing early is rare without some forward-planning. Because of this, many people (especially women) sadly leave consulting when they have a family and prefer to do something which fits around a more stable 9-5.

Have you worked long hours over the years?
I've been better than most of my peers. I feel strongly that it should be about the work you are doing, not about the hours you are spending in the office. I have had assignments that were 12-16 hour days, but when I have been finished at 5pm, I go home, I don't just sit there.

Have you had much fun over the years?
Yes, starting off in the big 4 was lots of fun, their graduate programmes are great, there is lots of socialising, you meet friends for life.

Would you be an advocate of a graduate programme?
If you don't know what you want to do, then it's good as you rotate around different departments and get a feel for what you like and what you don't like. They are good in that way.

Which would you prefer to work for: a small company or a big company, and why?

- I like working for a small company now, but also like the credentials from working with a big company, having that name on your CV.
- You'll get to see how processes should work if you start off with a big company first and then go small.
- Smaller companies can be harder work. With a smaller company, there is nowhere to hide. If you are having a good week, then great, everyone knows you are doing a brilliant job. If you haven't done something or missed something then everybody knows, which isn't so great.

Are you jealous of any of your friend's jobs?
One of my school friends is a professional adventurer, she rows across oceans, etc., but apart from that!

If you could start over and you were 22, but you know all you know now, would you do anything differently career-wise?
I would have left my first job after five years, as I stayed there for nine years and the last four I wasn't really learning anything.

What career advice would you give a young person now?
Don't settle for something that is not that interesting. You spend a lot of your life at work. You could do something with less pay, or longer hours, or less interest, but if you are passionate about it, then give it a go and see if you like it.

What advice would you give a young person who wanted to do what you do?
I would try and get into a top tier consultancy, to get into that you don't have to do a specific degree, you can do history or psychology, etc. However, when you go to an interview, you must demonstrate your knowledge of the business world. Read the papers and know your stuff so you can answer the competency questions in the interviews.

***

OLIVER, 33

78. Senior Business Analyst, Healthcare Organisation, London

What is your degree in?
Bachelor of Arts (Geography)

Why did you do the degree you did?
I didn't know what I wanted to do. I liked economics, geography, some of the human elements more so, and I liked being outdoors; so, geography seemed to make sense.

Why did you embark on the career you did?
I applied to several graduate programmes but didn't get any. I got a job with an independent phone company, working in the project management team, that's how I started in the projects world.

When you came out of university did you seek advice from anyone?
- I had a lecturer who was helpful in pointing me in the right direction.
- There was also a family friend who worked for a global IT company. She told me where to go, who to go to and how to prep for interviews etc. She gave me a lot of good advice.

Did you know what your day-to-day role entailed starting off in your career?
No, I knew there were methodologies. I knew from afar that project management encompassed a broad range of roles from your IT specialist to your managing consultants, and that appealed to me.

What percentage of what you learned in university have you used in your day-to-day roles?
- The soft skills - I still use these daily, i.e. stakeholder engagement, presentation skills, managing expectations. My university was very good at getting you up in front of people, making sure the subject matter was accessible and digestible to your audience.

- The theory - I can regurgitate the finer points of coastal erosion, but sadly it's no good to me at work.

With the benefit of hindsight, if you were 18 again now would you do anything differently degree-wise?
I'd change the modules in my second and third year, to the more human geography than physical geography.

Do you think you need to do a related degree (e.g. IT, construction) to become a project manager?
No, I don't think you need to study anything technical to be a project manager? The professional project management exams that I've done after university are all you need.

What are the jobs you've done since graduating? And what have they entailed?
2018 – 2018
Senior Business Analyst, Healthcare Organisation, London
Documenting the needs of various business units to ensure that they get reflected in new IT system implementations.
2015 – 2017
Senior Consultant, IT Consulting Firm, London
Ascertaining business requirements for projects and managing them from start to finish. Working with a range of clients from big blue chips to well-known household goods companies.
2013 – 2015
PMO Lead Consultant, IT Consulting, London
Flagging any project issues or risks and working with project managers to resolve them.
2011 – 2013
PMO Analyst, IT Consulting, London
Tracking milestones of projects, reporting on projects progress/issues.

What are the things you most like about your job, and the things you don't like?

Like:
1. The interaction with different cultures i.e. Poland, US, India.
2. The training and mentoring that you get from working with a big organisation.
3. The range of clients that you get to work with, pharma, government, cosmetics, etc.

Don't like:
1. The travel – as a consultant you can be sent to work anywhere, and it's often not glamourous.
2. Being seen as an outsider by the client you are working with. You may be working on the client site for several months trying to add value. Sometimes you can be treated with suspicion being an external consultant.

Which would you prefer to work for: a small company or a big company, and why?
I'd prefer a large company, the exposure you get, the ability to add value, I think the big companies have far more to offer.

Have you worked long hours over the years?
Consulting can be long hours, some weeks its 8am - 7pm.

Have you had much fun over the years?
- Yes, I've made a huge amount of contacts, and worked with and learned from some very smart people.
- Also, the projects that I've been on have always been very stimulating.

If you could start over and you were 22, but you know all you know now, would you do anything differently career-wise?
I stayed at one company a lot longer than I should have. I was a bit insecure in my skills. They were trying to pigeonhole me into being a public-sector specialist. I should have stood up for myself a bit more.

What career advice would you give a young person now?

I found myself wondering why my friends were getting graduate programmes and I wasn't. I started thinking "what am I doing wrong," and that then comes across in the interview process. I would advise them to take their time. Don't machine gun your CV out to lots of different companies. Be selective, be targeted in your approach. Spend more time researching companies and doing work experience to find out the type of company you enjoy and where you can add value.

What advice would you give a young person who wanted to do what you do?
Research all the firms – from the small boutiques to the big 4, they all have different styles and ways of working. Look at some of the white papers that they produce and some of the research that they carry out to see if it interests you. Most importantly go talk to consultants – they will be only too willing to help.

Which gets you further in a career – knowing people or being good at your job?
- Knowing the right people. I know people who have been delivering fantastically well and getting great client feedback, but if you are not exposed to the key decision makers then you're not in their mindset.
- There is an element of doing your day job properly but that's the bare minimum really, knowing the right people will really give you that extra advantage.

***

PETER, 35

79. Manager, Consulting Firm, London

What is your degree in?
Bachelor of Business Studies

Why did you do the degree you did?
I always had an interest in business, economics etc.

What percentage of what you learned in university have you used in your day-to-day roles?
50-60%

Did you know what you wanted to do career-wise?
I knew what I wanted to do, I wanted to do business strategy, international business, change management. I didn't know specifically the job, but I knew the topics that interested me. So, I went looking for a job that catered to those. I went to a big recruitment agent, here's my CV, here's what I'm interested in, and they put me in touch with a consulting company. 9-5 in the office is dull; I found a job that got me out and about all the time. I really liked it.

With the benefit of hindsight, if you were 18 again now would you do anything differently degree-wise?
Half of me would say no, the other half would say I'd go back and do philosophy, but I don't know what job I'd get out of it. I think today degrees are less relevant, a general degree can get you a general job. For example, people with an English degree can do what I'm doing in consulting.

Did you know what your day-to-day role entailed starting off in your career?
Not much, but I knew the areas that I was interested in.

When you came out of university did you seek advice from anyone?
- My dad was very good. He was always good at keeping me on the straight and narrow. A lecturer at university was also good; I could bounce ideas off him
- A lot of my mates all thought similarly, we were all interested in business.

What are the jobs you've done since graduating? And what have they entailed?
2016 – 2017
Senior Change Consultant, Consulting Firm, London

Heading up various change and transformational projects for big companies i.e. mergers, rolling out a new computer system etc.

2011 – 2016

Manager, Consulting Firm, London

Advising big organisations on how to put in place relocation programmes.

2008 – 2010

Project Co-Ordinator, Consulting Firm, London

Helping the project manager with relocation programmes of key staff for big companies.

2007 – 2008

International Assignment Consultant, Consulting Firm, London

Helping firms to relocate their staff to different countries around the world

What are the things you most like about your job, and the things you don't like?

Like:

1. Networking face to face with clients
2. Problem-solving
3. Not being at my desk all day long i.e. a mix of being in the office and out meeting clients

Don't like:

1. Clients – some of them can be a pain!
2. Situations where you are not backed up by your company.
3. Inflexibility, not sure where you are working and for how long.

Have you worked long hours over the years?

It can be long hours, but you must play the game, don't stay longer than you have to.

Have you had much fun over the years?

Yeah, would be a lot of fun, lots of nights out in these big consulting companies, and lots of people who are a similar age.

What career advice would you give a young person now?
- Speak to someone in the field of the area you are interested in, don't be afraid to ask them anything.
- Have a plan A, B, and C, as you mightn't get what you want, don't be narrow-minded. There is pressure on people to get a job, people just take what is on offer, take your time, is it the best possible job you can get?
- Also, if you can spot a path in the business and network with the right people on a social level, you just got to play the game a little bit and you can go far.

What advice would you give a young person who wanted to do what you do?
Go to all the top tier big consulting firms and apply for their graduate programmes. Be confident, but don't be an idiot, don't be an estate agent, don't be a sales-y, cocky so and so, be confident but be humble. People want confidence, but not arrogance. If you are an introvert, consulting is probably not the way to go.

Do a lot of people who start off in consulting, stay in consulting?
A lot of people go out on their own. They find their niche, build up their own client base, and then go freelance. They can then work in their local area or from home, and keep all the money for themselves.

Which gets you further in a career – knowing people or being good at your job?
It's a bit of both, but it's who you know, as they will be the people who get you places.

***

SARAH, 33

80. Programme Director, Big 4 Firm, London

What is your degree in?
Bachelor of Science (Information Management and Computing)

Why did you do the degree you did?
I had no idea what I wanted to do, but I was quite good at IT. I thought it was going to be more about making websites, etc. It was actually knowledge management, which I quite enjoyed, i.e. how you manage and access information.

With the benefit of hindsight, if you were 18 again now would you do anything differently degree-wise?
I probably wouldn't change, as I just usually go with the flow. I really admire people who know what they want to do, but that wasn't really me, it still isn't me. If I enjoy what I'm doing and learning that is the main thing for me.

Did you know what your day-to-day role entailed starting off in your career?
I was blind but was fortunate as I always had amazing managers and mentors. I quickly realised that a big 4 firm was the right environment for me. You need to ask yourself what is the right culture for me? What motivates you? What kind of people do you want to work with? Then the work almost doesn't really matter as the above factors are right for you and you can thrive.

What percentage of what you learned in university have you used in your day-to-day roles?
I always say university is about 80% life and 20% academic! I would say you use both in work! University is about life, who you are, and interacting with other people.

What are the jobs you've done since graduating? And what have they entailed?
2016 – 2018
Programme Director, Big 4 Firm, London
Doing a global refresh of our client experience programme.
2014 – 2016

Management Consultant, Big 4 Firm, London
Discussing with clients how to improve our customer journey. Performance improvement around customer experience.
2012 – 2014
Business Development Manager, Big 4 Professional Services Firm, London
Sales and marketing, identifying opportunities to develop the business and make more money.
2009 – 2011
Client Experience Mgr., Big 4 Professional Services Firm, London
Making sure people were asking their clients for their feedback and acting on that feedback.
2007 – 2009
Knowledge Consultant, Big 4 Professional Services Firm, London
Training people on where to access knowledge sources and how to share their knowledge.

What are the things you most like about your job, and the things you don't like?
Like:
1. The company I work for is a very innovative firm, very encouraging and output based.
2. The people I work with – you will have a problem to solve, then you have a host of brilliant people and a whole firm around you to try and find a solution.
3. Easy access to mentors available in your career.
4. How global my job is. Working across different countries, different industries, and how you feel connected to the whole organisation.

Don't like:
1. Nothing really

Have you worked long hours over the years?

Yes, sometimes, I would want to do a good job, so if I need to stay late, I do. On the flip side, if I want to leave at 3pm on a Friday, I don't feel guilty as I know over the years I've done the time.

Have you had much fun over the years?
Yes, lots of fun, some of the graduates are a tight group and are friends for life.

If you could start over and you were 22, but you know all you know now, would you do anything differently career-wise?
I would have tried to work abroad in a foreign country, i.e. take every opportunity you can.

What career advice would you give a young person now?
- Make sure you pick something you know you are going to enjoy, as work is such a massive part of your life. I remember my first job interview; I was asked 'Where do you want to be in five years?'. I said 'If I'm enjoying myself and learning all the time, then I don't mind', and that still applies 12 years later.
- Also, be committed and have the right attitude, as if you are engaged and passionate about what you do, you will do well.

What advice would you give a young person who wanted to do what you do?
Network via your parents, school, and university with as many people as you can, as it's all about relationships. Any opportunity or success I've had is from a relationship I've had, as opposed to a piece of work that I've done.

Which gets you further in a career – knowing people or being good at your job?
It's not all about knowing people, the two go hand in hand. I'm good at my job and that's important. What I'm really good at, is managing stakeholders. Figuring out what they want and making them look good.

Then they will really trust you and want to work with you and that's how you will really progress.

***

SEAN, 33

81. Senior Consultant, Consulting Firm, London

What is your degree in?
Bachelor of Arts (Modern Languages - French and Spanish)

Why did you do the degree you did?
It was the easiest option, as I'm half Spanish. I had done languages all my life and was always very good at them and very interested in them.

What percentage of what you learned in university have you used in your day-to-day roles?
10%

Did you know what you wanted to do career-wise?
I knew I wanted to move into business because it paid well, but I didn't know what exactly.

When you came out of university did you seek advice from anyone?
Not really, I had some friends that were in business, in banks, etc. so I talked to them a little.

Did you know what your day-to-day role entailed starting off in your career?
No, I was totally blind going into business. I had worked in the hospitality sector, my dad was a restauranteur, so I knew the value of hard work.

With the benefit of hindsight, if you were 18 again now would you do anything differently degree-wise?

Yes, I would study economics and history. I think it's important to study the past to understand the future. Economics helps you understand business.

What are the jobs you've done since graduating? And what have they entailed?

2016 – 2018

Senior Consultant, Consulting Firm, London

Helping clients implement their IT/strategic projects, with more responsibility.

2012 – 2015

Associate Consultant, Consulting Firm, London

Helping clients with IT communications and change management projects.

2009 – 2011

Business Analyst, Big 4 Professional Services Firm, Madrid

Helping businesses manage their talent.

What are the things you most like about your job, and the things you don't like?

Like:

1. Helping businesses solve their problems.
2. The brand image that comes with working for a big organisation, equating that with being a world-class professional.
3. The pay.

Don't like:

1. The politics – having to be false and not be yourself to get ahead.
2. The monotony – some roles can be quite tedious.

Which would you prefer to work for: a small company or a big company, and why?

- I'd prefer small. I think the best is to work for a big company when you start off your career, then small mid to late career.

- When you start, you want responsibility and more exposure, but the reality is you're not ready for it at that level. You need to get some experience learning the mechanics of an organisation to understand the bureaucracy, the politics, etc.
- Some people can handle lots at a young age. For example, the CEO of Lonely Planet and CEO of Heinz are both under 30, but these are the outliers!

Have you worked long hours over the years?
I did very long hours at the big 4, sometimes until very late at night doing very tedious work. In my current firm, the hours are not so bad, but it is not quite a tier 1 consulting firm yet.

If you could start over and you were 22, but you know all you know now, would you do anything differently career-wise?
I would realise the importance of networking, relationships and not burning bridges more. I'm more of a left-brain thinker i.e. logical and analytical. I've had to work on my emotional intelligence. Everybody tells you to 'grow your network,' but it's a harder concept to figure out when you are younger. In business, it's all about people and your relationships.

What career advice would you give a young person now?
- Try and find out about yourself, what type of person are you? What is your definition of success? I've just done a course online, 'What is Success and what it means to an individual?'
- There are two parts to the career path:
1. The inner life – self-awareness, and self-achievement.
2. The outer life - status, outward recognition.
Try to focus on your inner life first, as it's more permanent and sustainable, the outer life isn't and you can't control it.

What advice would you give a young person who wanted to do what you do?
Do a business degree. Make sure you've read widely across business and newspapers, and you are interested in business in general. You don't have

any experience at that point, so you need to leverage knowledge and desire when interviewing for roles.

Which gets you further in a career – knowing people or being good at your job?

I would argue one links to the other. If it's in professional services its knowing people, if it's in the big corporates it's being good at your job.

Coming from a non-business background, and another country, did you set yourself goals, and plot out your career in your 20s?

- I knew I wanted to learn about banking, law, etc. but wasn't certain I wanted to go down those routes.
- Consulting gives you the experience of different clients, the work may be menial at the start but the exposure to big corporates is fantastic. If you know you want to work in business, but are unsure what exactly, then consulting is a good option.
- I started out without a clear path, but with a sense I wanted to experiment. I've gone from being a generalist, to change management to more into ethical and behavioural consulting.

PROJECT MANAGEMENT

What I knew before the interviews:

- It is fast-paced and deadline driven.
- There is a lot of teamwork involved.
- It can be quite enjoyable all working towards a common goal.
- It can be good fun.

What I learned from the interviews:

- Get some project management experience early on, then add qualifications, i.e. finance to that.
- It suits people who get bored very easily.

DANNY, 33

82. Senior Associate, Project Management Firm, Sydney

What is your degree in?

Bachelor of Engineering (Civil)

Why did you do the degree you did?

- My dad taught building construction in secondary school.
- I was always interested in engineering.
- Physics was my favourite subject; I had a good physics teacher.
- He said civil engineering would be a good career path for someone who liked construction and physics.

Did you know what your day-to-day role entailed starting off in your career?

- While studying for my degree, I assumed that I would come out and work in an engineering firm. The way I saw it there were two routes:

1. Consulting engineer based in a design office.
2. Site engineer - building what has been designed on-site.

I got into the project management side of things accidentally; it was my first proper job. I always knew that project management was a facet of engineering. However, I thought you'd need to start doing design/site work first and build up a base of knowledge.

- All I knew starting off was the technical engineering stuff I learned in university, everything else I learned on the job.

What percentage of what you learned in university have you used in your day-to-day roles?

- 1%. What I studied in university is civil engineering theory, i.e. design, structures, concrete, etc. In my career, I've done zero design work. I've managed teams of design engineers.
- Moving to China, I was put straight into a management role, as I was the interface between the engineers and the clients who were foreign. When I first started, I was worried I'd skipped a step by going into management so quickly. I have fast-tracked my career by doing that, most

of the projects I work on now are more building construction jobs than big civil engineering jobs.

With the benefit of hindsight, if you were 18 again now would you do anything differently degree-wise?

If I had done something different, I wouldn't be where I am now. Having said that, I always wonder what if I did computer science? Computers and artificial intelligence is the way the future is headed. Who knows I might have been a multi-billionaire?!

What are the jobs you've done since graduating? And what have they entailed?

2017 – 2018

Senior Associate, Consulting Firm, Sydney

Advising companies on how best to manage their projects.

2013 – 2017

Senior Project Manager, Property Company, Shanghai/Sydney

Responsible for the successful delivery of multiple projects on-time and to budget.

2008 – 2012

Project Manager, Project Management Company, Shanghai

Responsible for the successful delivery of a project on-time and to budget.

2006 – 2007

Junior Marine Engineer, Ireland

Assisting more senior marine engineers.

What are the things you most like about your job, and the things you don't like?

Like:

1. The diversity of projects.
2. The travel element – experiencing different cultures.
3. The people management skills that I've developed, as they are very transferable.

Don't like:
1. The long hours.
2. Project management is probably the most thankless job I've had in the construction industry. No-one looks at a building and goes 'wow that must have had a great project manager.' If something goes wrong, the project manager is the first to be blamed.
3. The lack of creativity – there is no creating/designing in my role.

Which would you prefer to work for: a small company or a big company, and why?
- It depends on the company, I've got the small company blues right now as I'm working for a family business. I miss the big corporate, you get a nice office, company credit card, etc.
- Big corporates look after their staff well. A small company is more flexible because they don't have the governance and policies that a big company has. Also, with a big company, you get a lot more experience with a wider range of people. Small companies can be limited in terms of people and skills. I think I prefer a big corporate.

Have you worked long hours over the years?
8am – 6pm.

Have you had much fun over the years?
Serious fun, China was almost too much fun. In China, my company specialised in foreign investment, so there was a lot of entertaining foreign clients.

Would you be an advocate of going and working abroad?
In Ireland, I would never have got the experience that I got from moving overseas. In China, I built the biggest tyre company in the world.

If you could start over and you were 22, but you know all you know now, would you do anything differently career-wise?
I don't think I'd change anything. I'm pretty happy!

What career advice would you give a young person now?

- Every industry is going to have to change in the future with the advent of A.I.
- Law is going to completely change. Construction will be a very different landscape in the future. Steel design, structural design will probably all be done by computers. There will be whole industries that will cease to exist, so try and figure out which ones won't disappear in the future.
- Project management firms are always crying out for project managers. Don't just jump into the first company that offers you a job, do your research and make your selection based on the company. Will it look good on your CV when you go looking to leave that company? Or will it close doors to other prospective employers?

Which gets you further in a career – knowing people or being good at your job?

Being good at your job, 100% - I didn't know anyone in China, I still don't know anyone, and I've done fine!

***

GOSIA, 33

83. Project Manager, Consumer Goods Firm, London

What is your degree in?

Bachelor of Business

Why did you do the degree you did?

I wanted to be a trader and work on the stock exchange.

Why did you embark on the career you did?

I studied in Poland, and I came to the UK to learn English. When you come to the UK from Poland, you almost are a step behind, like starting over again.

What percentage of what you learned in university have you used in your day-to-day roles?

Quite low, maybe 30%, you do use the finance bit as you manage the budget, etc.

What are the jobs you've done since graduating? And what have they entailed?

2013 – 2018

Project Manager, Consumer Goods Firm, London

Responsible for delivering various projects.

2011 – 2012

Project Co-Ordinator, International Consumer Goods Firm, London

Provide planning support to the project team.

2008 – 2010

Procurement Specialist, Consumer Goods Firm, Poland

Selecting sources of supply, negotiating prices of raw materials.

2003 – 2007

Stock Controller, Construction Company, London

Managing stock movements from warehouse between all locations.

What are the things you most like about your job, and the things you don't like?

Like:

1. Negotiations – saving money for the company.
2. Strategy – figuring out long-term planning of the company.
3. Interacting with people and the variety of project work.

Don't like:

1. Politics – too much time wasted not adding any value.
2. Bureaucracy – sometimes changing things takes forever, not sure why people are so afraid to make decisions.

Which would you prefer to work for: a small company or a big company, and why?

I never wanted to work for big corporations, as you are just another number. However, now that I have worked for bigger companies, it's kind of cool, so there are pros and cons.

Have you worked long hours over the years?
Yes, long hours, there are peaks and troughs, but in general long hours.

Do you prefer projects or business as usual (BAU) jobs?
For business as usual (BAU) roles, each month is the same, whereas project work is so varied. Project work can be stressful, depends on who you are dealing with, what they want and when, how supportive they are, etc.

Have you had much fun over the years?
Yes, a lot of fun, lot of cool people, a lot of very knowledgeable people, you learn quite a lot in projects.

Do you find you work with a better calibre of people on projects?
You get more interesting types of people, they will be more specialised, whereas in BAU roles they will be more generalised.

If you could start over and you were 22, but you know all you know now, would you do anything differently career-wise?
No, I don't think so!

What career advice would you give a young person now?
Do what you like, forget about the money, follow your passion! It's so cliché! It's not easy. When you go working for a company it's very easy to fall in with what everyone else is doing. You quickly give up on following your passion.

What advice would you give a young person who wanted to do what you do?
No matter what you do, there will always be projects, get into an area you like, and then try out a project, and see if you like it.

Which gets you further in a career – knowing people or being good at your role?
I think it's a mix of both, you need to know certain things, but without knowing people you won't get that far!

***

NADINE, 33

84. Communications Manager, Consumer Goods Firm, London

What is your degree in?
Bachelor of Journalism and Public Relations

Why did you do the degree you did?
I enjoyed writing and thought that I'd become a print journalist.

With the benefit of hindsight, if you were 18 again now would you do anything differently degree-wise?
- I would think of what I would have liked to do, instead of what I was good at. I was very good at writing, but did I want to do it all day long? I'm not so sure. If I could do it again, I would have gone back and been a vet.
- The day-to-day of communications doesn't fill me with any joy.

Did you know what your day-to-day role entailed starting off in your career?
I decided I didn't want to be a journalist while in university. The degree course was very practical: developing papers/stories, student TV news broadcasts, camera segments, radio work, etc. In doing all that I decided it wasn't for me. It was too cut throat; there wasn't much writing.

What percentage of what you learned in university have you used in your day-to-day roles?
20%

What are the jobs you've done since graduating? And what have they entailed?

2014 – 2017

Communications Manager, Consumer Goods Company, London

Managing all communications for different countries/markets/senior stakeholders in a £1b IT transformation project.

2012 – 2014

Communications Manager, Infrastructure Project, London

Communicating with stakeholders/public about the project, what was happening, and that we were working within the statutory framework.

2008 – 2012

Communications Manager, Healthcare Company, London

Communicating about reconfiguring specialist services into fewer hospitals, managing communications to stakeholders.

2005 – 2008

PR Consultant, City Council, Brisbane

Worked with clients to develop pieces of communications work, i.e. fact sheets about their companies/projects.

What are the things you most like about your job, and the things you don't like?

Like:

1. You can be fun and creative i.e. videos, different ways of getting your message across.

Don't like:

1. Communications can be seen as pretty pictures and colouring in, i.e. just PowerPoint presentations. Whereas communications done properly should be involved at the start of a project at a strategic level, to help define scope, goals and communications journey, instead of just as a bolt-on nice fluffy piece.
2. It can often be quite long hours, as it's very reactive.
3. The amount of re-work you must do.
4. Everybody thinks that they can do comms, everyone has an opinion.

Have you worked long hours over the years?
Yes, it can be quite long hours.

Which would you prefer to work for: a small company or a big company, and why?
A big company, as there is more resource to do things.

Which would you prefer to work for? Public sector or private sector, and why?
I have enjoyed the public sector, you must be better with less, you must think more creatively, as you can't be frivolous with public money.

If you could start over and you were 22, but you know all you know now, would you do anything differently career-wise?
I would have asked for promotions earlier and understood my value in the market better (I was underpaid in a role for three years). Keep an eye on job adverts even if you are not looking to move, to understand your market value.

Have you ever wanted to change profession? Are you jealous of any of your friends' jobs?
One friend who was in communications with me, she has managed to negotiate flexible contracts where she works a number of days that suit her. She lives where she wants and had an awesome work-life balance.

What career advice would you give a young person now?
Go on a gap year – don't rush into university. I put a lot of work into high school, and because of that I completely ran out of steam, and had no energy in university. Then I didn't really take the time to figure things out for myself.

What advice would you give a young person who wanted to do what you do?
- Just get a job somewhere and start doing it.

- Don't be afraid to be vocal, as sometimes in communications they are slow to adapt to new ideas.

***

NATASHA, 32

85. Finance Project Manager, Utilities Company, London

What is your degree in?
Bachelor of Commerce

Why did you do the degree you did?
I wanted to do accounting but didn't want to do auditing. I saw a course where you could get a couple of credits for professional management accounting exams (CIMA), so thought that looked good.

What percentage of what you learned in university have you used in your day-to-day roles?
Very little. I only use the first principles of accounting that I learned in school, nothing that I learned in university has helped me in terms of my job.

With the benefit of hindsight, if you were 18 again now would you do anything differently degree-wise?
No, I wouldn't change anything. I never wanted to be an accountant, but I wanted to travel and I wanted to live in another country. It gave me that opportunity.

What are the jobs you've done since graduating? And what have they entailed?
2014 – 2017
Finance Project Manager, Various Companies, London
Managing, reporting and forecasting project costs.
2006 – 2013
FP&A* Roles, Various Companies, London

Responsible for month end reporting, budgeting, forecasting, ad-hoc queries.

(*FP&A stands for Financial Planning and Analysis)

What are the things you most like about your job, and the things you don't like?

Like:

1. Dealing with different cultures.
2. The variety of my roles.
3. Being able to choose what to do every day.

Don't like:

1. Being tied into month end every month.
2. Always looking back, accounting is very reactive.
3. Comparing one number with another number and figuring out why it's changed.
4. The politics – don't like to get involved with people running departments like empires.

Which would you prefer to work for: a small company or a big company, and why?

I like swapping between the two. I go big for a while and then small. Whenever I'm in one of them, I see the good sides and bad sides and then I switch to the other.

Have you worked long hours over the years?

Before I started contracting, I did very long hours. I had a bit of a re-think at 26/27 years of age and decided I wanted a better work-life balance. I haven't had a permanent role since!

Do you prefer permanent or contract roles?

I prefer contracting, because of the flexibility, the control over my own destiny. I have been tempted by permanent roles but just for a bit of a break. When you are a contractor you are constantly pushing yourself, and trying to impress and get a better contract, whereas in permanent roles you can take it easier.

If you could start over and you were 22, but you know all you know now, would you do anything differently career-wise?
- I would have tried to get out of finance earlier on in my career. When I was younger, I presumed you had to have a whole suite of financial roles under your belt before you could get roles outside of finance, i.e. FP&A, financial control. It turns out you don't; I think I waited too long to make a move out of finance.
- Go through the project management office (PMO) route. It's quite difficult to move into project management if you have too many years working in finance. I'd try getting some PMO experience and then adding onto that a good finance qualification i.e. ACA, ACCA, CIMA.

What career advice would you give a young person now?
- For any profession, I would say get out there and start working - don't fear making a mistake. I have a cousin who is scared to go out working. She keeps studying at university and it becomes worse the longer she leaves it.
- I think you have to try something. At least if you don't like your first job, you know what you don't like and can try something else.

***

RACHEL, 35,

86. Finance Project Manager, Media Company, London

What is your degree in?
Bachelor of Business, Economics, and Social Studies

Why did you do the degree you did?
I was always interested in history, politics, and I was good at finance.

Why did you embark on the career you did?
During my final year of university, the big 4 accountancy firms came to my university as part of the 'milk round.' I applied for jobs with each of the four firms; I didn't know anything about them, I didn't even know

what an auditor was! I got called for an interview with all of them and got offered two jobs. It offered a career path and was decent money starting off, so I took it.

What percentage of what you learned in university have you used in your day-to-day roles?

10%, some of the accounting maybe, in politics there is a lot of essay writing, so that helps with your communication skills. In finance and business partnering jobs, a lot of it is taking complex data and simplifying the message for non-finance people. My degree did help me a little with that.

With the benefit of hindsight, if you were 18 again now would you do anything differently degree-wise?

No, I wouldn't change my degree, as I really enjoyed it. My degree gave me no exemptions for my professional exams, so I had to do all the stages. Even if you said I could do a different degree offering more exemptions, I wouldn't change. I really enjoyed my course, the sociology, politics, it was a good broad range of subjects. My friends who did that degree all have totally different jobs now: HR business partner, journalist, economist, lawyer. It opened a lot of doors.

What are the jobs you've done since graduating? And what have they entailed?

2009 – 2018

Financial Controller/Project Manager, Various Companies, London

Lead a team of accountants that ensure month end processes and accounts adhere to accounting standards. Simplification of processes, assisting senior management with technical accounting issues, i.e. bonus schemes, payroll, pensions, acquisitions.

2003 – 2007

Audit Senior, Big 4 Accounting Firm, Dublin

Planned year-end audits, organised meetings with internal staff and client management.

What are the things you most like about your job, and the things you don't like?

Like:

1. The money.

2. The people side of it.

In business partnering roles dealing with the business/stakeholders. Even in the more financial control roles I've done, I really enjoyed managing teams as you are dealing with people.

3. Structure.

There is a defined path you can work your way up to financial controller or senior manager.

Don't like:

1. It's very repetitive.

With the audit, it's a different year but it's the same old questions, and with month-end, you start all over again every month.

2. Accounting isn't that inspiring. You don't wake up every-day bouncing out of bed.

Have you worked long hours over the years?

In the big 4, I managed to get away without doing long hours. When I was working in industry, it would only be long hours on occasion, at month-end or year-end only.

Have you had much fun over the years?

The big 4 is like a continuation of university, lots of people your own age going to lectures. There is a great social scene. All my companies were a lot of fun as everyone was young, i.e. under 40, you are surrounded by like-minded people. If you go into a firm where you are youngest by 20 years, it mightn't be much fun.

If you could start over and you were 22, but you know all you know now, would you do anything differently career-wise?

- I still would have done the training contract with the big 4, even though I hated a lot of it. It has opened so many doors; it has got me jobs in Australia and London.
- I would have been more confident and pushed for promotions more. When going for new roles guys will just go for it, and if they don't know they will just wing it, girls would be more hesitant.
- Girls tend to doubt themselves a bit more. If I see a job spec with ten tasks and see one thing I can't do, I won't apply for the job. Guys would look at the same job spec, and if they could only do one task they would go for it and chance it.
- Once you have a family, your career takes a backseat, and that's just the way it is, you can't commit to your career like you could when you didn't have kids. The way I look at it, having two young kids, for the next 10-15 years I can't give my career 100%. When I'm a bit older, I can go back and give it 100%. Interviewing for jobs now, I know I can do the job, but I know also that I have to leave at 5pm every day. I'd be stressed 24-7 juggling a job with long hours and family life.

What career advice would you give a young person now?
- I think you should research where the demand is going to be in the future. There is no point in doing a history of art degree if you can't get a job at the end of it.
- If you can get something that you like to do and pay the bills then great. Very few people get a job that they love and that pays well. If you get that you are really lucky. I'd really encourage you to think about how you're going to get money, how can you get a mortgage, where can you live, etc. Don't do a course for the sake of doing it, do it because you are trying to do something with it when you graduate.
- I would also urge young people to ask themselves do they need to go to university? I think apprenticeships are really undervalued, if you know what you want to do, they are just as valuable as university degrees. These days everyone gets a 2.1* or a 1.1*. and then does a Masters, don't underestimate doing something more practical.

(*2.1 is an upper second class honours and a 1.1 is a first class honours.)

What advice would you give a young person who wanted to do what you do?

Every company is looking for a qualified accountant.

There are two main routes:

1. You can do the ACA qualification and work in an accounting practice, or
2. do the ACCA qualification and work in a big company in industry.

My preference would be a big company. If you can get into a big 4 its great, because you can travel all over the world and get work with it. If you can't get into a big 4, go and work in a big multinational and get your ACCA exams and it will look great on your CV.

SALES/MARKETING

What I knew before the interviews:

- Marketing roles could get very busy around promotion times like Christmas.

What I learned from the interviews:

- There are always promotions to keep you busy.
- Working with cool brands and companies can be great

JOEL, 31

87. Analytical Consultant, Technology Company, London

What is your degree in?

Bachelor of Business Administration
Bachelor of Economics (Behavioural Economics)

Why did you do the degree you did?

- Economics: I have always been interested in how people make decisions, and how to help people make decisions. At the time, I thought the best way to help people was through fact, logic, and rationale. The one field of study that was closest to that was economics.
- Business Administration: All my other friends were talking about this program, so I said why not! It's probably been one of the things that has got me to where I am today.

Did you know what you wanted to do career-wise?

- I had no idea what I wanted to do. The real world seemed scary and confusing.
- I thought that I would be well suited to either consulting or economic research. I have tried all of those and turns out I'm terrible at all of them!
- Rather than having an idea about a profession, I looked at whether I believed in the work that's being done, whether I believed the company/team should exist. If I did, then I'm interested in exploring that and learning something new.
- My first job was doing research at an economic think-tank, which was researching how small business owners think, act and behave. It then sold that research to banks. I thought that was kind of cool, but after a couple of years, I became bored of it.
- For me it's been a lot less of me having a plan, it's been more about what seems interesting and exploring that for a while.

Did you know what your day-to-day role entailed starting off in your career?

I had been a research assistant for two years at university at that point so I had a feel for what it was and thought it'd be cool to get paid for it.

When you came out of university did you seek advice from anyone?
No, I didn't talk to anyone. I imagine if I had they would have talked me out of it or given me a much clearer idea of what was actually happening.

What percentage of what you learned in university have you used in your day-to-day roles?
25%. It's not the 25% I thought it would be, the technical stuff, the math, I use none of that, ever. What I do use are the softer skills, e.g. project management, presentation skills.

With the benefit of hindsight, if you were 18 again now would you do anything differently degree-wise?
I would do two things differently:
1. Instead of doing economics I would do computer science. The pace that I see A.I coming into the forefront, the people who understand that stuff will be at a huge advantage.
2. Instead of more technical skills like maths/statistics, I would have invested more time in softer skills. It would have been harder for me at the time, but it would have benefitted me more in the long term.

What are the jobs you've done since graduating? And what have they entailed?
2016 – 2018
Analytical Consultant, Technology Company, London
Helping design and measure the promotional relationships with global advertising agencies. I spend a lot of time designing deals and measuring performance against them.
2014 – 2016
Business Consultant, Technology Company, Toronto
Customer analytics product development. Looking at how you make it easier to do in market experiments in the real world.
2013 – 2014

Manager, Loyalty Program Company, Toronto

Working for a company that builds loyalty schemes, i.e. Nectar Card programmes. Looking at how you build the schemes to make them work in other countries.

2011 – 2013

Senior Business Analyst, Loyalty Program Company, Toronto

Economic modelling and tool creation for international projects within corporate development.

2010 – 2011

Research Analyst, Technology Company, Toronto

Designing surveys, analysing data.

What are the things you most like about your job, and the things you don't like?

Like:

1. Working with very smart people.
2. Working with a team that shares the same vision.

Don't like:

1. Every company I've worked for makes decisions slower than I would like.
2. The systems that have been used in all the companies I've worked for I have found frustrating, but usually, everyone does.
3. Decisions that I don't agree with or that frustrate me.

Which would you prefer to work for: a small company or a big company, and why?

A private company, although most private companies are big, I would prefer a small company. The advantage in working for a private company is the freedom and flexibility to make longer-term bets.

Have you worked long hours over the years?

- I've done 80-100 hour weeks. The long hour's culture in North America is the reason I've moved to Europe from Canada.

- I didn't have a good definition of success when I was growing up. From hanging around with my business admin buddies, I thought success was making lots of money, staying in the office all hours, having no life, never seeing your family, and travelling all the time. I wasn't keen on that lifestyle. I want something intellectually fulfilling, but that gives me the freedom to do what I want when I want, etc. Work is how you define yourself in the US, I don't think it should be that way.

Have you had much fun over the years?

- I've had a blast, I have taken jobs that I think will be interesting, I've travelled to the Baltics, Europe, London, India, sat in box seats at big sports games, etc.
- The best time I had was staying with my buddies from business school. We were all young, we all had good jobs, we were all having a great time. I'd never go back, never do it again and never tell stories about it, but it was a fantastic few years!

If you could start over and you were 22, but you know all you know now, would you do anything differently career-wise?

I would have invested in my soft skills more, try to get as much international experience, and breadth of experience as I could, and just figure it out as I go.

What career advice would you give a young person now?

- Get out of your comfort zone.
- Don't do the same thing your parents did.
- Don't stay in your home town; it will always be there if you want to go back.
- There's always a thousand reasons to not do something, take the risk, what's the worst that can happen?
- It's totally ok to not have a plan. Have shorter-term goals and aspirations and be able to pivot and change as you grow.

What advice would you give a young person who wanted to do what you do?

We have got too outcome orientated in our careers - make sure you know why you want that outcome. Start with the why, so you want to be the rich guy? Is it so you can travel? Figure out what you don't have in terms of skills and go about trying to get them.

Which gets you further in a career – knowing people or being good at your job?
- If people like you enough you can be bad at your job, that's a falsity. There is a basic competency level that you need.
- If you are the absolute best and you are irreplaceable then it's very hard to move, being more of a generalist can often work in your favour.
- It comes back to what you want, mobility and experience are what I want, so that's why I'm flexible.

***

LAURA, 30

88. Category Manager, Consumer Goods Company, Dublin

What is your degree in?
Bachelor of Business
Master of Food

Why did you do the degree you did?
- I was interested in history and politics, but my dad said they wouldn't get you anywhere. A business degree was broad and general enough to keep my options open, and it was more highly regarded than an arts degree.
- I came out of university with a very general degree. I thought I needed to specify, but didn't see the point in doing something business-related for a postgraduate degree. So, I did a Masters in Food, as I thought it would give me a good insight into the food industry.

Did you know what your day-to-day role entailed starting off in your career?

I had only a very limited idea. One module in my masters gave me some information, but I was completely blind as to the industry, and as to what FMCG* is and how it operates. FMCG is a whole different level; no one ever talks about it in university.
(*FMCG stands for Fast Moving Consumer Goods)

Why did you embark on the career you did?
When I graduated, I wanted to get a job, work for a few years and then go travelling. I spoke to the main lecturer in my masters, and he gave me some info on category manager roles. I didn't really know at the time what the role entailed, but I interviewed for a well-known company, who worked with big well-known brands. I got the job and headed down this path with a limited amount of knowledge.

What percentage of what you learned in university have you used in your day-to-day roles?
Hardly anything of the content. However, some of the softer skills have benefitted me, i.e. working as a group, working to deadlines, excel, putting a presentation together, etc. I'm not sure if I needed four years to pick up that stuff. The masters helped me a lot more in terms of preparing me for the working world. Also, doing work experience was really important, as it showed me what working in an office was like.

With the benefit of hindsight, if you were 18 again now would you do anything differently degree-wise?
- Yes, I would have picked a degree that would allow me to work outside Dublin. I would pick a career that was more lifestyle friendly, which would allow me to be closer to family and friends in the countryside. Having said that, I love the fast-paced nature of my job, love that it is constantly changing, that I don't know what's coming my way.
- Looking back now, I wish I had done an intensive career guidance assessment before I made my university choices. It's crazy that we don't do that if you think about it, they are such big decisions.

What are the jobs you've done since graduating? And what have they entailed?
2009 – 2018
Category Manager, Various Consumer Companies, Dublin
Accountable for management and strategy of pricing and propositions, new product launches, category management and trading performance. Alongside effective stakeholder management, planning and execution, and P&L responsibilities.

What are the things you most like about your job, and the things you don't like?
Like:
1. The cool companies and global brands I've worked with.
2. The opportunities that I've got – management roles, lots of exposure to very senior people in the business.
3. The pace of my job. Things are never the same; I get such a kick out of that. I get a lot of challenges and have to come up with the solution whether internally or to the retailer. That can be high pressure, but I love it, it's not the same boring old 9-5, my job is evolving constantly.

Don't like:
1. My job is very Dublin centric; you can't live in the countryside.
2. People not believing what the data is telling them.
My job is all about insights, looking at shopper behaviour and making recommendations based on that data. Sometimes you can present that data to people and they don't want to listen to the recommendation. That can be frustrating.
3. People underestimating the power of customer insights.

Have you worked long hours over the years?
Yes, crazy hours, it just comes with the territory, if you want to progress then you have to put in the hours.

Have you had much fun over the years?
Yes, lots of fun for several reasons:

1. The exposure to cool brands, the events, and the background info that you get.
2. Learning about consumer insights and behaviours is very interesting.
3. My job is always changing. If I were doing same thing every-day; it would drive me crazy.
4. You are always ahead of the trends, and you get to know what the next big thing is.

If you could start over and you were 22, but you know all you know now, would you do anything differently career-wise?
I'd think more about location. That is a constant battle for me. Even when you do try and move to the countryside, you don't want to give up the higher wages that comes with working in the city.

What career advice would you give a young person now?
- Put some thought into what career you want. People say 'oh you can change role and careers.' However, there are certain paths that you go down that are very hard to get out of.
- Get some professional career guidance.
- Approach some of the big companies and tell them you are interested in what they do, people will tell you what's it like, try and do one-week work experience.
- If you don't like something, don't waste away doing it for years, go and re-train as soon as you can.
- Think about what is important to you in your life, think about how transferable your job is, can you work abroad, can you live in the countryside.
- People who know what they want to do are lucky, as it is very hard, there are so many jobs out there that you don't know about that are cool jobs.

What advice would you give a young person who wanted to do what you do?
- Try and get into a small company first as you will get more exposure, it will make you a better category manager.

- Make sure you choose the company you go to carefully, what are the brands that they work with, what is the culture like etc.
- Ask yourself do you like to work under pressure and stress, as you will need to be able to handle both.
- Contact some of the big companies. I'd be very open to people coming in and seeing what a day in the life of a category manager involves.

***

MAURICE, 34

89. Senior Account Manager, Electronics Company, Dublin

What is your degree in?
Bachelor of Commerce (Marketing)
Master of Marketing

Why did you do the degree you did?
I didn't know what else to do. I was good at the business subjects in school, and wasn't great at maths, languages, etc.

Did you know what you wanted to do career-wise?
No, not in university, when I was 18, I knew I wanted to work in business, but didn't know what. I always knew that I'd always go and do a Masters.

When you came out of university did you seek advice from anyone?
- I went to a career guidance person and did loads of tests. They told me the ideal career for me was interior design. I didn't talk to the people who would really give me useful info, the people out in the workplace.
- I fell into recruitment, my aunt knew a person who owned a recruitment company, and that's how I got my first job.

What percentage of what you learned in university have you used in your day-to-day roles?
20-30%

With the benefit of hindsight, if you were 18 again now would you do anything differently degree-wise?

I would have done something computer related, as everything is computers now. The people who know programming and coding are the ones that are getting ahead these days.

Did you know what your day-to-day role entailed starting off in your career?

No, while the Masters was good in some ways, some of the theory is relevant. In reality, you go in and learn the role on the job. I've never heard of anyone who learned what they did at university and then applied it in their roles.

What are the jobs you've done since graduating? And what have they entailed?

2012 – 2017

Senior Account Manager, Electronics Company, Dublin

Plan the range, and the promotional cycle, deal with all the suppliers ensuring the product sales hits the necessary targets.

2007 – 2012

Category Manager, Consumer Electronics Company, Dublin

Planning and executing the promotional plan for all the stores in the country.

2007 – 2008

Recruitment Consultant, Recruitment Company, Dublin

Sourcing candidates to put them into jobs.

What are the things you most like about your job, and the things you don't like?

Like:

1. The sector I'm in, the product, I like electronics/gadgets, seeing the latest thing coming into the stores.
2. The control I have over the product, playing a key role in negotiations with suppliers.

Don't like:
1. Dealing with retail staff as they can be very negative, i.e. complaining about the promotions etc.

Which would you prefer to work for: a small company or a big company, and why?
In a big company, you are just another number, but with a small company, you're a bit more involved in everything. In my current role, I'm sitting at the boardroom table every week, so it depends on what you prefer.

Have you worked long hours over the years?
Yes, I do put in long hours, but at the same time, I have complete flexibility over my schedule, as whatever I'm doing my boss knows I'm on top of my work. If you are in a lull, then you are probably not on top of things, as there is always the next promotion to be preparing for.

If you could start over and you were 22, but you know all you know now, would you do anything differently career-wise?
If I were to go back and do it again, I wouldn't choose the path I did, but I don't know what I would do. It's something I think about a lot, and I still don't really know.

What career advice would you give a young person now?
- Try to get lots of work experience. That will give you that practical element that a lot of people just don't have coming out of university.
- I can't say my Masters made much of a difference to my career. I got my first job in recruitment due to a contact I knew. If you come out of university with a more general degree, then I think a Masters in a specific area would be valuable. For me, it wasn't.

What advice would you give a young person who wanted to do what you do?
- Get a graduate programme which will give you a good general view of the company. A friend of mine did one and got moved around in the different departments of a big multinational: brand, category, marketing,

channel management. At the end of the three years, he could pick the one he liked most to work in.

- I'd be wary of unpaid internships – we have a few unpaid interns, and they get given rubbish work and can be turned off the industry for good. I'd advise getting a good graduate programme, or a paid internship, that way the company will want to invest in you and train you up.

***

SARAH, 33

90. Marketing Manager, Consumer Goods Firm, London

What is your degree in?

Bachelor of Commerce (Marketing)
Master of Marketing

Why did you do the degree you did?

I liked business studies in school, so it made sense that I did a commerce degree. While doing the degree, I found the marketing side more interesting than the other subjects. I specialised in marketing in the final year but felt what I was learning wasn't specific enough. Also, I didn't feel ready for the working world. I thought it would be good to get more of an in-depth understanding of marketing and gain a bit of maturity before I had to get a proper job.

Did your degrees prepare you for working in marketing?

The marketing Masters was brilliant, but I'm 100% sure I would have gained more from it if I'd spent a few years working. What you learn is very abstract. It's difficult to relate it to real-world examples when you haven't worked anywhere. However, the risk is that if you get a job, you would get a bit of money in your pocket and you wouldn't go back to university. That's why I think it's so important to get work experience while at university.

Why did you embark on the career you did?

- My sister was in a marketing type of role. My older brothers worked in tech companies.
- I ended up working for an IT company in my first job as I thought that's where I needed to be. However, I didn't like it; it was business to business (B2B) marketing and not the big budget marketing that I was looking for. I spent a year there and it was so wrong for me. However, it was the best year of my career as I realised what I didn't want to do. It was an early blip but it was the best blip I could have had.
- What I do now is TV copy, big budget, creative marketing for big multinational firms.
- Some people might spend four or five years working in something and then realise that it isn't for them, but I found out after a year.

Did you know what your day-to-day role entailed starting off in your career?
- Marketing is so broad. You have the agency side, the client side, then within that there are all the different industries – fast moving consumer goods (FMCG), banking, etc.
- Nobody ever maps out the different career paths for you when you are at university. Even when you are doing a postgraduate degree when you would expect some guidance.

What percentage of what you learned in university have you used in your day-to-day roles?
80% - what I learned in university has helped me in my day-to-day roles. The human resources stuff helps me to manage a team of people now. The economics helps me understand why people make decisions. The accounting gives me the basics of managing a profit and loss (P&L) statement, as I'm responsible for managing the P&L of my brand.

With the benefit of hindsight, if you were 18 again now would you do anything differently degree-wise?
Not really as I'm in a good place with my career. The one thing I would do differently is I would get work experience while I was at university. It would have helped me to figure out what I liked and didn't like.

What backgrounds do your contemporaries have?

- Anyone at my level in a big multinational firm has studied marketing.
- The big companies look for someone who has a 2.1* in their undergrad, maybe a postgrad and has come from a similar firm. It's bad but people hire those who have similar backgrounds. I do it myself; I hire people like me as I want them to hit the ground running.

(*This is an upper second class honours.)

What are the jobs you've done since graduating? And what have they entailed?

2017 – 2018

Marketing Manager, Consumer Goods Company, London

Responsible for the top line brands in group HQ - trialling new ways of working and inventing new business models.

2015 – 2017

Senior Brand Marketing Manager, Consumer Goods Company, Dublin

Same as below only with more people management.

2013 – 2015

Brand Manager, Consumer Goods Company, Dublin

Same as below but for different brands.

2011 – 2013

Brand Manager, Consumer Goods Company, Dublin

Responsible for the seasonal advertising campaigns, ongoing content and media strategy, content creation, partnerships, events and store support.

2008 – 2011

Assistant Brand Manager, Consumer Goods Company, Dublin

Assisting the brand manager with marketing campaigns, events etc.

2006 – 2008

Marketing Executive, IT Company, Dublin

Working on marketing plans and campaigns.

What are the things you most like about your job, and the things you don't like?

Like:

1. The autonomy – you're given support, but ultimately you can drive your brand, manage your teams and make a real impact.
2. The changeable and fast-paced nature of my job – I like things to be different and keep me interested.
3. The scope for progression – the key question for me is 'am I still learning?'

Don't like:

1. The economic downturn was stressful; there were cutbacks, I survived a few rounds of redundancies. I know recessions will happen a few times in my lifetime, so you have to take it on the chin.
2. People that don't have the same attitude and work ethic as me. I'm quite ambitious, and some people aren't but I've learned to become more accepting of that.
3. The pace of change – technology changes so fast. For someone like me who likes to be in control, it can be a bit scary and exhausting.

Which would you prefer to work for: a small company or a big company, and why?

- I would prefer the bigger company; as there is better structure, hierarchy, training, bigger budgets, and you learn what's best in class. In a small company, you will get less opportunity to work on big deals. It can suit people who are more entrepreneurial, and don't need structure in place.
- I do think I would step down to a smaller company later in life. However, I'd advise starting big where you get the big budgets, the training, etc., then get one or two promotions and then move.
- When you are interviewing for marketing roles, it is all about what campaigns you have worked on. You want to work on the big ones that people will have heard of.

Have you had much fun over the years?

- Marketing is fun. The agencies take you out, you make a lot of fun advertisements. You are working with creative minds and interesting people, etc.
- You see a product in decline, then after a campaign that you do, people come back to it. It can be very rewarding.
- Check out the culture of the company that is the most important thing. Research it and talk to people who are working there. Several big well-known companies have approached me to work for them but I have turned them down as the culture wasn't right.

What is the difference between agencies and clients in marketing?
Agencies are the creative people who make ads for the products. I am the client who hires the creative agencies to make the ads. Even within that, there are other paths. There are people who just research, they sell the client what are called customer insights. The client then takes that to make a brief, which the agency then turns into a TV ad.

If you could start over and you were 22, but you know all you know now, would you do anything differently career-wise?
Nothing, as I always felt I was learning and progressing. There was a time during the recession that I was heading up a couple of brands that weren't doing well. Maybe I should have jumped ship and worked for someone else.

What career advice would you give a young person now?
- Before university, make sure you go to the best one you can and get your 1.1* or 2.1*.
- After university, go for big FMCG. They will have a checklist for new hires, a 2.1*, maybe a Masters, etc. Get a work placement, if you don't know anyone in the industry, ask your lecturers. They've seen it all, and they know all the top people, they will put you in contact with some good contacts.
- Also, make sure you have passion projects on the side, i.e. blogging, reading industry mags, marketing books. Try and demonstrate that you have passion.

- Don't worry if you do start off in the wrong career, if you realise you don't like it, then great! Your career will change so much in your lifetime; it's no big deal if you do something for a while that you don't love.
(*1.1 is a first class honours, 2.1 is an upper second class honours.)

What advice would you give a young person who wanted to do what you do?
If you are confused as to what type of marketing you should pursue, do your research, map out the different options. Ask yourself do I understand all of them, the hours, the typical day, the locations, the companies you would work for. If not, ask people! Once you build up some knowledge, there will be a sense of what you want to do? Then once you know that, get some experience even if it's helping out for a few weeks.

***

STEVE, 30

91. Hospital Account Executive, Pharma Company, London

What is your degree in?
Bachelor of Science (Biomedical)
Master of Marketing

Why did you do the degree you did?
Undergraduate: Mainly because I had an interest in the scientific method, discovering things. Finance and law were not for me!
Postgraduate: I did this to gain some business knowledge.

Would you be an advocate of doing postgraduate study straight after undergraduate?
I'm completely against doing a postgrad straight away after university. I think you should work for 18 months at least before you go back studying. Undergrads that do a Masters straight after university can't apply what they learn to real life, etc. I thought it was invaluable to have worked for a couple of years.

Why did you embark on the career you did?

- I'm a qualified clinical scientist. Your job is sitting in a lab all day long.
- At the time, there were not many jobs. The money was rubbish and you would be doing the same thing for 20 years unless you did a Ph.D. That's why I got into pharma, it changed my career dramatically.

Did you know what your day-to-day role entailed starting off in your career?

No, I didn't really know that pharma sales reps existed. At the end of the day, it's just sales, I had no idea in terms of what you did every day, i.e. the cold calling. I basically decide what I do every day, who I meet, where I go. People think it's really easy as you can choose your hours, but if you can't find any clients then you can't get any sales, that means no job!

When you came out of university did you seek advice from anyone?

- I spoke to a couple of careers people at university, but they weren't much help.
- A friend of a friend was a sales rep, so I had a coffee with her, then shadowed her for a day. In this job, you won't get a job unless you've done that, no-one will even give you an interview.

What percentage of what you learned in university have you used in your day-to-day roles?

- Science undergrad over 50%.

There are two types of sales reps:

1. Those who don't have the medical background, they get good training on the product, but that's all they know.
2. People who have science degrees and know much more than just the product they are selling.

- Marketing Postgrad 50%. Mainly because I get involved with the marketing stuff, the brand teams and product development. A lot of marketing is strategy, planning what we will do with the products this year, next year, etc.

What are the jobs you've done since graduating? And what have they entailed?

2015 – 2018

Hospital Account Executive, Various Pharma Companies, London

Selling infant nutrition products to hospitals (Secondary care).

2014 – 2015

Hospital Account Executive, Pharma Company, London

Selling asthma products to GPs and practice nurses (Primary care).

2009 – 2012

Medical Sales Rep, Pharma Company, London

Selling cholesterol products to GPs and practice nurses (Primary care).

Do you hit a ceiling as a sales rep in terms of career and progression?

If you are good, you get headhunted, and the biggest jump in salary you can get will be from moving companies. Also, if you stay at the same company too long, a lot will be expected from you, so there is a lot of moving around in sales.

What are the things you most like about your job, and the things you don't like?

Like:

1. In-depth conversations with doctors.
2. Seeing results with customers – people liking a new product.
3. Flexibility – you have plenty of free time to do personal stuff.
4. I've had days when I haven't left the house. If you are a good rep, nobody cares!

Don't like:

1. Cold calling – getting rejected constantly.
2. Flexibility – you got to find things to do for yourself. I've got no appointments but I need to sell products!
3. It's quite a cut-throat industry. People make big bonuses so they are willing to stab people in the back.

Which would you prefer to work for: a small company or a big company, and why?
I do prefer the big companies. There is more scope for progression, more products, everything is better. People say it's more like a family in a small company, forget it - give me a big company any day!

Have you worked long hours over the years?
No, the opposite in fact.

Have you had much fun over the years?
Yes, definitely. I got a free trip to New York the other week, with no work responsibilities, I've had a blast!

If you could start over and you were 22, but you know all you know now, would you do anything differently career-wise?
I would have gone into tourism, maybe hotel management, but they work you so hard.

What career advice would you give a young person now?
They put too much focus on your grades and what you've done at university. Good companies will train you up and invest in you. Work for a company where they are willing to invest in your skills and training.

What advice would you give a young person who wanted to do what you do?
Speak to sales reps, go out and shadow them. Make sure you demonstrate some sort of selling ability in your CV and interviews as employers look for potential.

SCIENCE

What I knew before the interviews:

- It doesn't pay that well.
- A lot of jobs involved you being stuck in a lab all day long.
- Academia is a well-trodden path in the science world.

What I learned from the interviews:

- Science and engineering are closely linked.
- There are fantastic careers available in pharma to people with science backgrounds.
- A lot of people who work in pharma are contractors. It can be quite lucrative.
- Ph.D.'s can be a lot of hard work without necessarily a guarantee of a job at the end of it.
- The biotech industry is a relatively young one and seems good fun to work in too.
- Dieticians play a very important role in people's recovery in the hospital.
- Careers in pharma can be quite lucrative.

COLIN, 33

92. Downstream Process Lead, Pharma Company, Dublin

What is your degree in?
Bachelor of Science (Biotechnology)
Master of Pharmaceutical Engineering

Why did you do the degree you did?
I got into more of the engineering side of things. I had business and IT as my first choices, but I realised I had far more interest in biology than anything else. I chose biotech as opposed to straight science, as it was a growing field that, it turns out, really exploded in Ireland. There were lots of high tech pharma plants built in Ireland as opposed to plants that just make a tablet.

Did you know what you wanted to do career-wise?
No, I had no clue. I graduated in May 2006; I had no idea what the inside of that pharma plant looked like. I had no idea about anything, to be honest. The course was more geared to a career in academia which I had no interest in. I wanted to get into industry. It didn't prepare you for the large-scale pharma operations. I had no idea what I wanted to do long term.

Why did you decide to do the Masters?
- It was always in the back of my mind that I'd go back and do a Masters.
- My first role was engineering. My second role was a science lab role, and my third role was more on the engineering side of things in Australia.
- To get into where I needed to be, I thought I might need a Masters. That Masters was purely geared towards the large-scale pharma industry. I learned a huge amount about large-scale manufacturing. I'm really glad I did it.

Would you be an advocate of doing postgraduate study straight after undergraduate?

Yes, I definitely think I did it the right way. There were 18 in my class, of which 12 were full time. I was the person who had spent the most time working. Most people were coming from science or chemical engineering degrees straight into it. I knew people struggled with some of the terminology and subject matter. I could appreciate the course that bit more as I didn't have to spend time working out what they were talking about.

When you came out of university did you seek advice from anyone?
- I talked to a few people I worked with in Australia, about where I wanted to go and how to get there.
- I would have leaned on the advice of people that I have worked with.
- I knew the Masters I wanted to do as it was really geared towards big scale pharma industry. That was where I wanted to be.
- I also would have talked to them about the types of companies they worked with.

What percentage of what you learned in university have you used in your day-to-day roles?
Undergraduate – 10%.
Postgraduate – 60%.

Are you happy you did a specific degree?
- I did a specific Masters and am completely happy with the choice I made. I think I knew it was the right choice as I had spent time out working and talking to people in the industry.
- As far as the undergrad goes, I do think people should be given a good base of chemical, civil, structural, etc. in their first year, and then be given the option to specialise in whatever they like best.

Did your degree prepare you for the working world?
- No, the undergrad doesn't prepare you for working, it prepares you for basic concepts of the biotech industry. I don't think any degree could have prepared me for a massive biotech manufacturing plant I was

working in straight after university. I would advise doing a degree that includes a year of work experience.

- I have a few interns working for me now who are doing a chemical engineering Masters. Their fourth year is a year in industry, last year I had three working for me, this year I have eight working for me, they are all fantastic. They come out with a Masters and a full year of experience, which will open so many doors for them - my company has already given some of them jobs.

What are the jobs you've done since graduating? And what have they entailed?

2015 – 2018

Downstream Process Lead, Pharma Company, Dublin

Managing a team of 11 engineers, managing the whole of the downstream manufacturing process.

2010 – 2014

Design/Commissioning Engineer, Pharma Company, Ireland

Testing all process equipment before handing over to production.

2007 – 2009

Validation Engineer, Pharma Company, Australia

Making sure all the new process equipment worked as per design.

What are the things you most like about your job, and the things you don't like?

Like:

1. The flexibility – you can work as a contractor (much more lucrative), or you can go permanent. Most of the people working in pharma in Ireland are contractors.
2. The travel – I've worked in Australia, the US, all around Europe visiting various sites.
3. The opportunities to grow - all throughout my career path, I've progressed quite quickly in my career.
4. Biotech is a relatively young industry. No-one is hanging around in the same role too long. There are good prospects for promotions.

Don't like:
1. You can get a bit comfortable in your roles and stay there too long.
2. Dealing with quality control can be difficult.

Which would you prefer to work for: a small company or a big company, and why?
A big company has more opportunities, and more challenges, you learn more than in a small company. In pharma, you have to be in a bigger company, as they are all global operators.

Have you worked long hours over the years?
It depends on the role, I probably average 45-50 hours a week and would have the laptop on most evenings. I'm at the level that you have to do that. Overall, I would say there is a very good work-life balance in pharma.

Has it been much fun over the years?
Yeah, very much so, there is a lot of young people in biotech, lots of nights out, great fun!

If you could start over and you were 22, but you know all you know now, would you do anything differently career-wise?
- I'd be more selective about what roles I took, instead of being of the mindset 'I've got offered this job so I better accept it.'
- I'd also be smarter about negotiating money and terms. You only find this out through experience though. If you are offered a job, the people want you, make sure you get the best deal you can. Negotiation is a difficult skill to learn. It's not something that comes naturally to most people. Ask as many questions as possible, and don't be afraid to go back to the recruiters and say you aren't 100% happy.

What career advice would you give a young person now?
Get your degree, work for a minimum of two years at home, then when you are 24/25 years old head off and travel. Engineering skills are so transferable around the world. The two years at home might be menial

work, do it and get it out of the way. It will build your confidence up and you'll be in a great place when it comes to getting a job abroad. Working abroad looks great on your CV, it shows you are not afraid to try different things.

What advice would you give a young person who wanted to do what you do?
I'd advise them to do a chemical engineering degree, as it will get you into big pharma, but it also leaves doors open to lots of other industries.

Which gets you further in a career - knowing people or being good at your job?
It's a bit of both, but you must be good at your job.

***

KEVIN, 33

93. Engineering Group Lead, Pharma Company, Ireland

What is your degree in?
Bachelor of Science (Physics and Electronics)
Ph.D. in Physics

Why did you do the degree you did?
I knew I wanted to go to university and knew I wanted to do something technical. I did physics for the A levels and liked the analytical side of it. I didn't want to do engineering as it was 40 hours of lectures per week. Physics and electronics were closest to engineering but without having to do all the hours.

When you came out of university did you seek advice from anyone?
I would have talked to a few lecturers but I didn't talk to any Ph.D. students – I didn't know anyone at the time. At university, you are quite siloed. You only mix with the people in your year – I'd really encourage young people to go and talk to older students.

Why did you embark on the career you did?

- I looked at companies that would hire physicists into engineering type roles. However, I didn't feel mature enough to leave university and go into the working world at the age of 21.
- The bursary was £1,000 a month to research something I was interested in, and a lot of my mates were thinking the same thing. I also wanted to challenge myself, I had attained a Level 8 (honours undergrad) and wanted to know could I get to a Level 10 (Ph.D.). My general mindset is how far can you get - doing the Ph.D. was more about challenging myself than my passion for the subject.

With the benefit of hindsight, if you were 18 again now would you do anything differently degree-wise?

No, if I'd have done something differently, I wouldn't be where I am today.

Were you envious of people going to work?

- When I started on the graduate programme, everyone was 22 and I was 26. Some of those guys were a lot more mature than I was when I was 22.
- The experience I gained doing the Ph.D. has really helped me to accelerate my development. I don't feel it hindered me in any way.

Did the Ph.D. prepare you for the working world?

The content of what I've researched, I use absolutely none of it. However, you develop certain skills. You learn to look at things objectively, problem-solving, presentation, communication skills, teaching undergrad students. These are all transferable skills into industry.

For a young person interested in doing a Bachelor of Science, does it matter what subjects he/she picks?

- It depends on what they want to do after their undergrad.
- When we are hiring people in work, I'm not hung up on what they have done in university. I'm more interested in their thought process and how they approach things.

Did you ever think about doing more research after the Ph.D.?
No, I wanted a job where I could earn some money, Ph.D.'s don't pay well and the job security isn't great as you are very reliant on academic funding.

What are the jobs you've done since graduating? And what have they entailed?
2017 – 2018
Engineering Group Lead, Pharma Company, Ireland
Engineering manager over one of the divisions of the company.
2016 – 2017
Senior Production Supervisor, Pharmaceutical Company, Ireland
Managing 30/40 operators and the production key performance indicators.
2015 – 2016
Manufacturing Engineer, Pharmaceutical Company, Ireland
Transfer of three manufacturing lines from the US to Ireland.
2013 – 2015
Operations, Pharmaceutical Company, US
Project managed $350m upgrades to manufacturing equipment.
2011 – 2013
Graduate Programme, Pharmaceutical Company, Ireland
Three different rotations, in three different locations.

What are the things you most like about your job, and the things you don't like?
Like:
1. Working with people.
2. The technical aspects of engineering.
3. The autonomy. Looking at the data available to me and making strategic decisions with that info.

Don't like:

1. Long hours – 50+ hour weeks, it wouldn't be sustainable if you had a family.
2. There isn't much that I don't like to be honest.

Have you had much fun over the years?
- Yes, it has been lots of fun, lots of people the same age.
- Manufacturing is good fun; there are lots of characters.
- Also, pharma is a great industry; everyone is very nice and helpful.

If you could start over and you were 22, but you know all you know now, would you do anything differently career-wise?
I wouldn't change anything. I've had lots of jobs in the last six years or so. I've never got bored, as I was constantly moving and doing something different.

What career advice would you give a young person now?
- I think getting an internship is key, six to nine months' experience. I didn't do one. The way we operate now, if we like the person, we will offer him a job after university.
- The best route in is via the graduate programme. It gets your foot in the door. It's geared to keep the people in the company for the long-term. They will invest a lot in you, and you will get lots of exposure to senior management. If you work hard, you will get a great chance to progress your career very quickly.

What are the pros and cons of living and working abroad?
- You get contacts out there. You can get a nice ex-patriate contract.
- You get a different perspective, you aren't siloed in your own manufacturing site, where people do things the same as they have always done.

***

MARK, 32

94. Life Science Specialist, Biotech Company, Dublin

What is your degree in?
Bachelor of Science (Microbiology)

Why did you do the degree you did?
I was good at science; there was no major thought process in terms of career. I found science easy in comparison to the rest of the subjects, and interesting.

With the benefit of hindsight, if you were 18 again now would you do anything differently degree-wise?
I would have put more thought into what jobs you could get out of your degree subjects - I didn't really research that. Find out what's important to you - is it money? Or lifestyle? Then try and tailor your career around that.

Did you know what your day-to-day role entailed starting off in your career?
I had no idea. There were good job prospects, and it was kind of interesting, apart from that I knew nothing.

Why did you embark on the career you did?
Again, there was no thought process. I knew there were people working in microbiology, but I had no idea if the jobs available would be suited to me, what kind of thing you did day-to-day, how much they paid, etc. - the key things that you need to know.

What are the jobs you've done since graduating? And what have they entailed?
2015 – 2018
Life Science Specialist, Biotech Company, Dublin
Marketing and selling clinical analysers to the life sciences market (universities and pharma companies who are conducting research)
2013 – 2015
Product Specialist, Medical Devices Company, London
Selling the equipment (clinical analysers) that I used as a clinical scientist.

2012 – 2013

Clinical Scientist, Clinical Diagnostics Lab, London

Studying clinical techniques and documenting my knowledge behind them.

2010 – 2012

Research Assistant, Medical Research Institute, London

Running experiments in the lab, developing vaccines.

What are the things you most like about your job, and the things you don't like?

Like:

1. I enjoyed the innovation of the research.
2. On the business side, I enjoy how it's fast-paced.

Don't like:

1. The stress of having to always improve your sales numbers.
2. Cold calling - annoying people trying to sell them products they don't want.
3. People complaining about what they have been sold.
4. The monotony and low pay of research.

Have you worked long hours over the years?

No, I don't do long hours and never have, my standard day is 9-5. Being in sales, I'm my own boss. I can go where I want, see who I want, set my own schedule. If I hit my sales targets no one cares where I am.

Which would you prefer to work for: a small company or a big company, and why?

A big company is better to work for in terms of training and getting to know how things should be done. However, a small company is more enjoyable to work for as you have more fun, and there is more of a sense of family to it.

If you could start over and you were 22, but you know all you know now, would you do anything differently career-wise?

Try and figure out what roles pay well, and then work backwards in terms of how you get there. For me, I didn't know that sales was one of the best paying jobs in science starting out. If I'd have known that I could have saved lots of time and gone straight into it.

What career advice would you give a young person now?
Try and figure out what careers are available and then get the necessary skills/techniques. Be much more career orientated, instead of just education orientated. Ask yourself how many doors will this open, and will I like the opportunities that it gives me?

What advice would you give a young person who wanted to do what you do?
Don't be afraid to get in touch with people who are currently doing the role. People are always keen to talk about themselves, say you are keen on doing what they do and ask them about it.

***

PAUL, 35

95. Chiropractor, Chiropractic Practice, Edinburgh

What is your degree in?
Bachelor of Arts (English and Drama)
Bachelor of Chiropractic

Why did you do the degree you did?
I was good at English but didn't put the work into my A levels. I thought I wanted to be an actor, but then in that course, I got really excited about the thought of having a craft. I got excited about learning again; my mum did chiropractic so I knew about it from her.

With the benefit of hindsight, if you were 18 again now would you do anything differently degree-wise?
I think I did it well, I did the first university course and got messing about out of my system. By the time, I did the second course, I was so much

more focused and wanted to get as much out of the learning experience as I could. I still had a blast, but I wanted to get more out of it.

Did you know what your day-to-day role entailed starting off in your career?
I didn't really know what the work entailed. The flip side of doing long training, i.e. five years, you think you come out of your course and be trained to do a job. In reality, you have no clue when you come out of university. There is lots of hard work after qualifying, but it's extremely rewarding. Chiropractic is one of the most rewarding things I've ever done.

When you came out of university did you seek advice from anyone?
I didn't do as much as I should have done, as my last year at university was messy and chaotic. I should have started thinking about where I want to work and started talking to people.

What percentage of what you learned in university have you used in your day-to-day roles?
25% is relevant on a day-to-day basis, 75% is good to know but you don't use, i.e. a patient has a malignant tumour and you need to refer him.

What are the jobs you've done since graduating? And what have they entailed?
2014 – 2018
Chiropractor, Edinburgh
Consultations, through to treatment and aftercare advice.
2013 – 2014
Chiropractor, Peru
Consultations, and some treating/adjusting.
2012 – 2013
Chiropractor, Isle of Wight
Learning my trade as a chiropractor.
2012
Chiropractor, London

My first job was with a guy I knew, but it was not how I wanted to do things. I found it a real learning curve. It was useful as it let me know what I didn't want to do.

What are the things you most like about your job, and the things you don't like?

Like:

1. Having some income, I didn't have any for about eight years through university.
2. Getting to meet so many interesting people.

Didn't like:

1. Working as a graduate in somebody else's practice, not liking how they did things. It's a good learning experience, but you are not completely free, and it can be frustrating.
2. The first five years were exhausting, as there was so much new stuff to learn.
3. Figuring out how I wanted to work as after I graduated it was a bit draining and confusing.

Have you had much fun over the years?

- I have so much fun every day. Once you prove to patients you are medically competent, you can have so much fun with them.
- I help people get well, and all my patients are amazing, lots of very interesting people.
- The having fun part only really comes once you've done a great job with your patients, where I am now I have fun all the time.

Have you worked long hours over the years?

It's more the intensity of the hours, my hours now are amazing!

If you could start over and you were 22, but you know all you know now, would you do anything differently career-wise?

Everything has come good. However, if I could go back in time I would have tried to get better A levels. I potentially closed a few doors on myself that I had to work extra hard to re-open later.

What career advice would you give a young person now?
- Have an appreciation that anything you want to do well, takes hard work.
- When you are 18, you think it all comes easy, but if you can, find something you enjoy so you won't mind putting in the hours!

What advice would you give a young person who wanted to do what you do?
Call/email a load of local chiropractors, speak to universities and try and observe. Try and look at someone who is a bit more leftfield to get a good overview as chiropractic is so varied - if you find a mentor along the way all the better!

***

SANDRA, 32

96. Dietician, Hospital, Dublin

What is your degree in?
Bachelor of Education (Science)
Master of Nutrition and Dietetics

Why did you do the degree you did?
My initial degree choice was veterinary, but I didn't get the results. I didn't get dietetics either, so science was the next thing I wanted to do. I thought a science teaching degree would be a good option. That was probably because I liked my science teacher in school. I also always wanted to work with people, I never wanted to just be in a lab on my own.

When you came out of university did you seek advice from anyone?
I did a year work experience while I was in school, where I shadowed a dietician. In university, I didn't know any dieticians. I always had an

interest in nutrition and food, but I didn't fully understand the role of a dietician until I did my postgraduate degree.

Did your nutrition and dietetics degree prepare you for a career as a dietician?

The course does prepare you because you have a full year on placement. If it didn't have that placement year and it was all theory, then it wouldn't have prepared me.

What percentage of what you learned in university have you used in your day-to-day roles?

- Nutrition and Dietetics 100%.
- The teaching not so much, but it did stand to me, as I teach people about food every day.

With the benefit of hindsight, if you were 18 again now would you do anything differently degree-wise?

- I only applied for courses where you got a title at the end of it.
- In hindsight, it might have been good to do a nutrition degree and then become a dietician.
- What I would say to young people now is to try and be open-minded when choosing their degrees.

What are the jobs you've done since graduating? And what have they entailed?

2016 – 2018

Senior Clinical Dietician, Heart and Lung Transplant Unit, Dublin

Preparing people for a transplant and the subsequent after-care.

2014 – 2016

Senior Clinical Dietician, Hospital Intensive Care Unit, Dublin

Managing people in intensive care, artificial nutrition, feeding people through tubes, etc.

What are the things you most like about your job, and the things you don't like?

Like:
1. Helping people.
2. Working as part of a team – everyone is very collaborative.
3. It can be quite rewarding.

Don't like:
1. Seeing people die.
2. People not taking your advice.
3. How the health system works.

Which would you prefer to work for: a small company or a big company, and why?
I'd always go with bigger hospitals, where there are more specialisms, and you are working with the best consultants and best teams.

Have you worked long hours over the years?
7:30am to 5pm. It is cushier hours than doctors and nurses' hours. There are no on-calls, no weekends, no nights.

Have you had much fun over the years?
- Yeah, great fun. We have a really good team here in the hospital.
- Yesterday there was a lady too sick to get married so she got married on the ward, and everyone helped and had different roles in the wedding, it was great.

If you could start over and you were 22, but you know all you know now, would you do anything differently career-wise?
- I would have been more confident, believed in myself more.
- I would have stayed in Australia longer, as the healthcare system is a lot better, and the pay is much better in Australia for dieticians.

What career advice would you give a young person now?
- Work and travel to get a different perspective, it's good to see how things work in other countries.

- Have a good mentor, always have someone you can discuss things with. It needs to be someone you trust, I've had some amazing mentors, they are the people I've learned the most from over the years.
- Don't worry about it. everything will always work out. When I didn't get into the veterinary degree, I wailed crying and thought it was the end of the world, but in hindsight everything has worked out fine!

What advice would you give a young person who wanted to do what you do?

Find an area of health you like. You need to experience a lot of different areas and hospitals before you truly know what you like and what you don't like. I always knew I never wanted to work in weight management. I loved intensive care, but what I learned in the intensive care unit was you don't get to know people and can't build up a rapport with them.

What jobs have your postgraduate classmates gone into?

There were only five people in my postgraduate course. Four are working as dietitians; one is working as a sales rep for a pro-biotics company. Of the dietitians, three are working in hospitals and one is working in the community.

TEACHING

What I knew before the interviews:

- Good hours, good holidays, probably good fun, but stressful, repetitive, and not paid that well.
- You are not confined to cities or countries. You can go and work as a teacher in a lot of places.

What I learned from the interviews:

- You can become the 'head of' if you work in a big school.
- You can travel the world as a teacher.
- The teachers I interviewed seemed pretty invested in the kids and seemed to really enjoy it.
- Dealing with the parents was a tricky part of the job which I never thought about!

AILEEN, 33

97. Primary School Teacher, National School, Dublin

What is your degree in?
Bachelor of Commerce
Higher Diploma in Teaching

Why did you do the degree you did?
I enjoyed the business subjects, and it was a good broad degree, I knew there were lots of career paths out of it.

Did you know what you wanted to do career-wise?
No, lots of things that I liked, but nothing that jumped out at me!

Did you know what your day-to-day role entailed starting off in your career?
Once I graduated, I looked at the specs of the different jobs, the job spec included working with figures and I really liked that so I went for that one.

What percentage of what you learned in university have you used in your day-to-day roles?
Undergrad not so much.
Postgrad 100%.

With the benefit of hindsight, if you were 18 again now would you do anything differently degree-wise?
I'd do the exact same thing, as I really liked my degree, and it gives you loads of options.

What are the jobs you've done since graduating? And what have they entailed?
2011 – 2017
Primary School Teacher, Ireland
Teaching a classroom of primary school kids.

2006 – 2008

Share Scheme Administrator, Dublin

In charge of the different share schemes in a company.

What are the things you most like about your job, and the things you don't like?

Like:

1. Work-life balance – When I was working as a share administrator, I found the hours long as I was commuting from my home town. Teaching has a much better work-life balance
2. Working with children.
3. I can work anywhere, can get a job close to home, don't have to commute.

Don't like:

1. There is a lot of extra work in it, i.e. paperwork, preparing classes etc.

Have you worked long hours over the years?

9am - 3pm, and then a bit of work outside of that, correcting, etc.

Have you had much fun over the years?

Loads, it is good, get a lot of laughs out of the kids.

If you could start over and you were 22, but you know all you know now, would you do anything differently career-wise?

I don't think I would, I went in with my eyes open, I tried working in an office, but it was commuting in and out of Dublin that I really didn't like. I quickly realised that city and office life wasn't for me.

What career advice would you give a young person now?

If you are not sure of what you want to do, do a good broad degree and you will have loads of different opportunities. Do work experience, and lots of different summer jobs and try and get a feel for what you might like and not like. Work experience is key.

What advice would you give a young person who wanted to do what you do?

- Apply to the local school for teaching experience. It depends on your location, it can be competitive in rural areas, but in built-up areas it's a lot easier. Try and get your foot in the door in a few different schools and then they will know you when it comes to interviewing.
- You used to have people from different disciplines giving up and becoming teachers but now not so much.

***

DECLAN, 33

98. Primary School Teacher, National School, Dublin

What is your degree in?

Bachelor of Commerce
Bachelor of Education.

Why did you do the degree you did?

I didn't really know what to do, thought I might want to do marketing or HR management, but I wasn't passionate about it. I just liked business in school, but I didn't know what to do at that stage in my life, so I did something general.

Did you know what you wanted to do career-wise?

I had done some teaching in my part-time job working in social care, and I enjoyed it. At that stage I wasn't sure if an office job was for me. I then did some substitute teaching to try it out and liked it and decided to pursue that path. It was primary as I preferred teaching younger kids, I found it less stressful than teenagers.

When you came out of university did you seek advice from anyone?

I asked my neighbour, who was a principal in a school, then I did a bit of subbing, if it's for you then you quickly find out.

What percentage of what you learned in university have you used in your day-to-day roles?

- Practically nothing from commerce.
- The teaching does give you some ideas, techniques, etc., maybe 50% from my teaching degree.

With the benefit of hindsight, if you were 18 again now would you do anything differently degree-wise?

Commerce was a bit of a waste of time as I haven't used any of it, but I had a great time and met some life-long friends.

What are the jobs you've done since graduating? And what have they entailed?

2010 – 2017

Primary School Teacher, Dublin

Teaching a classroom of primary school kids.

What are the things you most like about your job, and the things you don't like?

Like:

1. Good work-life balance, you only work 183 days of the year.
2. Good feedback from parents and kids, job satisfaction, nice to see kids happy.

Don't like:

1. It can be quite intense, 28 kids in a small classroom, 24 of them looking out the window, it can be stressful!
2. Big class sizes, if it were down to 15-18 kids, it would be a lot better.
3. Dealing with parents can be tricky, they see their son or daughter as perfect, and you must tell them they aren't perfect. (Some teachers might say dealing with parents is the worst part of teaching). Sometimes you meet the parents, and you see why the kids are the way they are!

Have you worked long hours over the years?

Start at 9:20am, and finish at 3pm, but I probably stay until 4pm. There is also correcting and preparing class work that you must do outside of classroom time.

Have you had much fun over the years?

Yes, good fun, staff are young, classes change every year, it can be good fun.

If you could start over and you were 22, but you know all you know now, would you do anything differently career-wise?

I'd probably have done the same. I'm not sure about general degrees. At least when you do teaching, you know you are going to be a teacher. It can be a long haul when you try and keep it so broad.

What advice would you give a young person who wanted to do what you do?

- If you are going to do teaching, try and do some substitute teaching, or if you can't do that just go in and observe a few classes. Talk to as many teachers as you can and find out the pros and cons from them.
- One thing to bear in mind is the money isn't great. My girlfriend is also a teacher, and we are looking at going to Dubai or Hong Kong, as the money is a lot better. It can be difficult to save up for a house if you are on a teacher's salary.

What is the career background of a lot of your teaching colleagues?

- A lot of teachers did something else and then went into teaching, nearly 50% have a stab at something else and then just give up and go teaching.
- When you see some of the university courses in prospectuses, they look cool. Then when you do the course you quickly realise it is rubbish. In my opinion, a lot of the university courses aren't well correlated to the well-paying jobs that there are available in the real world. When you graduate, there are the same kind of jobs on offer, finance, IT, teaching, etc.

What's the career path progression like for teachers?

You are going to be a teacher for the rest of your life, some people go off and work for the department of education. In general, you remain a teacher, you can apply to be a principal, but it's hard work to get picked. It's a very rigorous selection process. It's tough because you can't even move to a different school too easily, you're in that school teaching for the rest of your life.

***

MICHAEL, 33,

99. Head of Music, Secondary School, London

What is your degree in?
Bachelor of Arts in Irish Music and Dance
Higher Diploma in Education (specialism in Music)

Why did you do the degree you did?
I thought it would be practical and easy to do; it was the first year of the course. We were promised that you would study music, performance and get a degree out of it. Some people were apprehensive about doing it as there was no real career path out of it.

Why did you embark on the career you did?
When we started university, a degree was great, but when we finished university a degree became more of a stepping stone. I always thought that I would do a postgraduate degree. I picked the Higher Diploma in Teaching as I was doing a bit of substitute teaching at the time. I almost did physiotherapy but decided to go with teaching.

Are you specific to teaching primary and secondary schools?
They have started to do music specialism for primary, but I think I did secondary because I enjoyed working with older kids more.

With the benefit of hindsight, if you were 18 again now would you do anything differently degree-wise?

When you are 17 and you go to university, it's a starting point and you don't look for an ending point. I think it's much better to look for an end point and then try and work your way back. Looking back now, that was probably the best degree that I could have chosen to do. It was something I was interested in and I found it really engaging.

What are the jobs you've done since graduating? And what have they entailed?

2016 – 2018

Head of Music, Secondary School, London

I wanted to go back to teaching music.

2014 – 2016

Head of Key Stage group, Secondary School, London

Looking after the well-being of three years instead of one.

2012 – 2014

Head of year 10, Secondary School, London

Responsible for all Year 10 students' well-being.

2010 – 2012

Head of Music, Secondary School, London

Classroom teaching, responsible for exams, running of the whole department.

2008 – 2010

Teacher of Music, Secondary School, London

Day-to-day classroom teaching 11 to 16-year-olds.

What are the things you most like about your job, and the things you don't like?

Like:

1. Working with kids.
2. The holidays.
3. Working in an education facility is very inspiring.

Don't like:

1. The exam pressure.
2. The national league tables.

3. The socio-economic state of some of the school catchment areas.
4. Trying to raise aspirations, sometimes you nearly have to teach the family more than the kid.

Has it been long hours over the years?

Yes definitely, you do more hours as the years go on. As well as your own workload, you have to mentor others and line manage 10-12 people.

Have you had much fun over the years?

Yes, 100%, it's always easy to go to work when you enjoy something you do.

What are the pros and cons of teaching in a city?

- London schools have more cash to spend; some rural schools are disappearing as the people are no longer there anymore. There are also a lot more career opportunities as there are so many schools.
- If you are teaching in a primary school in Ireland and it's a permanent position, you can go on sabbatical for two years, come back and that job is still yours. You have people my age teaching back home, and they are still not permanent, it's a joke! In London, that's not really a problem, as there are so many teaching jobs.

If you could start over and you were 22, but you know all you know now, would you do anything differently career-wise?

When you are starting off you want all the money you can get. Then, when you get older, you get cynical and happiness becomes more important, all the money in the world won't give you that.

What career advice would you give a young person now?

- It's all about big steps and little steps.
- The big step is what do you want to do when you are older. This can be hard for a young person, so what I ask them is what do you not want to be when you are older, which is a little bit easier.
- It's difficult to figure out what you want to do when you are 20 when you are 16. So, once they have a list of careers they might be interested

in, what are the little steps involved to explore them further. Ask them what would they not like to do next year, and again it makes their decision that bit easier. Try and come at it from both angles – short and long term.

What advice would you give a young person who wanted to do what you do?
Before you start off teaching, ask yourself if you have a love of what you are going to teach. You also must have the patience to realise the students will not have the same love for or aptitude for the subject you do. Teaching is all about breaking up your knowledge into easily digestible size chunks of information so that anyone can understand it.

What's the background of all your contemporaries in teaching?
You would find people who have worked for a few years in their profession and then swapped over into teaching, i.e. banking to maths, engineering to science. Music teachers are generally people who have had music ever present all throughout their life.

Do you find teaching very rewarding?
Yes, it's very rewarding to see someone go from not being able to play an instrument to mastering it and really owning that instrument. It's very important to be aware of people's abilities though. You must celebrate the kid that can't play at all and learns 'twinkle-twinkle' on the tin whistle and the kid that plays at the London Palladium the same.

***

NEASA, 31,

100. Language Teacher, International School, London

What is your degree in?
Bachelor of Science (Speech-Language Pathology)
Master of Arts (Dance)

Why did you do the degree you did?

- I started off doing journalism, as I was good at English, all the adults around me said to go with your strengths! After a few months in, I decided it wasn't for me.
- I had a bit of work experience in speech therapy and fancied working in paediatrics/working with kids.

Why did you embark on the career you did?

- I wanted to get a qualification under my belt; once I had that I went back and did a Masters in Dance. I left the speech and language therapy world behind after I did the Masters. After graduating from the Masters, I went into an arts education charity helping young people, doing choreography.
- After that, I chose to move to France. It was more of a life decision more than a career decision. The most likely form of employment living in Paris was teaching English.

What have all your friends from the Masters ended up doing?

Most of us have dance on the side now, not as our main jobs, but I think we all have made money out of dance in some way.

When you came out of university did you seek advice from anyone?

Yes, the Masters was a massive financial undertaking so I asked people whether they thought I should do it. Most people said finish your degree and then go for it!

With the benefit of hindsight, if you were 18 again now would you do anything differently degree-wise?

I don't think I would. Did I need to do a Masters in Dance to get the jobs I did? Probably not. However, I definitely would recommend someone to go study something they are passionate about. The experience is incredible, if you have a calling for something I'd definitely pursue it. If it's something you feel very strongly about when you come out of school maybe even pursue it then. I'm very happy that I got my speech and language degree under my belt.

Do you think work experience would help a young person figuring out what they wanted to do?
I had some speech and language work experience before I even did my degree, so yes work experience is very valuable. For example, I had an idea of what journalism would be in my head but it was completely different studying it. I knew what working in speech therapy entailed. With dance, it is so diverse, but work experience can help you realise how many different options there are.

Could you do dance without an undergraduate? And go straight into performing/working?
- Yes, you could, however, if it's a technical style of dance then you do absolutely have to study it. What studying dance helps with is networking, it gives you more contacts which are so important.
- Also, I think the discipline and the life experience you get from going to university is so important. I think if I had forged a very successful career in dance but didn't do university I think I'd be lacking something.

What are the jobs you've done since graduating? And what have they entailed?
2013 – 2018
Early Years Bilingual Education Consultant, School, London
Co-ordinating the curricula for bilingual schools.
2011 – 2013
Primary School Teacher, Bilingual School, France
Developing classes and teaching young kids languages.
2009 – 2011
Operations Manager, Arts-based Charity, Scotland
Overseeing dance and media projects with kids who were disengaging with education.

What are the things you most like about your job, and the things you don't like?
Like:
1. Working with international, multicultural people.

2. Becoming bilingual and trilingual.
3. Leadership, getting more responsibility.

Don't like:
1. I'm very experienced in my job, but I lack the bits of paper to show that. 'I'm too niche' - I'm very employable by a small group of employers around the world, but I don't have the formal qualifications in education.

Have you worked long hours over the years?
The huge plus is that I'm always on holidays, it's a bit of a running joke. Working in primary education is a nice deal, in terms of hours and holidays.

Have you had much fun over the years?
Yes, I specialise in early years, so it's great. I'm not at a desk, I'm in a very fun and energetic environment.

Is your job less stressful than a normal teaching job?
- As I work in a fee-paying school, my stresses are more about what gets escalated to the senior management of the school. We're a business model with the parents being our clients. So, there is a constant dilemma between satisfying the parents and going above and beyond for the kids.
- In a state school, the stresses are the behaviour of the kids, the big classes; we don't have those issues as much. For me, the only school I can work for is fee-paying as they are the real bilingual ones.

What advice would you give a young person that couldn't decide whether to follow their passion or just settle for a well-paying job to cover the bills?
- My hippy heart would want to say just go for it, if it goes well that's amazing! If it was my child, to be very honest with myself, I'd want them to secure a qualification at university.
- In terms of timing, I'd say go straight into university and get it out of the way. Ideally, you'd do both at the same time, pursue your

qualification, but have your artistic interests on the side. At university, you will meet like-minded artsy people, through clubs, societies, etc.

If you could start over and you were 22, but you know all you know now, would you do anything differently career-wise?
I'd like to go back and have some qualification in education, but it's tougher now as I'm a little older.

What career advice would you give a young person now?
- I think we waste a lot of time and energy thinking about things. Just try something and if it doesn't work, it doesn't work. Don't wait around for the perfect opportunity or the perfect job to come calling.
- I think of other friends, and I admire the brave ones. They put themselves out there all the time, make their own opportunities and get great jobs.

Would you encourage young people to go abroad to live and work?
Yes. I think just the whole experience, it's terrifying when you do it, but it's also hugely character building. Living and working in a different culture is really valuable for your character, confidence, and independence. It's terrifying in the beginning, but it would top the list of my recommendations to any young person.

'The only source of knowledge is experience'

Albert Einstein

PART 2: THE ADVICE OF 100 GRADUATES

There is some amazing advice in this book. A lot of the interviewees cared passionately about helping a younger generation and offered several pointers which add up to several hundred pieces of advice.

I wanted to condense the advice given into some takeaways, so I've collated all the most often mentioned tips, sorted them in descending order, and grouped them. I didn't want to include every piece of advice offered, so only tips offered by three or more people are outlined below. However, some of the best advice was the odd nugget given here and there usually by very smart people who think a little bit outside the box. So, make sure you read the interviews to get the most benefit out of this bank of knowledge and advice.

UNIVERSITY:

The more work placements you do, the better, as you can compare roles and companies and find out what you like/don't like.

(Giulia #49, Paul #73, Katie #26, Natalie #33, Shane #42, Niall #40, Nasir #47, Sarah #90, Kirstine #52, Oisin #67, Taj #59, Ashling #69, Ronan #74, Maurice #89, Kevin #93, Declan #98, Aileen #97, Neasa #100, Laura #88, Gareth #30, Linda #56)

Research the jobs/career paths available to you from your degree; what graduates of that degree end up doing ten years later, and what is the long-term earning potential.

(Rick #58, Suzanne #35, Niall #40, Sarah #90, Taj #59, Michael #72, Eoin #71, Mark #94, Laura #88)

Make sure you get good grades. They will stay with you for life.

(Jennifer #62, Oisin #67, Rachel #86, Eoin #71, Paul #73, Sarah #90, Caroline #1, Neasa #100, Emma #44)

Work experience allows you to figure out quickly if you don't like something, instead of wasting 18 months - 2 years in a permanent role.

(Richie #14, Asaf #17, Niall #40, Nasir #47, Hawwa #45, Nadine #84)

Work placements often get you jobs, because if you do well and a company likes you, they will offer you a permanent role.

(Conor #25, Freya #11, Kevin #20, Darragh #36, Jennifer #62, Kevin #93)

The more practical your degree the better, especially if it has a full one-year work placement as it will give you insights into what a future career might entail.

(Nadine #84, Suzanne #35, Darragh #36, Rick #58, Maurice #89, Sandra #96, Emma #44)

Work experience puts you a step ahead of your peers when applying for jobs.

(Michael #72, Jennifer #62, Stuart #22, Georgie #31, Colin #92)

Choosing a broad degree that has a few different options to specialise in at the end of it is a good option.

(Giulia #49, Conor #25, Michael #72, David #70, Aileen #97)

Doing several work placements will give you a better education than university.

(Asaf #17, Paul #13, Rick #58, Shaun #34)

Try to get a craft or a skill out of your degree, e.g. accounting, medicine.

(Aya #43, Kathryn #51, Ashling #69, Declan #98)

CAREER:

Go live and work abroad. You will experience different cultures, get a different perspective, and get great life experience.

(Jess #12, Claire #24, Darragh #36, Nicola #66, Lorcan #38, Colin #92, Mark #39, Sandra #96, Niall #40, Colm #9, Moira #4, Neasa #100, Niamh #65, Emma #44, Colin #8)

Don't be afraid to step out of your comfort zone/take risks/ask people for something. What is the worst that can happen? You end up back where you were with a lot more experience gained and no regrets. You will always find a million reasons not to do something.

(Paul #5, Kevin #20, Nicola #66, Colin #92, Joel #87, Richie #14, Chris #18, Asaf #17, Katie #26, Wayne #6, Paul #13, Colm #9, Peter #79, Natasha #85, Dan #54, Linda #56, Neasa #100)

Do something you enjoy doing. You will excel at it; as you won't see it as work.

(Gemma #77, Gosia #83, Kathryn #43, Sarah #90, Asaf #17, Sam #21, Padhraic #41, Tom #15, Isla #32, Louise #3, Amy #29, Gareth #30, Julia #46, Linda #56, Neasa #100)

Research the possible career paths available to you. Research the different professions, industries, companies, and jobs. Don't just take the first job offer. Research the different departments in that company, and the company itself. Talk to people who work there; they will tell you how it really is.

(Nicola #66, Danny #82, Marcus #63, Paul #73, Oliver #78, Natalie #33, Sarah #90, Paul #73, Maurice #89, Steve #91)

Don't stay in the same role/company if you are not learning anything new.

(Nadine #84, Aya #43, Kevin #20, Eoin #71, Feidhlim #37, David #48, Wayne #6)

The pros of a graduate programme:
1. You have an instant network and make friends for life.
2. Gives you great exposure to different parts of the company, and to senior management.
3. They are good if you are unsure what to do.
4. They are a good transition from university to the working world.

(Fearghal #10, Conor #25, Rachel #86, Chris #18, Maurice #89, Gemma #77, Stuart #22)

The cons of a graduate programme:
1. The learning curve can be quite shallow.
2. They can be poorly run, and you can get stuck in one department.
3. It can be very dependent on who your manager/client is.
4. The candidates who are picked are not necessarily the best ones; assessment days can tend to favour the loudest people.

(Fearghal #10, Chris #18, Stuart #22, Gemma #77)

Reasons to aim to work for the best company you can:
1. The best people work for the best firms. The better the people you learn from, the better you will be.
2. Once you get a top company on your CV; it's easier to get other jobs.
3. The training and processes will be much better than in a small firm.

(Freya #11, Gemma #77, Peter #79, Jess #12, Steve #91)

Have confidence in yourself, be brave. Apply for roles; what is the worst that can happen?

(Georgie #31, Rachel #86, Nadine #84, Sandra #96, Linda #56, Neasa #100)

If you are passionate or good enough at something; you can make a living out of it.

(Kevin #20, Colm #9, Tom #15, Sarah #90)

You need to decide in your 20s which motivates you more, is it money or is it what you love to do?

(Kim #27, Suzanne #35, Tom #15, Claire #24)

Put yourself in positions where you feel uncomfortable. Don't be afraid to do things no one else is doing; ask people for advice. The best learning is under pressure.

(Paul #13, Tony #23, Colm #9)

Stepping out of your comfort zone or doing a role that is difficult may be tough at the time. However, you will look back and be so glad you did it as you will have learned so much.

(Paul #13, Conor #25, Colm #9)

SKILLS:

Don't be afraid to get in touch with people who are currently doing the role. People are always keen to talk about themselves, say you are keen on doing what they do and ask them about it.

(Mark #94, Shane #42, Warren #60, Marcus #63, Eoin #71, David #48, Claire #24, Natalie #33, Declan #98, Oliver #78, Feidhlim #37, Michael #72, Paul #73, Steve #91, Sarah #90, Louise #3, David #70)

Take the time to invest in relationships, build a good network. You'll be surprised how much it will benefit you.

(Isabella #50, Sarah #90, Darragh #36, Kim #27, Sean #81, Paul #73, Andrew #16, Ashling #69, Dan #54, Emma #44, Gareth #30, Caroline #1)

If you can spot a career path in the business, network with the right people on a social level. Try to get a mentor or someone who brings you up through the organisation.

(Peter #79, Brian #7, Asaf #17, Sandra #96, Tony #23, Kathryn #43, Oisin #67, Niamh #65)

Don't underestimate the value of your personality and soft skills in getting you opportunities. They play a huge part in career progression. The better you can communicate with people the more successful you will be.

(Kevin #20, Conor #25, Lorcan #38, Joel #87, Dan #54)

Be adaptable. Jobs and industries will change dramatically over the next 20 years, try and future proof your job.

(Danny #82, Shaun #34, Tony #23, Niall #64, Joel #87)

Get involved in extra-curricular activities as it can make the difference on your CV and in interviews.

(Paul #5, Mary #2, Hawwa #45, Eoin #71, Sarah #90)

Reach out to people you don't know for advice. Some won't reply, but lots will. Ask them for a coffee, you have nothing to lose.

(Isabella #50, Freya #11, Giulia #49, Paul #73)

WHAT NOT TO DO:

If you don't know what to do, don't worry. You will find your path. Try different things out; it may take a few years to figure out what you like, but it will all work out in the end.

(Georgie #31, Suzanne #35, Giulia #49, Chris #18, Niall #57, Sandra #96, Christian #19, Padhraic #41, Hawwa #45, Niamh #65, Natasha #85, Sarah #90, Neasa 100, Louise #3, Linda #56)

Keep your options open. You never know what you might want to do when you get older. Be open-minded and don't shut doors on yourself.

(Eoin #71, Rick #58, Niall #57, Peter #79, Paul #95, Fearghal #10, Oisin #67, Andrew #16, Charlotte #61, Katie #26, Shane #68, Sandra #96)

Take your time. Don't rush into decisions. Make sure the degree/job/company is right for you.

(Warren #60, Aya #43, Padhraic #41, Oliver #78, Eoghan #55, Claire #24, Niamh #65, Eoin #71)

CONCLUSION

In the introduction, I talked about three reasons why I think young people are underprepared for the working world. To conclude, I want to revisit those reasons and give you some key takeaways to help you be more prepared.

University versus the working world:

Earlier in the book, I talked about how university and the working world are very different; and how students didn't realise they were starting all over again in their first job.

The way to make this transition as smooth as possible is either **do a practical degree, or get work experience, both if possible.** The people in this book who did work experience were so much more clued in when it came to choosing a career path. The more practical/work experience you get, the sooner you will be able to figure out how jobs and companies work. This will make your life so much easier. Some of the interviewees who didn't do any work experience have spent years figuring out what they wanted to do.

The advice young people get:

I also discussed how the advice that young people get mightn't be the best advice, and how that can lead to them making poor decisions.

Another key takeaway which will help you avoid making poor career decisions is to **seek advice from people who have gone before you.** If you are pursuing a career as a solicitor, and you don't know any solicitors ten years older than you, it's very hard to know what lies ahead of you. Seek these people out. Ask them about their roles, the pros and cons, the work-life balance, the pay. Don't get stuck in a career that you don't like.

Your parents and friends might give you advice, but they won't know as well as someone who has lived it. People ten years ahead of you will only be too willing to help. Research their roles and ask them good questions. I use ten years because those people will remember being in your position and facing the same decisions.

Lack of defined path:

My last point in the introduction was about the lack of a defined path that young people are used to after their school years.

One of the strong messages coming out of this book is **don't worry.** As long as you are learning, developing your skills/experience, and enjoying yourself things will work out. You might feel like you don't have a clue what lies ahead or wonder if you've made the right choice. Lots of the 100 interviewees felt the exact same way, and they have turned out just fine!

Having a defined path works for some people, but I think what this book has shown is that following those defined paths are not for everyone. People have spent years qualifying as lawyers and accountants only for them to not like their job. Try not to shut doors on yourself so that when you figure out what you want to do, you can go and do it!

As a final word, while writing this book, I've been inspired to look at my career differently. If it inspires some young people to research a career more, think differently about their career path, or ask advice from a person they wouldn't have before, it will have been a worthwhile effort!

FEEDBACK

Reviews:

Word of mouth is crucial to getting more people to read this book. If you enjoyed the book, I'd be really grateful if you left a review on Amazon, even if it's just a couple of lines.

Corrections:

I want this to be the best read it can be. If you noticed a mistake, or have any suggestions for improvements, please email me about it so I can fix and include in updates.

Questions:

If you have any career questions, please do email them to me and I will try to answer them as best I can.

careeradviceforyoungpeople@gmail.com

Blog Newsletter:

If you liked the book and want to get more exclusive content, please do sign up to my newsletter. You'll find the sign-up form at the end of all my blog posts.

www.1000yearsofcareeradvice.com

35646516R00208

Printed in Great Britain
by Amazon